Public Inquiries into Residential Abuse of Children

Public Inquiries into Residential Abuse of Children

*Brian Corby, Alan Doig
and Vicky Roberts*

Jessica Kingsley Publishers
London and Philadelphia

First published in the United Kingdom in 2001 by
Jessica Kingsley Publishers Ltd
116 Pentonville Road
London N1 9JB, England
and
325 Chestnut Street
Philadelphia, PA 19106, USA

www.jkp.com

Library of Congress Cataloging in Publication Data
A CIP catalogue record for this book is available from the Library of Congress

British Library Cataloguing in Publication Data
A CIP catalogue record for this book is available from the British Library

ISBN 1 85302 895 9

Printed and Bound in Great Britain by
Athenaeum Press, Gateshead, Tyne and Wear

Contents

Introduction

In September 1996, the North Wales Tribunal of Inquiry held its first hearing into the abuse of children in residential care in Clwyd and Gwynedd. Under its terms of reference, the inquiry was required to examine all allegations of abuse said to have taken place in residential homes in these two counties between 1974 and 1996. In all, there were approximately 650 complaints to consider made by over 80 individuals, and allegations of abuse were received from ex-residents of 38 of the 84 homes which were in operation between the years in question. Just over two-thirds of the complaints made were about physical assaults and the remainder about sexual abuse.

This Tribunal of Inquiry came at the end of a long list of inquiries into child abuse – we estimated that there had been 72 such inquiries between 1945 and 1996, all but 2 of which took place from 1973 onwards (see Corby, Doig and Roberts 1998). Between then and the beginning of the year 2000 there have to our knowledge been 9 other inquiries (see Appendix 1 for full details). Most of these inquiries were concerned with the deaths of children physically abused while living with their parents or carers in the community. However, in the 1990s concerns about the abuse of children in residential care gained increasing prominence. The trend was clear. Only 4 of the 50 inquiries held between 1945 and 1989 were concerned with the abuse of children in residential care. By contrast, since 1990 residential childcare has come under the scrutiny of public inquiries in roughly equal measure to that of field social work, though to some extent this is accounted for by the introduction of a less public means of investigating serious child abuse in the community in 1991 under Part 8 of the *Working Together* guidelines which were implemented that year (Department of Health (DoH) 1991a).[1]

The types of residential establishments which have been inquired into are varied. They include approved schools, local authority community homes of varying kinds and residential schools for children with learning difficulties and/or behavioural problems. Common features of all these establishments have been that residents were from the older age groups of childhood (mostly 11 and above) and largely, though not exclusively, male. The North Wales Tribunal of Inquiry, as noted above, received complaints from 38 homes, including local authority community homes with and without education on the premises, hostels for young people of working age, observation and assessment centres and also a large privately owned set of establishments for older children – Bryn Alyn. It should be noted that inquiries have also been carried out into abuse of younger children in day care settings (see Hunt 1994) and that this form of abuse has been the subject of much debate and controversy particularly in the USA (see Finkelhor, Williams and Burns 1988; deYoung 1997). In addition, we know that children are at risk of abuse in a wide range of other settings including public boarding schools, hospitals, nurseries, youth clubs, Scouts associations and sports centres (see Utting 1997; Gallagher 1999a). There are particular concerns about the potential for child abuse in foster care situations, which are currently preferred options for children needing extrafamilial placements (Utting 1997). However, for reasons of space and focus, these situations are not considered in any detail in this book.

In addition to the inquiries themselves, there have been extensive joint police and social work investigations into allegations of residential abuse in other parts of the UK (see Gallagher 1999b). Furthermore, in response to these inquiries and investigations, there has been a series of government-sponsored fact-finding and policy development reports (Utting 1991; Lady E. Howe 1992; Warner 1992; Utting 1997) and, most recently, highly publicised government initiatives, backed by a considerable body of research (DoH 1998a), to improve the quality of residential care and ensure better monitoring and accountability (DoH 1998b).

Residential childcare is, therefore, very much in the public gaze at this moment in time. The establishment of the North Wales Tribunal of Inquiry, the most formidable instrument of government available for investigating allegations of negligence or wrongdoing at a cost of £12 million, was a clear reflection of the degree of concern felt about the abuse of children in residential care. As the then Labour Welsh affairs spokesman, Rhodri Morgan, put it before the commencement of the North Wales Tribunal hearings: 'The residential care system of this country is now on trial' (see Webster 1998, p.11).

Aims and objectives

This book has several key aims in relation to abuse of children in residential care and public inquiries into such mistreatment.

Weighing up the facts

The first of these aims is to collate knowledge about abuse of children in residential care using material mainly from the public inquiry and government reports referred to above, but also drawing on literature on institutional abuse and newspaper reports about police investigations and the prosecution of offenders, which continue to occur almost daily.[2] In collating this information, some attempt will be made to estimate the size of the problem and to analyse the forms of abuse presented and the situations and circumstances in which they occur.

Context of residential childcare

A second aim is to consider key contextual issues in relation to abuse of children in residential care. In order to do this, an historical account of such provision in Britain is offered. It will be argued that institutional care of children and other forms of substitute care, such as fostering or boarding-out, have at all times been last resorts for the children of the poor and destitute, and that, as a consequence, for the most part they have been characterised by very low standards of care provided as cheaply as possible and often with a minimum of external scrutiny. In the light of this, it may seem surprising that prior to the 1990s there have been so few scandals about abuse. However, it will be argued that to a large degree the natural preference of the state for families to rear their own children and the stigmatisation of those who failed to meet this requirement meant that, except in the most extreme cases, harsh treatment, which we would now term abusive, was a relatively normal (and therefore unremarkable) experience for children in residential care certainly up to the mid-1940s.

Consideration is given to shifts in thinking about childhood which have led to greater attention being paid to the emotional care of children, or more accurately, to the prevention of their abuse, from the 1960s onwards and to how this shift in thinking has impacted on residential care, particularly during the 1990s.

Role and impact of public inquiries into residential abuse

A third aim of this book is to consider how the state has responded to the rising concerns about abuse of children in residential care with particular focus on the role played by public inquiries into these matters. The way in which inquiries are used by the state in general and their functions and dysfunctions are subjects that could fill a book alone. Nevertheless, in the space available, it is important to understand the politics of inquiries (i.e. how and why they are established, what form they take and what constraints there are on their findings and recommendations), and the impact that they have on public policy. Child abuse in particular (as has already been pointed out) has been subjected to considerable public scrutiny by means of inquiries and much of the development of systems and laws for dealing with child abuse has been greatly influenced by their findings. Residential care is now very much under the microscope and it is important to analyse how inquiries have impacted and will continue to impact on public perceptions of such institutions and on the response of the state with regard to substitute care arrangements for children in the future.

North Wales Tribunal of Inquiry

A fourth aim of the book is to provide a detailed account and analysis of the North Wales Tribunal of Inquiry. Thanks largely to the geographical proximity of the venue for the Tribunal to Liverpool, we were able to be present for a large part of the 18 months in which it conducted its hearings. We had access to transcripts and other written material and we were able to conduct interviews with legal personnel acting on behalf of complainants and those complained against and with the chairperson of the Tribunal. We did not attempt to approach complainants, as we were acutely aware of how difficult and stressful making statements to the police and giving testimony to the Tribunal had been for many of them. We did not wish to exacerbate these difficulties. We did, however, hold discussions with some other key persons who gave evidence at the Tribunal.

In our view, the North Wales Tribunal provides an excellent case example of the working of inquiries and is, therefore, an important event to report on and analyse. Consequently, we devote three chapters in the book to its operation. The first of these describes and comments on events leading up to the establishment of the Tribunal. The second focuses on the process and conduct of the Tribunal, looking at the problems and difficulties of establishing the truth about highly sensitive and contentious issues in a court-like procedure. The third looks at the findings and recommendations of the Tribunal and analyses how it came to the conclusions reached.

The future

Our final aim is to make some recommendations based on our findings for better methods of inquiring into abuse of children generally, but particularly in relation to that which takes place in residential care. In our view, it is important to find ways of ensuring that responses to abuse in residential childcare are considered and effective ones. While it is without question that any abuse of a child in residential care is unacceptable, it is important to ensure that the whole enterprise of residential care is not jeopardised in the process of rooting out such abuse and preventing its reoccurrence in the future. There are dangers that this may happen, and that the findings of the North Wales Tribunal of Inquiry will provide further evidence to support such a trend. It is our intention to have some impact on this process by providing a balanced and objective account of the interplay between child abuse, residential care for children and inquiries, set within a clear social, political and historical context, and by pointing to improved ways of seeking the truth, which both meet the needs of victims and maintain the viability of residential care for children.

Notes

1   It should be noted that Part 8 Reviews were preceded by part 9 Reviews in the 1988 *Working Together* guidelines (DHSS1988). Further discussion of Part 8 Reviews takes place in chapters 4 and 10

2   For instance, at the time of writing, yet another fairly typical case is reported as follows:

A former social worker admitted sexually abusing children at a Merseyside Orphanage.

John Carroll, 50, admitted 35 offences against 12 boys as young as 8 while working as a supervisor at St Edmund's Orphanage, Bebington, Wirral and in Lambeth, south London.

The Merseyside home was run by Catholic nuns and priests and is now closed.

Liverpool-born Carroll was originally charged with 76 offences against 14 children to which he pleaded not guilty. When charges were put to him again today he admitted almost half of them. The others were ordered to lie on file.

The case was adjourned until July 30 for sentencing.

The charges included serious sexual offences, indecent assault and gross indecency between 1966 and 1991.

Carroll ... was sacked by Lambeth Social Services in 1991 after an investigation into financial irregularities.

His arrest in 1997 followed a complaint by a victim.

Carroll claims he was sexually abused as a child at St Edmund's Orphanage.

Some of his victims, now grown men, were visibly upset at today's hearing. (Peter Harvey, *Liverpool Echo* 5 July 1999, p.10)

CHAPTER 1

Setting the Context
A Brief History of Residential Care for Children

Introduction

At one level the issue of abuse of children in residential care can be seen as a straightforward one. It is simply a matter of vulnerable children being exposed to sexual, physical and emotional ill-treatment at the hands of adults in whose care they have been placed by the state. It is a clear case of misuse of power, the potential for which lies within all adults, and it requires a firm response and watertight safeguards to prevent its occurrence in the future.

Yet this explanation seems to be patently insufficient. There must be more to help us understand why abuse to the extent and degree that is currently being discovered could have taken place in residential establishments set up to meet the welfare needs of deprived and disadvantaged children.

In order to achieve this type of understanding, it is important to consider a range of economic, political and social issues that influence policy and practice in regard to the provision of substitute care for children separated from their families. Abuse of children in residential care needs to be understood in terms of the value placed by society upon children in general, in terms of the value placed on poor children, and finally in terms of the value placed on poor children whose parents cannot maintain their care. It also needs to be borne in mind that not all children who come into residential homes do so as the passive poor in need of care. Many are perceived as actively problematic to society because of their antisocial and offending behaviours.

One means of gaining a better understanding of this context is to take a historical view of the use of residential care. It is often easier to evaluate the significance of events in the past than those of the present (though one must always be careful not to judge the past by today's standards). Key lessons can be learned from looking at the past. It is possible to judge whether problems are specific to one period of time or whether they are perennial issues that seem to persist across all ages.

The following outline of key events in the history of residential childcare is undertaken with this in mind. The emphasis, therefore, is on matters such as the following:

- the type of child seen to be in need of residential care over time
- views about the type of care that should be provided for these children
- the aims of residential care in relation to the children placed within it
- the quality of residential care workers
- issues relating to punishment and forms of mistreatment.

To reiterate, the aim of this historical review is to provide a background to help understand revelations about residential childcare in the 1990s. It should be noted that the concern is to aid understanding and the following analysis should not in any way be construed as providing a justification or defence for the extent of abuse currently thought to be prevalent.

From the Middle Ages to early Victorian times: making provision for poor and indigent children

One could be forgiven for thinking that society's concerns about its responsibilities towards abandoned, deprived, neglected and delinquent children were a relatively recent phenomenon. In fact the institutional care of children has a much longer history than might be expected.

Pinchbeck and Hewitt (1973a, 1973b), Heywood (1978), Boswell (1990), Shahar (1990) and Cunningham (1991) provide excellent secondary sources for considering the period from the Middle Ages to 1850, and for this reason this section is derived mainly from material in these accounts.

Pre-Reformation

In the Middle Ages, England was a predominantly rural society and in the country areas where most people then lived 'the manor' (presided over by the local gentry) made provision for the poor and impotent residing within its area of influence, including children who were abandoned, orphaned or born out of wedlock. The approach was communitarian – a child without parents was considered to be a child of the people (see Heywood 1978, p.1).[1] Most often children in these circumstances would be reared by relatives or by child-poor families; it should be noted that able-bodied children in those times were of greater economic benefit to adults than children of today because by the age of 7 most children of the rural poor were working as agricultural labourers.

This state of affairs had been formalised in 1388 by the passing of the Statute of Cambridge, which sought to impose a legal obligation on the 'manor' to make the provision that it had previously carried out on a 'voluntary basis' (see note 1). Another key player in the care of deprived children up to the 1500s was the Church. Monasteries and nunneries provided support for poor families and provided care for orphaned and abandoned children (see Boswell 1990; Shahar 1990).

In the towns which were developing at a very fast rate in the late Middle Ages, the destitute poor were more likely to be housed in hospitals. These hospitals undoubtedly included children, but they would normally be admitted along with family members. Mortality rates among infants in these establishments were very high. Children who survived would be apprenticed to local tradesmen and artisans at an early age, such apprenticeships being paid for out of local taxation.

The Reformation

The period of the Reformation, dating roughly from the early 1500s, saw a revolution in the rural economy with a shift from crop production to animal husbandry and a consequent diminution in the need for farm labourers. This led to a population drift into towns and to a massive increase in vagrancy and begging. Matters were made worse by the assault on the powers and resources of the Church by Henry VIII, which greatly reduced its influence on provision for the poor.

These events led to the passing of the first Poor Law in 1531 which was followed by further legislation in 1536. A strong element of coercion came into play with regard to the treatment of destitute children – local authorities were authorised to round up child beggars and vagrants and to put them to work in apprenticeships.[2] Severe penalties could be imposed for non-compliance. Apprenticeships were the preferred option for destitute children well into the eighteenth century. This form of placement could be seen as an early prototype of modern-day boarding-out or foster care. However, unlike today, where fostering is seen as more likely to meet children's developmental needs than placing them in residential care, the motive at this time was based on cost, pragmatism and the notion of work as the antidote to idleness and mischief. In fact boarding-out was a risky business for the children concerned and of highly variable quality.

Residential care at this time was not really an option. It was perceived as expensive and its proponents were seen as being too concerned with children's spiritual and educational needs. For instance, in 1535 William Marshall, drawing on continental models, advocated that children be educated in residential schools rather than put to work, but his ideas were not well received (see Pinchbeck and Hewitt 1973a, pp.94–95).

CHRIST'S HOSPITAL

The problems of urban vagrancy continued to increase and in 1552 in London the solution opted for was the establishment of four Royal Hospitals, one of which (Christ's) was to cater specifically for destitute children. This was the first true childcare residential establishment to exist in England. It took in 380 children as soon as it opened its doors (see Pinchbeck and Hewitt 1973a, p.95). It provided wet nurses for infants, and lodging and education for older children. The extent of poverty outside of the Hospital made it grossly oversubscribed. This led to concerns about costs and resulted in measures to control the intake of poor children including the provision of outdoor relief to prevent the break-up of families that were deemed to be respectable despite their poverty. Not surprisingly the material and health standards in the Hospital were considered high relative to those found in poverty-stricken families in the community.

Hospitals on the model of Christ's were founded across the country throughout the sixteenth century, but by the middle of the seventeenth century such institutions had been put to other uses and no longer provided care for destitute children. The reason for their decline was largely lack of money.

Workhouses in the seventeenth century

The Poor Law Act 1601 confirmed the duty of the parish to provide for the indigent and needy and further legitimised the raising of local taxes to defray expenses. Outdoor relief, provision of wet nurses and enforced apprenticeships were the main means of dealing with poor children in need of parental care. The residential experiment was reintroduced in London following the passing of an Act in 1647 for the Relief and Employment of the Poor in the form of workhouses (see Pinchbeck and Hewitt 1973a, p.146). Initially these were for adults only, but by the end of the century children were being admitted to such establishments and, soon after, some workhouses were set up specifically for children. The key concerns of such establishments were to train children to be industrious and to ensure that they were equipped to be economically self-sufficient. They were different from earlier forms of residential provision by virtue of the fact that children could be compulsorily detained there and were subjected to more systematic forms of discipline and control.

As with the hospitals in earlier times, concerns were raised about costs and oversubscription. By 1725 it was estimated that there were 129 workhouses across the counties of England (see Pinchbeck and Hewitt 1973a, p.166). Most of these establishments contained children and adults; some were for children only. Standards of care were very variable. For the most part, there was little in the way of education – the focus was on equipping children for a life of menial labour. Health standards for infants were appalling. According to the social reformer, Jonas Hanway, half of children admitted under the age of 3 years were likely to die in the first few weeks of their stay (see Pinchbeck and Hewitt 1973a, pp.177–178).

London Foundling Hospital 1741

The workhouses by no means provided for the size of the problems created for the rest of society by the children of the destitute poor. Abandonment, particularly of illegitimate children, was a constant occurrence, especially in urban areas. It was the sight of children left dead in the streets of London that moved Thomas Coram to start his 20-year campaign to establish the London Foundling Hospital (McClure 1981). In 1741 when it opened, the Hospital was inundated with referrals, reflecting the extreme seriousness of the deprived conditions experienced by the London poor.[3] The Hospital was funded as a charitable institution and, early on, ran to very high standards in a way not dissimilar to that of Christ's Hospital two centuries earlier. Infants were sent to wet nurses in the country and by this means mortality rates were kept lower than was the case in the workhouses. In these early days, the Hospital was careful to select those children for whom success was most likely to result, i.e. those with the least health problems. Within a few years, however, the Hospital ran into financial difficulties and was forced to depend on public funding, as a result of which it was required to relax its selective admission policy. It soon became grossly oversubscribed resulting in soaring mortality rates and a steep decline in the quality of provision offered. Only by a return to the policy of greatly reducing and carefully selecting the children it admitted was it able to function successfully again, which it did until well into the twentieth century.

Children cared for by the parishes in workhouses and by other forms of provision, such as being placed with wet nurses or with apprentice masters, generally fared a lot less well than those placed in an establishment like the

Foundling Hospital. Some attempts were made to raise standards in the London area by setting up means of regulation and inspection of wet nursing arrangements which were notoriously variable (Hanway's Act 1767), but they had little long-term impact and no such measures applied in the rest of England. By the end of the eighteenth century philanthropists like Thomas Gilbert were advocating that children should be excluded from workhouses altogether (see Pinchbeck and Hewitt 1973a, pp.192–193). His wishes were not realised, however. The Poor Law Act 1782 retained both mixed and children-only workhouses, many of which were prison-like with only a few honourable exceptions to the rule.

Young offenders

Prior to the middle of the eighteenth century there is little mention of child offenders or criminals in relation to the provision of residential care, except in the case of children whose parents had been convicted of crimes. Essentially, until this time, children under the age of 7 were not much differentiated from adults in this respect; the emphasis was on their criminality not their age. It was assumed that they were fully aware of the fact that they were doing wrong, and poverty and destitution were clearly not taken into account in making judgements. There was, therefore, no specialist childcare route for young offenders; they were not placed in such childcare establishments as there were.[4] That there was some awareness of youth offending as a special category is evidenced by the fact that children were rarely sentenced to death for offending (see Parsloe 1978).

Summary

It is almost impossible to do justice to developments in the state care of destitute children over a 300-year period in such a brief overview. However, it is possible to point to some general trends and ideas which are relevant to the problems and issues which substitutes for family care raise for us today.

It is obvious how social upheavals and economic change impacted on the state's arrangements for supporting the poor and their children. Urbanisation and changes in the agrarian economy, in the sixteenth century in particular, saw a shift from localised and more individualised community-based responses to destitution, to provision of more large-scale block provision based around more extensive geographical areas.

Three other key features stand out:

- a reluctance to use residential care for children (until the latter half of the eighteenth century)
- the importance attached to making deprived children work for a living
- a preoccupation with costs.

There were notable examples of attempts to provide good standard residential care for children with greater emphasis on education and reasonable health and material standards, but these were the exception rather than the rule. The normal means of substitute care for children – wet nurses, apprenticeships and latterly workhouses – were generally of low standards and characterised by high mortality rates, boredom and drudgery.

There is little firm evidence of gross mistreatment of children cared for outside their families (one exception being court records of cruelty cases brought against apprentice masters (Pollock 1983)), but there are many clues pointing to harsh discipline and poor living conditions. The high infant mortality rate both in residential establishments, and to a lesser extent among children placed with wet nurses, could be seen as an indicator of cruelty and neglect, but such a judgement must be weighed against the original poor state of health of the children when placed and the general high death rates across the UK. Evidence of complaints of ill-treatment in hospitals and workhouses is rare. McClure (1981) paints a rosy picture of the London Foundling Hospital in this respect between 1741 and 1777, but refers to the use of solitary confinement as a punishment thereafter. However, the Foundling Hospital in its early days was something of a showpiece and cannot be used as a typical example of residential provision for destitute children of the time.

Another area which is little commented on is that relating to children who committed offences. While in the nineteenth and twentieth centuries the issue of whether or not to treat delinquent children in the same way as the destitute became a central concern for those providing substitute care, it did not arise in the previous three centuries because young criminals were not greatly differentiated from adult criminals and were subject, therefore, to the same treatment. Put simply, until the 1800s child offenders were not perceived as children, except by social reformers such as Hanway and others (see note 4) and, therefore, were not considered as in need of the type of solutions offered to children of destitute families.

From the model workhouse to the children's home: providing residential correction, training and education

Poor Law Amendment Act 1834

The Poor Law Amendment Act 1834 was introduced at a time of considerable hardship in Britain and increased rates of pauperism. To stem what was seen as the rising tide of begging, dependence and idleness, a tougher approach was advocated making explicit the divide between those deserving of help and those not. Outdoor relief which had been seen as growing to unacceptable levels (and increasing indolence and lack of independence among those receiving it) was to be severely restricted. Families unable (but usually deemed unwilling) to cope were to have no alternative but to enter workhouses and be confronted with harsh and rigorous conditions and standards of treatment which in theory would create in them the will to leave as soon as possible and become self-sufficient again.

The impact of this legislation was to increase the numbers of children in workhouses. In 1838 there were 42,767 children in workhouses. Two years later the number had risen to 64,570, well over half the total workhouse population (see Pinchbeck and Hewitt 1973b, p.500). Figures such as these created great concern among the Poor Law Commissioners, who reacted by ensuring the provision of at least three hours' basic education within the workhouse per day. Soon after, it was agreed that there was a need to create separate educational facilities for children outside the confines of the workhouse. From the 1840s onwards, more and more schools were built – some in the grounds of the workhouses they served, some entirely separate. The latter usually served the needs of two or more Poor Law unions. These schools all had their own residential facilities; thus, children were separated from their families and contact with them was confined to weekends or visits at even longer intervals. District schools (or Barrack Homes), as they were called, could contain as many as 1500 children. Standards of health and education were poor in many of these establishments and regimes were harsh. Even so, up to 1870 when compulsory schooling was introduced, there were frequent complaints voiced about the fact that Poor Law children were receiving education when their age counterparts outside the workhouse were in all likelihood receiving none.

It is interesting how in the second half of the nineteenth century, education had taken over as the key activity for poor children in place of work. For instance the use of apprenticeships following the 1834 Act greatly diminished. This could be seen as progress. A more cynical view is that it reflected changes in the work economy. Put simply, there were fewer requirements for children to work from an early age than in previous eras: they were less and less an economic asset. The standards and qualities of care and education outlined above should also serve to dispel over-positive interpretations of developments between 1834 and 1870.

From 1870 to 1908

The Education Act 1870 which made schooling compulsory for the general child population saw a shift away from Poor Law schools. Children housed by the Poor Law unions could now more easily attend local elementary schools and there was less need for large-scale residential institutions. At the same time, the Boards of Guardians came under the auspices of central government and there was a shift away from the less eligibility ethos in respect of children. Greater attention was paid to providing more child-centred care.

Cottage homes were introduced and renewed emphasis was placed on boarding children out. However, the changes were sporadic and some of the new developments did not lead to markedly better standards of care or less stigmatisation. Most cottage homes, for instance, retained an institutional atmosphere – they housed large numbers of children, albeit in smaller individual units. They (and as a result the children who lived in them) were easily identifiable. Several of these types of establishments still retained schools on the premises with poor educational standards exacerbated by the fact that their teachers were isolated from professional colleagues in the community.[5] As a whole, therefore, they did little to help their young residents to become integrated into the community and little to equip them with the means of coping independently once discharged from their care.

More positive aspects were the development of scattered homes as in Sheffield in 1892, followed by similar schemes in Leeds and Cardiff. Greater use was made of boarding children out with families during this period but, according to Middleton (1971), the standards of substitute care were low. This was largely as a result of narrow perceptions of who should provide such care – only poor families were seen as fit carers for poor children – and the heavy-handed and intrusive nature of the Poor Law inspection system, which acted as a deterrent to those who might have been willing to come forward to help.

The Majority and Minority Reports of the Poor Law Commissioners in 1909 gave an indication of the varied picture existing in the Poor Law system at the turn of the century. In 1903 there were 62,426 indoor pauper children, of whom 16,221 were still being maintained in mixed workhouses (see Pinchbeck and Hewitt 1973b, p.536). Beatrice and Sidney Webb, the authors of the Minority Report, employed their own Children's Investigator, who found that the vast majority of children coming under the purview of the Poor Law were grossly deprived physically and psychologically. Contrary to the views expressed in the Majority Report, the Webbs argued that significant change in terms of the education, health and social needs of children in Poor Law care could not come about under the then existing administrative arrangements (Webb and Webb 1909). They advocated the abolition of the Poor Law guardians and for their duties to be taken over by local authority health and education departments; their view was that these departments had operated to the benefit of children living in the community, and that Poor Law children had been excluded from these benefits by virtue of being under the management of separate bodies unable to divest themselves of the 'less eligibility' principles that had been established nearly a century before. It was not till 1929 that the Minority Report goals were achieved spreading the Poor Law functions between Health, Education and the newly formed Public Assistance Committees.

Dealing with young offenders

By the end of the eighteenth century concerns about young criminals were beginning to exercise the minds of those in power. The Philanthropic Society was the main player. Formed in 1792 in London, this society was one of the first to make special residential provision for young delinquents and thereby divert them from conventional punishments such as imprisonment and transportation. The society seems to have had a chequered history in its early years, dogged by financial problems, the demands of a challenging and unruly clientele, lack of suitable staff and muddled management.

In 1841 the Reverend Sydney Turner took over as chaplain and manager. He was committed to raising standards of education and providing a more humanitarian regime. He was also committed to assessing which children were most likely to benefit from attempts to reform them and to providing different types of regime on the basis of his assessments (see Pinchbeck and Hewitt 1973b, pp.468–469). His overriding message was the need to work strategically with young offenders, to give them responsibility, work training and decent domestic facilities. Turner's views were a major influence on the acceptance of the need for wider and better provision for young offenders outside the penal system for adults. Other influences were protagonists such as

Mary Carpenter, leader of the Voluntary Reform Movement, who was a vigorous critic of the prison system and the Prison Service itself which in the years between 1800 and 1850 had made some attempt to improve its provision for young offenders, most notably in setting up a specialist institution in Parkhurst on the Isle of Wight (Pinchbeck and Hewitt 1973b, pp.471–477).

REFORMATORY SCHOOLS

In 1854 the government in the face of soaring numbers of children in prison (11,348 in 1844: 1 per 300 of 10–20-year-olds in the population) accepted the need to make general provision for young offenders outside the prison system. It passed legislation enabling courts to send such children to reformatory schools. Soon after, in 1857, it made further provision for children over the age of 10 who were on the streets but not convicted of offences to be sent to industrial schools. Both sets of schools came under the supervision of inspectors based in the Home Office (Parsloe 1978). Thus, the separation of older destitute children from the workhouse system was set in train, as was the distinction between offenders and non-offenders, an issue which was at the heart of debates about the use of residential care throughout much of the twentieth century. Regimes in both reformatory and industrial schools were variable, but hard labour, disciplinarianism and corporal punishment were staple features. Despite the report of a Royal Commission in 1884 recommending greater focus on education and less punitive regimes, there was little evidence of change.

As with many developments in residential care for children, attempts to make improvements and to develop more enlightened approaches were only partially successful. Reformatory schools were better overall for children than imprisonment, but created a new set of problems. As with establishments for destitute children, the concern was that standards of care and provision inside residential establishments should not exceed those outside. In particular, young offenders should not appear to be rewarded for their crimes. Pressure to reform children could lead to excessive zealotry.

This combination of factors laid the foundations for regimes which were potentially highly abusive. Rimmer (1985) provides evidence of riots and arson in reformatory schools on Merseyside, events which often arose from and were responded to by harsh physical mistreatment. Mahood (1995) provides similar evidence from Scotland. The inquiry into the use of punishment at the Heswall Reformatory School in 1911 (Masterman 1911) and the subsequent parliamentary debate give some flavour of the quality of the regimes.[6] The harshness of the treatment of children in reformatory (and also industrial) schools to some degree reflected the standards of outside society at the time; it is worth remembering that the birch was in use for young offenders up until the passing of the Criminal Justice Act in 1948. It also reflected prevalent views about the natures and needs of children, i.e. they were largely seen as potentially evil and in need of firm, even severe, handling to ensure that they adhered to the path of righteousness. The influence of religion in this respect is hard for those of us living in more secular times to grasp, but this was the driving force behind such beliefs. Finally, it has to be remembered that the recipients of this approach were all children of the poor. Such children have always been more exposed to advocates of discipline and hard labour than their more privileged peers.

CREATION OF APPROVED SCHOOLS

The Children and Young Persons Act 1933 saw the end of reformatory and industrial schools. Both were suffering a lack of clientele. In the case of reformatory schools, after a rise in juvenile delinquency during the First World War, there was a decline throughout the 1920s and also greater use was being made of probation orders. In the case of industrial schools, the problems of vagrancy had by then greatly reduced; children of the street were a much rarer sight than before. These schools were replaced by approved schools, which were to admit both young offenders and other older children from deprived and neglectful backgrounds, though they tended to cater more for the former. Approved schools remained under the aegis of the Home Office. Many inherited the same sites and buildings as the schools they replaced. However, where they differed most from their predecessors was by placing greater emphasis on education and craft training than on labour and discipline.

Children in care 1908–45

This period, and particularly that between the two world wars, saw the gradual breakdown of the Poor Law system. In the 1920s and 1930s there were more varied sources of support being developed for families in the community, such as pensions, unemployment assistance and health insurance. However, until 1929 the Poor Law system still existed for families and their children who could not maintain an independent life, and the quality of provision for the large numbers of children brought into care as a result did not greatly improve. Even after 1929, it took time for the Poor Law ethos to be less pervasive, as ex-Guardians often took over their former responsibilities in the local authority departments that succeeded their Boards. The poor quality of care was clearly in evidence in the findings of the Curtis Committee report of 1946 which will be considered in more detail in the next section (Curtis 1946). For some children, there had been no changes at all – in 1946 there were still 6500 children in general wards of workhouses (Curtis 1946, para. 32), while 10,000 children continued to be housed in 'Barrack Homes' between the wars. Middleton (1971), in his review of this period, shows that even for children in the more family-type institutions that had evolved, life was dull and unrewarding, dominated by household chores and routines and characterised by a lack of child-centred activities. Worst of all, very little effort was made to enhance contact with birth parents or extended families; indeed, in many places this continued to be actively discouraged.

Both Middleton (1971) and Hendrick (1994) are at pains to point out that in this, as in earlier periods, physical punishment was also a characteristic of residential care. Control and discipline were maintained by the use of birching, particularly in the case of older children. Boys were most at risk of such punishments, but girls were by no means excluded. In one senior approved school for girls, the Curtis Committee found that there had been 34 registered beatings over a 12-month period (Curtis 1946, para. 304).

Summary

In contrast to events in the preceding period, the nineteenth and twentieth centuries saw little reluctance to use residential care for children. For much of this period Poor Law and other provision was made for around 100,000 children, nearly four times the rate for children today. The bulk of these children were looked after in homes, schools and workhouses.

Many of the children were the victims of the state's treatment of their poverty-stricken parents. Residential care was used as a deterrent to those who could not maintain themselves in the community. Fear of the workhouse was used to force families to manage on low wages, low levels of outdoor relief and charity. Children in workhouses were treated in the same stigmatic and insensitive way as their parents. They were subjected to poor living conditions, boring labour routines, poor standards of education and harsh discipline where necessary, and they were cut off from the community. They were easily identifiable as workhouse children and stood as a race apart from others. Children who broke the law were also subjected to residential treatment. For them this was seen as an improvement on pre-existing conditions. Nevertheless, conditions in reformatory schools were generally harsher than in workhouses in terms of punishment and discipline.

It was in this context that the foundations of modern residential care for children were set. The rationale for residential care for children was to make living conditions worse inside than out; these were essentially places of punishment for being poor or places of reform for being bad. Residential staff and teachers in these establishments were generally of poor quality. Their attitudes were in general both patronising and punitive. Children were expected to be grateful for the provision received and punished if they did not toe the line. Keeping down costs was another feature of these establishments.

While in the last third of this period there were developments of a less punitive and more child-sensitive nature, e.g. the attempt to provide smaller homes with more of a family atmosphere, these developments were for the minority of children and by no means always successful in achieving these goals.[7]

Family homes, fostering and prevention: 1945 to the present

Catalysts for change in the 1940s

A series of events during and around the Second World War had a major impact on thinking about the provision of residential care for disadvantaged children.

The first of these was the impact of child evacuation from city to country areas to protect against the effects of enemy bombing. According to Parker (1983), government committees were meeting as early as 1943 to consider potential substitute care needs for large numbers of evacuees who it was feared were likely still to be displaced by the end of the war. It was clear even then that the existing forms of residential care, dominated by large voluntary and public assistance homes, would be unacceptable in post-war society.

Professionals in the fields of child psychology and welfare (mainly female) were pointing to the emotional needs of evacuees and the impact on them of sudden separations from their parents (see Burlingham and Freud 1942). Their views emphasised the need for substitute care of a far more sensitive kind than had previously been available.

Another major factor in the shift in thinking about new forms of residential care was the pioneering work of Lady Allen of Hurtwood, who led a publicity campaign in 1944 to establish a committee of inquiry to look into the issue. She received massive encouragement from the large numbers of letters sent to her by former children's homes residents. She stressed that she had 'had only one letter from an individual telling me of her happy childhood in a Home' (Allen 1945, p.3). The main features of the accounts she received were as follows: monotony, strict discipline, stigma, poor material and dietary standards, poor quality of staff, inappropriate placements and lack of contact with birth families.

By early 1945 the government was committed to setting up the sought-after inquiry into the needs of children separated from their parents. This decision was further vindicated by the findings of two highly publicised inquiries which reported in February and May of the same year: the Vick (1945) report, which examined the circumstances of a 7-year-old girl placed in a London County Council Remand Home for girls aged 14 to 17 and the Monckton (1945) report into the killing of Dennis O'Neill, a 13-year-old boy placed in a foster home in Shropshire. Both strongly emphasised the lack of coordination between the numerous bodies which shared responsibility for the welfare of children in the care of the state.

CURTIS COMMITTEE REPORT 1946

Dame Myra Curtis and James Clyde were appointed to head the two resulting committees of inquiry (for England and Wales, and Scotland respectively), which reported in 1946.

The Curtis (1946) report provides a similar picture of residential care to that painted by Lady Allen of Hurtwood:

> Our impression was rather that the lack of understanding of children's needs led with the best of intentions to a dreary uninteresting life in many of the Homes, and that this showed itself in a lack of liveliness and vigour in the children. (Curtis 1946, para. 210)

Hendrick (1994) infers that the committee was too keen to provide a balanced picture, and dodged the issue of cruelty and excessive punishment particularly in regard to approved schools, which also came under its inquiry remit. Whatever the case, the committee placed its emphasis on the future rather than on the past. Its aim was to ensure

> that all deprived children have an upbringing likely to make them sound and happy citizens and that they all have chances, educational and vocational, of making a good start in life that are open to children in normal homes. (Curtis 1946, para. 435)

Its key recommendation in pursuit of this goal was the formation of new departments dedicated to providing for the care needs of deprived children – children's departments.

After much internal wrangling within central government (see Parker 1983), the Home Office emerged ahead of Education and Health as the department that would oversee the work of this new initiative. Its main claim to this lead role was a rather dubious one – its experience in organising inspections of approved schools. Nevertheless, it presided until 1971 when social services departments took over the responsibilities of the children's departments under the aegis of the Department of Health and Social Security. Arguably, the period between 1948 and 1971 was one of the most successful eras in the history of residential care for children.

Replicating the family: 1948 to 1971

From the start of this period there was a new sense of optimism and a determination to give prime consideration to the welfare of children when making provision for them to be cared for away from their families.

Following on from the work of the wartime psychologists referred to above, Bowlby (1952) developed his maternal deprivation theory. This had a telling influence on the new developments in the childcare field, resulting in boarding out and family group homes becoming the two main cornerstones of substitute care.

Boarding out with foster parents came to be seen as the most desirable resource for children needing care away from their own families, and much was done to ensure that the proportion of children cared for in this way was raised over time. In 1949 the percentage of children boarded out was 35 per cent. By 1969 it had risen to 48 per cent, the high point during this period being 52 per cent in 1965.

Small group homes were seen as the next best thing, homes which could create near-family environments for children separated from their birth parents. Such homes were used increasingly in the 1950s and 1960s, but in 1969, for all the expressed concerns, they still accommodated only about a quarter of all children in statutory care. They did not become the main mode of residential care until the 1990s by which time, as we shall see, the numbers of children living in such establishments had reduced dramatically.

Homes with large numbers of children, which were common in the voluntary sector, began to be viewed with increasing disquiet; they were seen as too institutional. Cottage homes in particular fell into disfavour: not only did they house large numbers of children but also they were easily identifiable and therefore created the potential for stigmatisation. Such establishments continued to be in use in some areas well into the 1970s, though every effort was made to make them more like family homes by breaking them down into separately run units with particular staff dedicated to small groups of children.

PREVENTING THE NEED FOR CARE

There can be little doubt that this period saw significant improvements in the quality of care compared with the provision offered up to the end of the Second World War. However, there were growing concerns that too many children were coming into care unnecessarily; in fact although the absolute numbers were rising, the percentage of the child population in care remained fairly constant because of the rising birth-rate (see Table 1.1).[8] Nevertheless, their admissions were increasingly coming to be seen as preventable by social work professionals provided families could be supported with casework and material aid. This was made more possible following the findings of the Ingleby Committee in 1960 and the subsequent Children and Young Persons Act 1963 which empowered local authorities to allocate resources to preventive work (Ingleby 1960).

Table 1.1 Numbers and rates of children in care (England and Wales) 1949–70		
Year	Numbers	Rate per 1000 children under 18
1949	55,255	5.5
1954	58,987	5.6
1960	61,729	5.0
1963	64,807	5.1
1966	69,157	5.3
1970	71,200	5.2

figures from: Dingwall and Eekelaar (1984)

APPROVED SCHOOLS

One area of residential care where significant changes did not take place during this period was that of approved schools. These establishments were not viewed in the same way as other residential homes. They were essentially schools to reform young offenders. Their emphasis was on character- training, instilling discipline and providing education. They stood apart from mainstream residential care both in terms of aims and in terms of values and ethos.

In 1949 approved schools had 9000 residents and in 1969 just prior to their closure they had 7000. In 1960 they came under the scrutiny of the Ingleby Committee (referred to above) which was set up in the light of growing juvenile delinquency rates. This committee recognised linkages between neglect and offending and, therefore, that many children in approved schools came from deprived backgrounds, not dissimilar to those of children in other forms of residential care. Nevertheless, it did not recommend substantial changes to the administration of approved schools.

By the end of the 1960s, however, it was clear that these schools had run their course. The links between deprivation and delinquency were constantly stressed in a stream of government White Papers and this new style of thinking pointed to the need for less authoritarian and more therapeutic types of intervention (see Hendrick 1994, pp.229–235).

The Court Lees inquiry which condemned excessive use of corporal punishment in a school in Surrey (Home Office 1967) seemed to symbolise the issues.[9] A more measured child-centred approach was seen to be required in a society where there were signs of growing affluence and challenges to older orthodoxies.

CHILDREN AND YOUNG PERSONS ACT 1969

The outcome was the Children and Young Persons Act 1969 which, when implemented in 1971, abolished approved schools and replaced them with local authority administered community homes with education on the premises. These new establishments (mostly revamped approved schools) were intended to transform into establishments that worked with individual children to resolve emotional and social problems. They were to be social worker-dominated rather than teacher-dominated establishments.

Issues arising in the 1970s

NUMBERS

The numbers of children in care appeared to rise dramatically during the first half of the 1970s and to stay at that level in the second half of that period (see Table 1.2).[10]

**Table 1.2 Numbers and rates of children in care
in England and Wales 1971–80**

Year	Number	Rate per 1000 children under 18
1971	87,400	6.4
1974	95,900	6.9
1976	100,600	7.3
1980	100,200	7.8

figures from: Dingwalls and Eekekaar (1984)

The number of children in all kinds of residential homes remained between 40,000 and 45,000 until the late 1970s. About 9000 children were in small group homes, about 14,000 were in larger homes or assessment centres, 6500 were in community homes with education on the premises, 5500 in voluntary homes, 2000 in homes specifically for children with disabilities and 1500 in residential nurseries. The boarding-out rate hovered at around 40 per cent of the total numbers of children in care.

CARE AND CONTROL

Residential childcare in the 1970s presents a mixed and ambiguous picture. In broad terms, it was a decade in which a more child-centred approach was aspired to; certainly there was an attempt to adopt this type of approach with older children and particularly those who had committed offences, replacing the more disciplinarian approach of the approved schools. How successful this was in practice, however, is another question. Of growing concern as the decade proceeded was the need for appropriate methods of containing young people with difficult and challenging behaviours under the new regimes. Staff training should have been one of the obvious answers, but even by the mid-1980s little had been done to improve the quality of residential workers. Social work qualification rates were at about 4 per cent throughout the decade. Many of the staff seconded to social work courses turned to the more prestigious activity of fieldwork once they had received their certificates.

FOSTERING AND ADOPTION

Two factors account for increased importance being attached to fostering and adoption and a resultant decline in interest in residential care. First, there were growing concerns about the emotional needs of large numbers of younger children in residential homes. Rowe and Lambert's (1973) influential study pointed to the need for a more assertive and proactive use of permanent fostering or adoption in order to solve this problem. Second, there was the problem of cost. Following the monetary crisis of 1976, local authorities were forced to consider cost-cutting exercises after a decade of growth. Residential care was a relatively expensive part of the childcare budget. Thus, fostering and adoption were seen both as cheaper and more professionally desirable ways of providing substitute care for children. The belief that fostering was the best form of substitute care for children whose parents could not cope was not (as we have already seen) a new phenomenon. However, the cost element was, and it added fresh urgency to the drive to find families to foster.

The 1980s: diversion from care

By the early 1980s social services departments were beginning to reduce the number of children coming into care and divert more and more of those that did enter care into fostering and adoption. As regards the former, research carried out at Lancaster University had an enormous impact. Thorpe (1980) found that large numbers of children brought into care for offending did not meet the 'in need of care and protection' criteria set out in the Children and Young Persons Act 1969 and, therefore, were not in need of residential care. Another fact to be taken into account was the high reoffending rates of children in care. In other words residential care was both ineffective and unnecessary for this type of youngster. This capped the factors already outlined above.

Some local authorities started to make drastic cut-backs. Warwickshire took the most extreme position, closing all its residential facilities, relying instead on community measures and the use of out-of-county residential resources in extreme cases. Staffordshire Social Services Department, which later on in the decade was the subject of a major child abuse scandal, cut its residential facilities by nearly half at the beginning of the 1980s. It placed great reliance on family centres which were part community and part residential facilities (see Staffordshire County Council 1991). The result of these kinds of changes in many local authorities was one of chaos and confusion. Staff morale was lowered. Those that were retained within the residential services sector often found themselves working with unfamiliar age-groups and in very different regimes from those to which they had been accustomed. The closure of homes often took place in an abrupt manner and with no prior consultation with the children concerned. As can be seen in Table 1.3, the reduction of the children in care population continued throughout the 1980s with the major shrinkage taking place in the residential sector.

Table 1.3 Numbers and rates of children in care in England and Wales 1984–89		
Year	**Number**	**Rate per 1000 children under 18**
1984	78,900	6.5
1985	73,300	6.1
1986	70,900	6.0
1987	69,200	5.9
1988	67,800	5.8
1989	65,400	5.6

figures from: Childern in Care in England and Wales 1989. Dept of Health

By 1989 the boarding-out rate had risen to 55 per cent (from 40 per cent in the late 1970s). There were 1500 children in children's homes with education (compared with just under 6000 in 1979). In all there were about 19,000 children living in some form of residential accommodation, fewer than half the number in 1979.

The 1990s: more of the same

The 1990s saw a continuation of the trends in the 1980s. The number of children in care only in England in 1997 was 51,600, having reached a low point of 49,300 in 1994. This represents a rate of 5.0 per 1000 children under 18. Approximately 65 per cent of these children were boarded out and 10,500 were in residential care. There were just over 1200 children's homes in operation, about two-thirds of which were local authority managed. The 1990s saw a large increase in private homes, there being approximately 200 in 1997. Large children's homes have virtually become a thing of the past – only 46 homes in 1997 accommodated more than 20 children. It is notable that 13 local authorities had no residential establishments which they managed within their own boundaries (see DoH 1998a).

There have been two recent significant reports about residential care. The first of these looked at the whole picture of children living away from their own homes (Utting 1997). This report highlights the fact that children in residential care facilities form only a small proportion of all those children living away from home; there are larger numbers in hospitals (12,000), boarding schools (84,000) and residential special schools (21,000). It stresses the need for greater awareness of the welfare and protection needs of all these children. However, it reaffirms the importance of residential care and its utility particularly for older children from deprived backgrounds. It warns against further cut-backs, arguing the need for there to be sufficient variety within local authority and regional areas to enable children to be placed appropriately in terms of their needs and not too far from their family homes.

The second report, *Caring for Children Away from Home* (DoH 1998a), summarises a series of government-sponsored research projects into the quality of residential care. A picture emerges of small homes with older children, many of whom have experienced deprived and abusive home lives prior to coming into care. These children present a range of challenging behaviours (violent and sexual) to staff. About half of the homes provide reasonably positive atmospheres, but there are problems in many homes with bullying, meeting educational needs and providing adequate leaving care facilities.

Summary

The second half of the twentieth century has seen many significant changes in the provision of residential care for children. The most notable of these have been in relation to the following:

- The size of the population looked after in homes and residential schools care – the numbers have reduced considerably, particularly in the 1980s and 1990s.

- The size of the homes themselves – small children's homes are now the norm. It was clear, even in the late 1940s, that smaller children's homes were most likely to provide the best atmospheres for care because they most replicated 'normal' family life.

- The ages of children accommodated – boarding out gradually became the standard form of substitute care for younger children. In the 1980s and 1990s children's homes became almost solely the province of older children.

In terms of ethos, the whole period has been characterised by seeing care as a last resort in the case of family breakdown. With regard to young offenders, this last resort philosophy has also been in evidence particularly since the late 1970s. Control of children in care has been a constant problem – this was seen as a particular concern for approved schools and community homes with education until the early 1980s. As general children's homes have been required to take on older children with more challenging behaviours, the issues of containment and punishment have become more central. These issues will be considered more fully in the following chapters. For the moment, it should be noted that control and discipline have been regulated centrally by means of community homes' regulations. Corporal punishment, which figured largely in approved schools, was still permissible in children's homes until 1990. In reality, however, nearly all local authorities had prohibited its use by the early 1980s.

One area where there had been little progress until the 1990s was the quality of staff. Residential workers in childcare have for the most part remained poorly qualified and ill-equipped to carry out the tasks required of them. It is notable that even today in a much smaller and more specialised service, rates of relevant qualification remain as low as 15 per cent. It is only recently as a result of several concerning public inquiries (see the Introduction) that there has been a concerted effort to examine recruitment policies and practices (Warner 1992).

So, while residential childcare services have improved considerably since the dark days of the Poor Law, the changes have been less dramatic than might have been expected. Residential care has always suffered and continues to suffer from being a service for the children of the poor, and from being seen as a last resort measure for children separated from their families.

Concluding comments

This historical tour has looked at how the ambivalence of the state with regard to providing out-of-home care for children has affected the provision of residential care. In earlier times issues of cost and fears of undermining the will and motivation of families were the main reasons for not ensuring high standards of residential care for children. While these factors persist to some degree, they have taken second place to concerns about the need to pay more attention to meeting children's emotional needs by supporting families to prevent admissions and placing more children in foster homes. In the midst of all this, residential care has tended to be overlooked and given low priority. As we shall see, it has taken major concerns about child abuse in the wider society to draw attention to this neglected sector of childcare policy and practice.

Notes

1   It should be noted that the communitarian approach we have described was underpinned by the economic and political realities of the time. The rural economy was totally under the control of the 'manor' and there was no alternative labour market. Both adult peasants and their children were labour commodities. Thus what might seem to be an enlightened community response to the problem of destitute children is not the full picture.

2   A distinction was made between disabled children who were perceived to have a right to beg and the rest who were regarded as 'sturdy beggars' and therefore capable of work (Pinchbeck and Hewitt 1973a).

3   McClure's (1981) account of the opening night of the Foundling Hospital makes fascinating reading. She quotes from the Hospital's minutes:

> About Twelve o'Clock the House being full the Porter was Order'd to give Notice of it to the Crowd who were without thereupon being a little troublesome. One of the Govrs. went out and told them that as many Children were already taken in as Cou'd be made Room for in the House and that Notice shou'd be given by a Publick Advertisement as soon as any more Could possibly be admitted... On this Occasion the Expressions of Grief of the Women whose Children could not be admitted were Scarcely more observable than those of some of the Women who parted with their Children, so that a more moving scene can't well be imagined. (p.50)

4   Notable exceptions were provided by the work of Sir John Fielding and Jonas Hanway, who had previously contributed to the establishment of the Foundling Hospital. They were concerned to make provision for the reform of young prostitutes. The Magdalen Hospital set up by Hanway and another reformer, Robert Dingley, provided for 2851 girls and young women between 1758 and 1793 (Pinchbeck and Hewitt 1973a, p.120).

5   As we shall see in Chapter 8 this issue was still in evidence in children's homes with education in the 1970s and 1980s; it was a concern for the North Wales Tribunal of Inquiry in respect of Bryn Estyn. Research in recent times has highlighted the poor educational achievements of children in care and this is a centre-point of the standards now being set by the Department of Health (see DoH 1998b).

6   Two former members of staff of the Heswall Reformatory School (also known as the SS Akbar, the name of the ship moored in the River Dee which housed the original school) alleged that there had been excessive use of birching and that boys had been gagged and muffled to prevent their cries being heard outside the school grounds. There were other allegations including keeping children standing still beside their beds throughout the night, and drenching them in freezing water. The deaths of two boys were said to have been linked to excessive punishment. The Masterman inquiry found no real substance to these allegations. The debate following on from the report being presented to Parliament shows how for the most part severe punishment was thought to be acceptable for young offenders. The Member of Parliament (MP) for Wirral, the constituency in which the SS Akbar school was situated, 'reminded the House of the class of boys the superintendent had to deal with, and the necessity for severe discipline. If there had been any mistakes in the infliction of punishment, the publicity of the inquiry and the report would be security against a repetition of the punishments' (*The Times* 24 February 1911).

7   The Curtis Committee report provides some contrasting pictures of children's homes:

Some of us saw with distress thirty toddlers at a Convent Home, who were being cared for by a woman of very low mentality who had been a girl in the home and was then 28 and incapable of working outside. The children rushed at us, pulled, petted, clung and felt our clothes and possessions ... In striking contrast to this Home was a small villa Home for girls aged 5 to 14. When we visited some of them were getting ready to have tea in the garden (a pleasant large garden with plenty of grass). Some were playing with a see-saw and the old dog, others had toys, balls and other games. They all appeared happy and occupied and took no notice of visitors in whom they were not in the least interested. (Curtis 1946, para. 264)

8   It should be noted that there were significant numbers of children in voluntary residential and foster homes not technically recorded as children in care. In 1949 there were 28,000 such children and in 1970 there were 8000. If one takes these figures into account, then the absolute numbers of children being cared for in residential homes away from their families is fairly constant over this 20-year period and in fact represents a decline in the proportion of under-18 children in such situations.

9   There were two inquiries into approved schools predating Court Lees. The first of these (at Standon Farm) was concerned with the shooting of a staff member and the second (Carleton) with a riot (Home Office 1947, 1959). While neither of these inquiries was directly concerned with ill-treatment of young residents, they nevertheless give some insight into the quality of the regimes of the period.

10   On closer examination it appears that the rise in numbers results more from statistical changes than from a sudden intake of additional children into care from the community. The leap in numbers between 1970 (see Table 1.1) and 1971 can be accounted for by the transfer of large numbers of children from criminal to care statistics. By 1974 all the children in approved schools were incorporated in children in care statistics. Also all children in voluntary care were included in children in care statistics following the implementation of the Children and Young Persons Act 1969. Any actual rises that took place in the 1970s is accounted for by Dingwall and Eekelaar (1984) as the result of conservative practices in regard to discharging of orders. Nearly a fifth (18,700) of 'children in care' in 1979 were in fact living at home under statutory orders.

CHAPTER 2

Children, Society and Child Abuse

State ambivalence towards residential care of children

It is clear from a reading of Chapter 1 that the state has always been ambivalent in its use of residential care for children. Early on in history, such provision was seen as an expensive option and one with a potential for undermining the responsibilities of poor families. Later, it was used in a punitive way to deter families from breaking up, and as a means of training and controlling young offenders. In more recent times, because of concerns about its potential for exacerbating emotional deprivation, residential care has been seen as an option of last resort with prevention of family breakdown and the use of foster care and adoption as preferred options – a reasonable judgement in some ways, but not without negative consequences.

Underlying the state's ambivalence has been its reliance on the family as the natural means of bringing up children. As a consequence, there has been a lack of sustained concern to ensure the maintenance of high standards of practice in residential care, as evidenced by indicators such as the low qualification rate of the vast majority of those working in children's homes (Crimmens 2000). Arguably, another indicator of this indifference has been a lack of emphasis on careful monitoring of the treatment of children in residential establishments. As we noted in the Introduction, it was not until the early 1990s that concern about maltreatment of children in residential care truly came on to the social policy agenda.

In the research we carried out into the history of residential institutions, there was very little written about efforts to monitor the standards of treatment of children in state care. Surprisingly few official concerns were raised in the period between 1800 and 1950. For instance, in a review of reports in *The Times* into official concerns about the ill-treatment of children in Poor Law institutions between 1834 and 1900, only a very small number of cases were found. There was minimal public concern raised about reformatory and industrial schools throughout the whole of their existence between the 1850s and 1933; the Heswall Reformatory School case referred to in Chapter 1 was the only major case inquired into. The only other case raising national concern during the whole of the period in question was that concerning the placement of the young girl in a remand centre in 1945 (Vick 1945).

Moving on, we found evidence of only six formal inquiries into residential care between 1950 and 1990. Three of these were in approved schools, and have already been referred to (Home Office 1947, 1959, 1967). As noted in Chapter 1, technically only one of these, the Court Lees inquiry, was directly concerned with child abuse. In the 1980s there were two inquiries into the sexual abuse of young people (Department of Health and Social Security (Northern Ireland) (Lewisham 1985; DHSS(NI)) 1986) and one into the excessive use of physical restraints in an establishment for older girls (Social Services Inspectorate 1988). None of these six inquiries raised general concerns about the standards of care being provided more widely in the residential sector. Most were seen as isolated incidents of abuse confined to the particular establishments where they occurred. There was no general examination of the standards of residential care for children by the state after the Curtis Committee, which reported in 1946 (Curtis 1946), until the Wagner (1988) report, which was concerned with determining indicators of good practice in residential care for all client groups.

As we pointed out in the Introduction, this was in stark contrast to what happened in the 1990s. The aim of this chapter is to try to explain the reasons for this wave of concern about institutional abuse after so many years of apparent unconcern. In order to do this, we will look at events and changes in relation to notions about childhood in the wider society and in particular at the development of concerns about child abuse from the late 1960s onwards.

Physical child abuse: 1962–87

There are several useful and informative accounts of the growth of concern about child abuse in Britain in recent times (Parton 1985; Corby 1993; Merrick 1996; Parton, Thorpe and Wattam 1997). The emphasis here, however, is on why the concerns took the form that they did with a view to understanding the impact they had on thinking about children in residential care.

It should be noted that concerns about the abuse of children in their own homes by their parents and caretakers is not purely a modern issue. The late Victorians were just as determined to tackle child physical abuse as we have been in recent times. The 1880s and 1890s saw the formation of the National Society for the Prevention of Cruelty to Children (NSPCC) and the passing of a series of laws to enable the state to intervene more effectively into families to protect children (Behlmer 1982). This was a period of alerting society to the problem of child maltreatment across all classes and of pressurising for reforms and changes of attitude. The momentum of these developments persisted until the First World War, but subsided after that. While the NSPCC carried on its child protective work throughout the whole of the period between then and the late 1960s (when child abuse became a major public concern again), it did so in a much less overt way than before. By the 1920s and 1930s its focus had come to rest more on poor standards of childcare among deprived families.

In the 1960s, therefore, there was limited public awareness of the abuse of children in families in Britain. This was also true of the USA. However, in 1962, Henry Kempe, an American paediatrician, first raised the issue by asserting that a high percentage of babies who were presented to hospitals as having experienced accidents had in fact been assaulted. By use of X-ray techniques, it had become possible to detect older, healed fractures in babies brought to clinics with new injuries in suspicious circumstances (Kempe *et al.* 1962). Kempe argued that these injuries were often inflicted by parents who lacked the emotional capacity to care adequately for their infants. He went on to argue that early identification of problems allied to temporary removal of the child and therapeutic treatment for the parents was the answer.

Kempe's ideas about battered babies were taken up in Britain in the late 1960s. Indeed, both in the UK and in the USA, from this rather narrow initial focus, concerns about the ill-treatment of children spread wider and wider. In 1974, the case of Maria Colwell hit the headlines. This little girl of 7 had died as a result of being beaten and neglected by her stepfather and mother after having been in the care of the local authority. A public inquiry was held (DHSS 1974), which was highly critical of the lack of coordination between different health and welfare agencies and recommended the establishment of more formal inter-agency systems for dealing with cases of child abuse, a recommendation which was implemented almost immediately across the UK.

This inquiry, though not quite the first of this era, took strong hold on the public imagination and the issue of physical child abuse was firmly established. It was followed by a host of other inquiries in the second half of the 1970s, all concerned with physical abuse and neglect of babies and young children mostly already known to welfare agencies prior to their deaths. The 1980s saw little let-up in these developments; in particular in the second half of the 1980s there were several highly publicised inquiries which captured the headlines, most notably those relating to Jasmine Beckford (Brent 1985), Kimberley Carlile (Greenwich 1987) and Tyra Henry (Lambeth 1987). The findings of these reports were in similar vein to those in relation to Maria Colwell in the previous decade. The main concerns were about a lack of coordination between agencies and a lack of focus on the needs of children as distinct from the rights of the parents. While there was now a more formal system for responding to child abuse situations, it was not producing results. One of the problems rarely identified in any of the reports was the increased referral rates as professional (and, to a lesser extent, public) awareness took hold, and the fact that resource allocation to the problem was not commensurate.

Accounting for the new wave of childcare concern

How can we account for this massive upsurge in concern about abuse of children in their own homes during this period? Various reasons have been put forward.

Professional self-interest has been argued by some. Pelton (1978) was of the view that the paediatric profession in the USA was searching for a new role as child disease and mortality were reducing. Parton (1985) has argued that the NSPCC, who were influential in transferring Kempe's ideas to the British scene, were searching for a new role, as their mainstream work with children and families had been increasingly taken over by state social work services. Nelson (1984) in the USA and Parton (1979) in the UK pointed to ways in which politicians used child abuse to promote campaigns and policies. In the British case, Parton argued that the then-Conservative government saw child abuse as a means of targeting services to those most in need, a policy it was pursuing with the intention of reducing welfare costs.

However, while these accounts undoubtedly have some explanatory value, they are not sufficient because they do not take into account broader societal changes from the 1960s onwards which created the climate in which child-sensitive initiatives were more readily adopted. Increasing affluence, particularly in the USA, and higher standards of living were the major factors behind the development of greater attention being paid to children during this period. Another major contributory factor, linked to that of increased affluence, was the shift towards smaller families as a result of decreases in infant mortality rates, greater control over childhood diseases and wider access to contraception. As a consequence of these developments, individual children gained more importance than before and their parents invested more in them. Greater attention was paid to a wider range of children's needs than before, particularly to their emotional needs. Childcare manuals, such as those of Dr Benjamin Spock (1966) encouraged more intimate relationships between parents and children, in contrast to the emphasis on greater discipline which had been advocated by childcare experts until the early 1950s. Greater focus was being placed on the notion of childhood as a protected time in which children should enjoy freedom from the sorts of responsibilities that surely awaited them in adulthood.

It was in this atmosphere that Henry Kempe's concerns about baby battering were raised (Kempe *et al.* 1962). The effect was one of considerable outrage. The fact that at a time when children were becoming increasingly more important as individuals to their parents, some were being seriously and fatally abused by them, was patently unacceptable.

A broadening of concerns

Kempe's model of abuse with its focus on emotionally deprived parents lacking the ability to nurture their own children kept the focus of concern on child abuse within the family. This model of thinking considerably influenced British thinking about child abuse from the mid-1970s to the mid-1980s. Until the mid-1980s, in Britain the term 'child abuse' essentially meant physical abuse of children within their own families. Little consideration was given at this time to the possibility of abuse of children in residential or substitute care. While residential homes were seen as a last option for children who were considered to need to be in families to ensure their emotional well-being, they were not perceived as possibly abusive environments. The family, despite being generally seen as the best means of rearing children, was also coming to be seen as a potentially dangerous place for a growing minority (see Gelles and Cornell 1985).

In the middle to late 1980s in Britain, there was a widening of concerns about abuse of children. Child protection statistics showed a massive increase in registrations during this period, mainly in areas other than physical abuse (see Corby 1993). Neglect and emotional abuse had come on to the child abuse agenda – and most importantly, so had child sexual abuse. This broadening of concerns had taken place somewhat earlier in the USA where the child abuse industry developed at an exponential rate throughout the 1970s and early 1980s. Researchers into child abuse in the USA during this period were taking a much broader perspective and placing more and more emphasis on the emotional quality of children's lives and not just on their physical treatment. Particular attention was given to the consequences of abuse on individual lives. This was an outstanding feature of the development of child sexual abuse as a social problem.

The underlying reasons for these developments continued to be the prizing of childhood, but strong impetus came from the feminist movement which spread through the USA and the UK in the 1970s and early 1980s. Sexual abuse of children was seen by feminists as a gendered crime caused by patriarchal structures and relationships in society (Rush 1980; Dominelli 1986). They placed far less emphasis on individual pathology as a reason for such abuse taking place. Again the focus was mainly on intrafamilial abuse, but more attention was paid to sexual abuse outside the family than had been the case with physical abuse and neglect. This is because women's accounts of sexual abuse often involved both forms of abuse (see Russell 1984).

By the beginning of the 1980s in the USA there was common agreement about some core factors in relation to child sexual abuse. First, it had become accepted that such abuse was far more widespread than had previously been thought, both within and outside the family (Russell 1986). Second, it affected a wider range of children (including some at a very early age) than had previously been considered to be the case (Macfarlane and Waterman 1986). Third, it was becoming more accepted that children tended not to lie or fantasise about being sexually abused (Miller 1985). Fourth, the long-term consequences of sexual abuse were seen as potentially extremely debilitating and damaging (Finkelhor and associates 1986).

These ideas initially took hold rather spasmodically in Britain. In London, Ben-Tovim and his colleagues (1988) developed techniques for treating intrafamilial sexual abuse. In Leeds, practitioners were starting to work on extrafamilial abuse carried out by paedophile rings (Wild 1986). However, concerns about intrafamilial sexual abuse came to a head in Britain with events that took place in Cleveland in 1987. There, 121 children were made the subject of emergency care orders within a period of six months based largely on the evidence of a controversial physical test for anal abuse. The ensuing report (Butler-Sloss 1988) did not reach clear conclusions as to whether the children concerned had all been abused, but focused instead on the poor quality of interprofessional activity and on the insensitive treatment of both parents and children. The key significant factor about Cleveland was its concern about what the inquiry panel saw as overzealous intrusion into family life. It posted a warning that there was a limit to the forms of action to be taken in regard to protecting children. This did not necessarily represent a reduction in the prizing of childhood, but rather it placed question marks on the strategies being adopted to ensure what was in the best interests of the child.

Taking the focus off the family

Following on from Cleveland, therefore, there was greater uncertainty about how to deal with child abuse within the family. Despite the prizing of childhood which characterised the 1960s and 1970s and despite the vast increase in knowledge about the extent, range and consequences of child abuse which it generated, the methods used by professionals to protect children within families were beginning to be seen as excessive and unacceptably intrusive. On the other hand, child abuse persisted and was no less acceptable than before. Indeed, there were several key inquiries into the deaths of children living at home following Cleveland, the most notable of which were those relating to Doreen Aston (Lambeth, Lewisham and Southwark 1989), Stephanie Fox (Wandsworth 1990) and Sukina (Bridge 1991).

The problem for the state in the 1990s was how to resolve this dilemma, i.e. the need to do justice to the prizing of children without alienating the key instrument of child socialisation, the family. The answer adopted has been to reframe the issue, so that instead of seeing parents as abusers from whom their children need protection, they should, except in the worst circumstances, be worked with and provided with help and support to ensure that their children are not exposed to further risk. This shift in focus has been promoted by a variety of mechanisms.

Children Act 1989 and Working Together guidelines 1991

First, the Children Act 1989 introduced the new legal concept of parental responsibility and a raft of new family support measures. At the same time it retained and extended child protection measures and increased somewhat the rights of children.

Second, new Working Together guidelines introduced in 1991 reflected the shift to working more cooperatively with parents involved in child protection procedures (DoH 1991a). In particular these guidelines emphasised the need to involve parents and children (where appropriate) more fully in decision-making processes, most particularly at child protection conferences and subsequent planning meetings.

Messages from Research 1995 and beyond

A third factor influencing the shift in thinking about and responding to intrafamilial child abuse in the 1990s has been the findings and interpretation of research sponsored by the Department of Health following Cleveland. This research was summarised in 1995 in a document entitled *Child Protection:*

Messages from Research (DoH 1995), which has had a major impact on child protection policy and practice.

The key findings of this research were that the child protection system was dominated by and geared towards dealing with families where serious physical and sexual abuse was suspected, but that in fact these types of cases formed only a very small part of the total number of referrals. Most of the children referred to the child protection system were only at moderate risk of actual abuse, but many of these were subject to low standards of parental care and in some cases neglect. By and large these cases were not given particular attention despite research pointing to the fact that persistent neglect can have some of the worst effects on children's development of all forms of child abuse. The parents in many of these families were seen to have multiple problems and difficulties, but rarely received ongoing services and support because of the focus on more serious abuse. The *Messages from Research* document argued for a change in thinking about child abuse, for greater awareness of the needs of a wider range of children and for a shift of focus away from abuse towards families' needs for support, except in the most serious cases.

Finally, following on from *Messages from Research* there has been a series of more family-supportive measures introduced in 2000, including new *Working Together* guidelines (DoH 2000a) and broader assessment tools to enable social workers to assess a wider range of children's needs in families than just those relating to protection (DoH 2000b).

Thus, the 1990s have seen major changes in thinking about child abuse. There has been no diminution of concerns about children. Children are as valued in the 1990s as they were in the 1960s – probably even more so. Writers such as Beck (1992) have argued that, as western societies become more technologically advanced, expectations of gaining control over our environments increase and we become more and more preoccupied with reducing and eliminating risks. Applying this sort of thinking to children, we see a trouble-free and protected childhood as the norm. In this climate, child abuse is increasingly unacceptable. The issue is not whether to intervene to protect children at risk, but how. There is now much greater circumspection about tackling all but the most serious forms of abuse within families in a head-on fashion, i.e. using the methods of intervention which were encouraged throughout much of the 1970s and 1980s. The officially required approach to moderate intrafamilial abuse, poor standards of care and neglect in the 1990s is a more strategic one that is aimed at supporting and developing the strengths of parents. This way of thinking is clearly not without its critics and there are many that feel that such strategic approaches could put more children at risk of serious abuse (Bridge 1998; NSPCC 1999).

Extrafamilial abuse: paedophile rings, ritual abuse and child prostitution

When one considers the issue of abuse of children outside the family in the 1990s, the position is almost reversed. The moral outrage felt about paedophiles, organised and institutional abuse, and most recently child prostitution, during this period at times reached fever pitch. Is it too fanciful to suggest that these forms of abuse have filled a vacuum left by the rethinking that has taken place in regard to intrafamilial abuse?

Concerns about paedophiles, though not an entirely new phenomenon, made a major impact on the public consciousness as a result of the Jason Swift case in 1985. This 14-year-old boy had been living on the streets and performing sexual acts for money for some time before his death. He was drugged and slowly suffocated to death while being sexually abused by four men, who were later convicted of manslaughter. The idea of children being plucked off the streets to be sexually abused and killed has taken a strong hold on the public imagination, and has led to a series of measures being passed to monitor the movements of offenders after leaving prison. In some places these ex-offenders have been 'outed' by the press, leading to protests by those living in the same neighbourhoods. However, fears about this type of paedophile seem to be greatly exaggerated. Bibby *et al.* (1996) estimated a national incidence rate of organised abuse as a whole to be 278 cases a year, but only a small proportion of these cases involved organised extrafamilial rings. Thus, the notion of a large network of evil people preying on vulnerable children outside the family is not supportable. However, in a society preoccupied with the elimination of all risk, even such small odds are unacceptable.

Organised abuse was identified as a concern in the mid-1980s and is included in the 1991 *Working Together* guidelines (DoH 1991a). Defined there as abuse involving a number of abusers and a number of abused children, it covers a wide range of abuse situations, including paedophile rings, ritual abuse and abuse by more than one family member. It is largely used in relation to sexual abuse. Concerns about extra- and intrafamilial ritual Satanic abuse were raised in Congleton, Rochdale, Manchester, Liverpool and Nottingham in the late 1980s and early 1990s. By 1994 (see La Fontaine 1994, 1998) there was much circumspection about the existence of the Satanic and ritual elements in this form of abuse. In the Orkneys case which led to a public inquiry, as with Cleveland, the efforts of child protection professionals to safeguard children at risk of abuse were seen as overzealous and overintrusive into families (Clyde 1992).

The main pattern of abuse found in many of these cases was of children from deprived families being exposed to sexual abuse within their extended families and in some cases neighbourhoods.

In the late 1990s, the issue of child prostitution became a cause for concern. Research carried out by voluntary agencies showed that many young girls were inveigled and later coerced into prostitution. In the new *Working Together* guidelines (DoH 2000a) it is proposed that such children should not be viewed as offenders, but as victims of abuse.

Extrafamilial abuse: abuse of children in residential care

Concerns about institutional abuse had taken hold by 1990 and guidance on how to investigate allegations of such abuse was included in the 1991 *Working Together* guidelines. The inquiries into the Leeways (Lewisham 1985) and Kincora children's homes (DHSS(NI) 1986) had both found evidence of prolonged sexual abuse of boys in children's homes by senior residential staff. Poor training, lack of proper monitoring and managerial oversight were seen as key issues. In the Leeways case there was additional cause for concern because the abuser had a prior conviction. These cases alerted professionals to institutional abuse and to the need to develop systems to prevent and detect it. They did not, however, at this stage, lead to the widespread investigations that characterised the 1990s. To some degree this may be explained by the fact that attention was still being centred on intrafamilial abuse in the mid-1980s and the time was not right for a more dramatic shift of focus. In the USA, there was considerable concern about the abuse of children in day nurseries in the 1980s (see Finkelhor *et al.* 1988), but no concerted attention paid to child abuse in residential institutions.

Summarising the debate

The details of the concerns about abuse in British children's homes in the 1990s is the subject of Chapter 4. We will conclude this chapter by elaborating on and summarising the reasons for the unprecedented upsurge in concern about abuse of children in residential care.

As we have seen, there were several important contextual factors behind the growth of concern about childcare and child abuse in the early 1960s which still persists. The key factor was that of increasing affluence in the USA and in the UK. Another factor was medical advancement which impacted in two ways, first in relation to birth control, and second, in relation to more successful treatment of childhood illnesses. Family sizes, as a consequence of both these developments, have reduced dramatically over the last three generations or so. The nature of childhood has changed too. Changes in the work market have led to an extension of the period of childhood and the need for more education as a preparation for work. Greater affluence has created markets for more child-focused industries (leisure, clothes and entertainment). The expectation of childhood is that it should be a protected and fun-orientated time. The price to pay for this, for there always seems to be one, is that children must also work hard at education in order to be well placed to do well in the more rigorous world of adulthood. For our purposes, however, the expectation that childhood will be a protected time is the key issue. Children are expected to be protected from illness, from accidents, from harm from outsiders and, where necessary, from harm in the home. The key word here is 'expected'. Parents in the Middle Ages, Victorian and pre-Second World War period of the twentieth century would mostly have wanted these things for their children had they considered them possible. However, since the 1950s, because of scientific developments and wealth creation in the western world, it seems that anything is possible including a risk-free society (Beck 1992). This is evidenced by the strength of reactions to illnesses like meningitis, the deaths of children by drug overdoses and the deaths of children by abuse.

These developments, therefore, provided the context in which the work of Henry Kempe and later child protection protagonists had its impact. As we have seen, the initial concerns were about physical abuse and spread to a much wider range of types of abuse with particular emphasis on the emotional damage that they could cause. Child abuse became associated with health and the future, almost in the same way that cigarette smoking has. Its elimination was seen to be universally desirable. However, it has proven to be a tough nut to crack. The issue of sexual abuse which came to the fore in the mid-1980s posed particularly difficult problems. Social work intervention into families in order to protect children alleged to have been sexually abused proved to have a major divisive impact, largely along gender lines (see Campbell 1988). To some degree, the acceptance of child sexual abuse as harmful to children has been more ambivalent than in the case of physical abuse. While the evidence of its deleterious short- and long-term effects is well documented (Beitchman *et al.* 1991, 1992), and there is far more awareness and sensitivity about it as an issue than ever before, there is still uncertainty about how best to respond, particularly in the case of intrafamilial abuse. As we have seen, this ambivalence is now not confined to sexual abuse allegations. After 20 years of unidirectional policies in relation to physical abuse of children, there has been a shift in certainty about how to intervene in families particularly with regard to less serious assaults and neglect. Some have gone so far as to describe this process as a backlash (Myers 1994).

These ambivalences do not exist so strongly in relation to abuse of children outside the family. We would not wish to argue that our more child-focused society has turned away from intrafamilial abuse as a result of the difficulties of intervention to extrafamilial abuse because it is easier to tackle – that would be too simplistic an analysis. Nevertheless, there is some interrelation between these two developments. It is through intrafamilial abuse that concerns about the emotional impact of child abuse has gained hold in society. This has heightened attention to a wider range of children in need and to their experiences in a wider range of settings.

Concluding comments

Physical abuse and neglect of children in residential care has simply not been a major consideration in history. Excessive cruelty in such institutions has only rarely been subject to external response over many centuries. This is probably because in the past harsh regimes were thought to be necessary and no more than children deserved. Poor and unstimulating environments were very much in evidence in the findings of the Curtis Committee in 1946. While there were no doubt improvements in the quality of residential care after that, it is somewhat surprising that between 1945 and the late 1980s there was only one public inquiry into physical ill-treatment of children in care – at Court Lees in 1965. It is of course possible that little such ill-treatment existed. However, it is more likely that there was a fair degree of acceptance of physical means of control of a kind which is now no longer seen to be acceptable in care settings and is contrary to regulations.

There is little evidence of sexual abuse of children in residential care prior to the 1980s. However, Mahood (1995) found accounts of such abuse in Scottish homes in the 1930s. This is perhaps less surprising than in the case of physical abuse. Prior to the recent 'discovery' of such abuse in the community, the chances of being believed if one were to make an allegation of sexual abuse would have been very low. By 1990 because of what had happened in relation to intrafamilial child sexual abuse, such abuse was no longer thought to be rare and children's allegations were more likely to be received with greater credibility.

Thus, the relatively late arrival of residential child abuse on to the social policy agenda is probably accounted for by the heavy focus on intrafamilial abuse throughout most of the 1970s and 1980s and the relatively low level of visibility of children in residential care for a variety of reasons. However, without the prior focus of intrafamilial abuse, there would have been little chance of abuse of children in residential care coming to light at all.

In the chapter that follows, we switch our attention to the key instrument of social policy development in the child protection field – the inquiry.

CHAPTER 3

Public Policy, Public Inquiries and Public Concern

Introduction

This chapter will examine the role played by inquiries and commissions in the development of public policy in general, and particularly in relation to the failure of public policy. It will:

- outline the range and type of inquiries available within the policy-making process, pointing to their different roles and procedures

- consider the role of inquiries in allaying public concern about the actions and behaviours of state officials and examine the efficacy of administrative and regulatory systems and structures

- consider the conduct of inquiries with particular emphasis on powers, issues of fairness, styles and rules of procedure – for example whether inquisitorial or adversarial, whether private or public. In particular reference will be made to the Royal Commission chaired by the Rt Hon. Lord Justice Salmon which in 1966 considered and made recommendations for the conduct of Tribunals of Inquiry that have since become generally accepted as the ground rules for most types of public inquiries (Salmon 1966).

By this means we aim to set the general framework for examining inquiries into child abuse both in the community and in institutions which form the subject of Chapters 4 and 5. In particular we will consider how the principles and ideas reviewed here are relevant to the North Wales Tribunal of Inquiry.

A confused landscape: the types and roles of inquiries

One of the issues touched on by the North Wales Tribunal in its report was whether or not legislation or guidance was needed for public authorities 'to institute inquiries into matters of wide concern' (Waterhouse 2000, p.486). The Tribunal itself noted some of the issues facing the Jillings inquiry, which had been set up by Clwyd County Council in 1994 to establish the facts of child abuse there.[1] It particularly emphasised Jillings' lack of powers to compel witnesses and to have the right of access to documents from all the agencies concerned. These shortcomings contributed to its lack of success and the subsequent need for a Tribunal of Inquiry.

Wraith and Lamb (1971; see also Woodhouse 1995) in their analysis of inquiries established for, within or by the state, outlined the extensive range of their functions, their institutional nature, structural forms, legal powers and purposes, and suggested that their work essentially fell into four broad categories:

- inquiries into appeals against administrative decisions of public authorities
- inquiries into objections against intentions of public bodies
- investigations in advance of a decision
- post-mortems into accidents, scandals or other matters of public concern.

It should be noted that many of these inquiries have the force of statute and the powers endowed by statute but this is not universally the case. Any public body or government department may initiate an inquiry into issues which it considers to be of public concern. However, inquiries established by this means must rely on the cooperation of individuals and agencies concerned and, as in the case of the Jillings' inquiry referred to above, their findings may not have the status of a full-blown judicial inquiry with the full range of statutory powers.

In the following sections we shall be considering three types of government-sponsored inquiries: administrative inquiries, fact-finding inquiries and investigative inquiries, moving on to consider where child abuse inquiries fit into this general picture.

Administrative inquiries

The first category is discrete, covering a myriad of statutory bodies charged with adjudication and redress responsibilities (broadly administrative justice), some of which have substantial roles (see Table 3.1).

Table 3.1 Tribunals for redress and adjudication

Tribunal	Legislation	Number of tribunals	Number of cases: England and Wales*
Child support maintenance	Child Support Act 1991	3,155	8,563
Industrial tribunals	Industrial Tribunals Act 1996	20	34,905
Valuation tribunals	Local Government Act 1988	56	274,000
Social security appeals tribunals	Social Security Administration Act 1992	42,374	263,009
Disability appeals tribunals	Social Security Administration Act 1992	14,102	54,575

*Note:** figures for 1997: (Council on Tribunals 1998)

As with appointed bodies in general, such administrative bodies operate at the interface between the public and the state – usually in relation to the welfare role of the state. Their functions are to provide:

- a means of redress of grievance
- adjudication of dispute
- recognition of the rights of the individual.

Their advantages are that they offer a quick, cost-effective, independent decision-making process which is not overly legalistic. They were meant to counter concerns that politicians and officials on their own may not necessarily

devise procedures or decision-making processes which will ensure fairness in interest representation, fairness in procedure, avoidance of arbitrariness, accessibility and meaningful participation for interested members of the public or effective accountability where the exercise of power and broad discretionary decision-making are involved. (Birkinshaw 1985, pp.6–7)

The business of these administrative tribunals is supervised under the terms of the Tribunals and Inquiries Act 1971, itself a successor to the 1958 Act which followed the Franks Committee report (Cmnd 218, 1957). The focus is on speed of resolution, cost, expertise, throughput, accessibility and flexibility (see Wade and Bradley 1985). The procedures of the various tribunals are overseen by the Council on Tribunals whose functions, set out in the 1971 Act, include dealing with complaints concerning the operation of tribunals, and advising on the setting up of new tribunals and the tribunal structure as a whole. There have been concerns about the increasingly legalistic nature of some procedures and the growing complexity of organisational structures, but the overarching focus has been on trying to deliver Franks' objectives of openness, fairness and impartiality. The main mechanisms for achieving these objectives are the use of chairpersons with legal experience, the clarity and uniformity of procedures (including the right to legal representation), publication of the reasons for a decision and the right of appeal.

Fact-finding inquiries

Barker (1994 p.329) suggests that there are seven categories of what we term fact-finding inquiries, those which are intended to:

- discover or create new information or analysis
- clarify and organise existing, confusing information
- establish some new subject or approach in policy-making
- legitimise or confirm information or policy already favoured by government (or established opinion)
- reject or delegitimise such information or policy which is officially disfavoured
- recommend a possibly controversial decision, including development and environmental issues
- investigate 'serious system failure' ('policy disasters', major accidents, scandals).

This final category, which we term an 'investigative inquiry', will be considered in more detail in the next section. Barker's analysis would also suggest that setting up an inquiry has a number of political functions such as:

- removing an issue from the political arena
- giving the appearance of governmental concern

- buying time to allow public concern to abate
- offering a semblance of independence with a degree of control through the inquiry membership.

This fact-finding and fact-sifting role which forms part of the state's endless quest for information as part of the ongoing policy process (and the inclusion of interested parties in anticipation of policy formulation) is carried out through a number of forms, such as advisory non-departmental public bodies, Royal Commissions, *ad hoc* departmental committees and non-statutory official inquiries (see Butler and Butler 1987). There is little systematic basis for distinguishing between these forms of inquiry in terms of the subject matter they deal with, and there is considerable variation in their procedures and outcomes. On the one hand, they are highly flexible, and they can be seen to be impartial and independent. On the other hand, they are often lengthy (a Royal Commission takes on average over two years and a departmental committee over one year, to report), their membership lies in the hands of ministers who invariably rely on Establishment figures (Hennessy 1986) and their report's fate 'can range all the way from ... total disregard ... to wholesale acceptance and implementation of its recommendations' (Cartwright 1975, p.204). Royal Commissions fell out of favour during the 1980s and 1990s when only a handful were established compared to previous decades, and their role has now been largely usurped by the Labour government's Task Forces and Reviews.

Investigative inquiries
DISASTERS

Public inquiries also exist to examine 'failures', such as accidents (for example, civil aviation crashes, deaths at sea, etc.). They have a role in opening up the policy arena to a wider than usual range of voices and they may have an impact on the legislative process. Writing about the role of public inquiries and the British offshore safety industry, Simon Thompson (1993) noted that

> the role of a public inquiry as a gatherer of information is of great importance. The supply of information to the inquiry is considerably greater than the supply of information to the day-to-day policy community. Diverse and alternative viewpoints are heard, and examined. Information is obtained from groups which are normally excluded from the policy community, and is included into the policy making process. (p.20)

A study of those who gave evidence to the Taylor inquiry into the Hillsborough Stadium disaster confirms this (Taylor 1989). They included bodies as diverse as the Football Supporters Association and the British Greyhound Racing Board. The inquiry also benefited from Taylor's own discussion with architects, stadium designers, police forces and football club managers. As a consequence, the final report made wide-ranging policy recommendations against a background of previously ignored reports.

ROUTINE FAILURES

Where lesser-level but more regular 'failure' exists, the inquiry process may be more routinised and professionalised as is the case with planning inquires or Department of Trade and Industry (DTI) inquiries into company affairs. Their existence has largely been driven by the growth of legislation which has to be policed. The DTI appoints inspectors (lawyers or accountants) to go into companies on

> fact-finding exercises to examine whether there is cause for public complaint and for its intervention and, if there is, to fix responsibility. There may be some general issues of corporate governance and professional responsibility which are revealed by investigations, and it may be important to draw these to the attention of the business world and the general public. (Levi 1993, p.62)

While both planning and DTI inquiries are subject to rules and regulations on procedure and are essentially outside any political influence, it may be argued that public inquires where failure is less 'routine' can become 'a non-political mechanism for dealing with essentially political issues' (Cane 1986, p.301). This concern was expressed about the committee of privy councillors under Lord Franks, which was asked by the Conservative government in 1982 to sit in judgement on that government's culpability over the invasion of the Falkland Islands (Franks 1983), and about the Le Quesne inquiry into the Barlow Clowes affair,[2] where the inquiry's terms of reference were written to ensure that it could not allocate blame. (Le Quesne 1988)

SCANDALS

A third type of investigative inquiry is that which is concerned with deviant, pathological and/or criminal behaviour with political implications, determining the cause of a scandal or matter of significant concern where the pursuit of the truth may require specific resources and powers. Thus, while Royal Commissions and parliamentary committees have on rare occasions in the past undertaken investigations into specific allegations or individuals, both they and departmental committees lack any statutory powers that could be essential if the inquiry or investigation required access to people and papers which might not otherwise be forthcoming. There are examples where such means of inquiry have worked in potentially controversial areas and received the required assistance without recourse to powers of compulsion.[3]

The Tribunal of Inquiry: In a Class of its Own?

The Tribunals of Inquiry Act 1921 was quickly passed to deal with allegations of corruption over armaments contracts in the Ministry of Munitions. The need for this legislation was based on the susceptibility to political influence of pre-existing methods of inquiry, and a dearth of statutory measures at the time to deal with problems in particular policy areas. The 1921 Act placed greater reliance than before on quasi-judicial processes. It allowed for a Tribunal to be established on the order of both Houses of Parliament to investigate 'a definite matter of urgent public importance' (Section 1 (1)), with the powers of a High Court that included taking evidence on oath, and compelling the availability of witnesses and documents.

Until the establishment of the North Wales inquiry Tribunals of Inquiry had been held on at least 19 occasions (see table 3.2 on p.58).

Despite the primary criterion of a definite matter of urgent public importance, there has been no pattern to the use of Tribunals. Their establishment may often have derived from the status of the complainants or the lack of a suitable alternative. It is notable that in the 1920s complaints involving the police dominated the work of Tribunals. Statutory provision for inquiries under subsequent legislation have channelled these sorts of cases elsewhere. The introduction of alternative methods of dealing with some definite matters of public concern explains the relative rarity of Tribunals of Inquiry since 1962. During this period, those Tribunals that have been held seem to have been concerned either with matters at the heart of the political establishment or with matters which have generated enormous public emotion or concern.

Tribunals' powers and procedures

Tribunals have been noticeable for the width and flexibility of their approach. The 1933 Tribunal into corruption in the Corporation of the City of Glasgow did not restrict itself to those departments where bribery was alleged but looked at the workings of the council as a whole. It was also the first to place advertisements inviting evidence of corruption and offering witnesses immunity before the Tribunal; a similar method of inviting evidence was used by the North Wales Tribunal of Inquiry. The 1978 Crown Agents Tribunal of

Table 3.2 Tribunals of Inquiry up to the Establishment of the North Wales Tribunal

Date	Subject
1921	Allegations concerning the Ministry of Munitions
1924	Royal Commission on Lunacy and Mental Disorder (which had powers granted under the Act)
1925	Allegations against the Metropolitan Police
1925	Allegations against the Chief Constable of Kilmarnock over the dismissal of two officers
1926	Mining subsidence in Doncaster
1928	Allegations against the Chief Constable of St Helens by the Watch Committee
1928	Allegations of the conduct of the Metropolitan Police toward a former MP's girlfriend
1933	Allegations of corruption against Glasgow Corporation
1936	Allegations of a budget leak by a government minister
1939	Sinking of the submarine Thetis
1943	Conduct of a juvenile court case in Hereford
1944	Allegations of misuse of office by a local government official in Newcastle upon Tyne
1948	Allegations of corruption by a government minister
1957	Allegations of a bank rate leak by government ministers and/or civil servants
1959	Allegations against Caithness Police
1962	Activities of John Vassall, Russian spy
1967	Aberfan disaster
1972	Bloody Sunday march in Derry
1972	Collapse of the Vehicle and General Insurance Company
1978	Corruption and misconduct in the Crown Agents
1996	Dunblane shootings

Inquiry argued that 'each tribunal must have some flexibility to adapt its procedure to meet its own circumstances' (Winetrobe 1997).

Vassall Tribunal 1962

The extent of the Tribunal's powers have always been a matter for concern. Tribunals of Inquiry are endowed with some powers of the High Court, such as the compelling of witnesses, the production of evidence and the facility to certify a contempt to the High Court; there is an expectation that the proceedings will be held in public. Such concerns came to a head at the Vassall inquiry in 1962 following the conviction of John Vassall, an Admiralty clerk, on charges of espionage. For security reasons the hearings were held partly in private. This need to depart from the expressed view of Parliament led to the subsequent establishment of the Security Commission to inquire into security issues related to the public services. This was also the first time that a Tribunal had used its powers to certify a contempt in respect of three journalists, who refused to disclose the sources of their stories to the inquiry. Two of the journalists were imprisoned for their pains and the affair inevitably triggered a round of indignation among the press, illustrated by the following *Times* comment:

> these powers are exercised without the protection afforded by the normal rules of procedure, no charges are preferred, there is no justiciable dispute between the parties, ordinary rules of evidence and relevance do not apply throughout. It is like a powerful locomotive running without rails. (26 April 1963)

This and other sources of concern over the application of the Tribunals of Inquiry Act 1921 led to the establishment of the Royal Commission under the chairmanship of Lord Salmon in 1965 to consider whether the Act should be retained and, if so, to make recommendations as to any desirable changes. The Royal Commission reported in 1966, recommended that the 1921 Act be retained but made 50 proposals to improve its application. The recommendations centred on the concerns about procedural safeguards for those embroiled in such inquiries and its 'six cardinal principles' formed the hub of the reforms he suggested.

Salmon report 1966

The Salmon report confirmed that there was a role for inquisitorial inquiries that dealt with issues which 'occasion a nation-wide crisis of confidence'; that had the power to compel witnesses; that were seen to be independent; that offered an opportunity for those who were criticised to be heard; and that were open to the public.

> It is only when the public is present that the public will have complete confidence that everything possible has been done for the purpose of arriving at the truth. (Salmon 1966, p.38)

The Royal Commission thus proposed a series of reforms that focused on:

- witness immunity
- the absence of any appeal from a Tribunal's findings
- legal representation and any costs incurred
- access to criminal records
- general rules on counsel presentations
- the composition of the Tribunal membership.

It established the 'six cardinal principles', which covered the right of anyone affected by the Tribunal's work:

- to know the substance of any allegations against them
- to have the right of legal representation (both for witnesses and for those at risk of being 'prejudicially affected' by the inquiry)
- to have the right to address the Tribunal and be examined by his or her legal representative
- to have the right to cross-examination
- to have enough time to prepare any case
- to have the right to call any material witness.

Salmon came down against any statutory rules of procedure for Tribunals of Inquiry. His argument was that the application of rigid rules would inevitably become the subject of legal challenge. This would undermine the need for flexibility and speed implicit in the inquisitorial and constitutional functions of such a Tribunal.

The upshot is that, subject to their adhering to the spirit of Salmon's guiding principles – the six cardinal principles – tribunal chairs and their fellow members are free to conduct hearings in whatever way they feel will help them to fulfil their terms of reference and elicit the maximum information from witnesses and parties. A key instrument in this process is what has become known as the Salmon Letter, whereby those who are likely to be criticised during the course of a Tribunal are informed of any allegations or complaints likely to be made against them, thus giving them an opportunity to prepare a response prior to the actual hearing.

In 1973 the government responded in a short report that accepted many of the Royal Commission's recommendations, including those concerning the grounds for establishing an inquiry, the need for public hearings, the six cardinal principles, the right of legal representation and cross-examination, and the absence of any appeal from the findings of a Tribunal (*Government Views* 1973). It is, however, worth noting another review of inquiry procedure and practice which followed the non-statutory Scott inquiry, set up as a direct result of the abortive prosecutions in the Matrix Churchill case.

Salmon and Scott: politics and procedures

The prosecution in the Matrix Churchill case highlighted some alleged discrepancies between the government's public stance on the sale of arms and related equipment to Iraq and the implementation of export control policies by ministers and civil servants. In order to prove their claims that they had received unofficial encouragement from the government to export their wares, the defendants sought disclosure of government documents which was resisted by the use of Public Interest Immunity (PII) certificates signed by ministers in four departments of state. An application (heard in October 1992) to have the PII certificates set aside was successful and, on the basis of evidence from civil servants and Alan Clarke, a junior Conservative minister, which would appear to suggest that there was a clear divergence between government policy in public and in private, the trial collapsed. Fuelled with documents which seemed to confirm the defence case, media interest continued to the point where, in November 1992, the Attorney-General made a statement to the House of Commons in which he promised a full and independent inquiry by Sir Richard Scott into the events surrounding the case, the terms of reference to be discussed with the judge.

Scott was given a wide-ranging brief and unprecedented access to papers, ministers and civil servants, together with an undertaking that if he were to feel at any stage that he was receiving less than complete cooperation from departments and potential witnesses, he could be assured that a request from him that the inquiry be converted into a Tribunal of Inquiry (1921) would be acceded to. Scott sat alone, without fellow panel members or assessors, and the proceedings were managed very much in an inquisitorial fashion. This, and Scott's liberal interpretation of the Salmon principles, attracted considerable criticism from Lord Howe in particular.

Although Scott went to great lengths to ensure that parties were made aware of allegations, had the opportunity to address them, and had access to successive drafts of sections of the report to amend if necessary, there remained significant criticism, notably by Lord Howe, that the Salmon principles were being flouted by the chairman. Lord Howe's complaints surrounded the lack of legal representation for witnesses attending the inquiry and the perceived inability of witnesses to tell their own story to their own counsel and to cross-examine or comment on the testimony of other witnesses. The procedure adopted of inviting a series of written comments from witnesses on their and others' evidence was deemed inadequate to ensure fair treatment of those who could be prejudiced by criticism during the public hearings and in the final report of the inquiry. Another strand to the complaint which, given the procedure adopted, was said to have jeopardised even further the protection of individuals' reputations, was the fact that this was a single person inquiry panel and, in particular, no assessors had been appointed to advise Sir Richard Scott of the 'way things worked in Whitehall'.

As a result of the disquiet over the conduct of the Scott inquiry, the Lord Chancellor initiated a consultation exercise on procedures to be adopted in future. Among those consulted was the Council on Tribunals, which concluded that no single set of rules would address the requirements of every inquiry but that each inquiry should conduct itself with a view to ensuring effectiveness, fairness, speed and economy. The Council considered that fairness and effectiveness were paramount. The way in which the inquiry is set up, the powers it is given and the procedures it adopts will determine the achievement of these key objectives. In what follows we outline the Council's key judgments:

- In setting up an inquiry a minister needs to recognise the implications of doing so, e.g. the possibility that the inquiry will generate more questions than answers and that there may remain a number of unresolved issues.

- The conduct of the inquiry must be for the inquiry chairman to decide in consultation with any other members of the inquiry in the light of the particular circumstances of the case.

- It is not possible to draw an absolutely hard and fast distinction between the inquisitorial and adversarial modes. The presence of Counsel to the Inquiry may introduce an adversarial element into the proceedings. Features characteristic of adversarial litigation may properly be introduced into the inquisitorial process if that assists in the fair and efficient conduct of the inquiry.

- Salmon Letters should be regarded as indicative of the sorts of issues which may be raised rather than firm 'charges' against individuals.

- Laborious exchanges of drafts for comment may be excessive to ensure fairness. Flexibility is the key to guaranteeing this.

- The full gamut of legal representation may not be necessary in all cases to ensure fairness but should be a matter for the panel to decide in every case.

All these were to be issues that impacted directly and indirectly on the North Wales Tribunal.

North Wales Tribunal of Inquiry

In this concluding section we shall look briefly at the reasons for adopting the Tribunal of Inquiry in preference to other forms of inquiry to consider events in North Wales, and the decisions made by the Tribunal in relation to the process to be followed in the light of the issues raised in the fall out of the Scott inquiry.

The reasons for adopting the Tribunal form were both practical and political. In practical terms it has to be recognised that there had already been two abortive attempts in Clwyd to conduct an authoritative inquiry into the events in question and to produce a publishable account (Cartrefle and Jillings). These had signally failed. By the time this failure was finally accepted, the old county structure in Wales had been dissolved. What had been two counties were now six. If the Secretary of State were to make a direction for a statutory inquiry, to whom would he address the direction? Furthermore, the new unitary authorities which had previously made up the county of Clwyd made representations to the Secretary of State for Wales about the costs involved in a directed inquiry which would fall on their council tax payers. The allegations of physical and sexual abuse had been rumbling around North Wales for ten years before matters came to a head in 1996. There was a strong political imperative to put the matter to rest and only the authoritative status of a full judicial inquiry would do the job. These issues are dealt with in detail in Chapter 6.

Process

In contrast to Scott's approach (as we shall see in more detail in Chapter 7), that adopted by the North Wales Tribunal adhered much more closely to Salmon's cardinal principles. It was conducted in a much more legalistic fashion with considerable emphasis placed on cross-examination of witnesses, use of

Salmon Letters and submissions by counsel. This is understandable to some degree in that its task was much more complex, more prone to dispute surrounding the facts, and possibly therefore, more suitable for adversarial treatment. The facts were by no means easy to establish; the events and allegations to be investigated by the Tribunal related to a 20-year period; homes had closed or changed function; what records had originally been available had been either dispersed or destroyed; systems were such that there could be no reliable version of events on record. Thus oral testimony would be as important as documentary examination in trying to establish the 'true' facts surrounding the experience of care in North Wales children's homes during that period. The sheer number of witnesses involved and the emergence of substantial numbers of new allegations, too, would have rendered Scott's system of written notice and response, which underpinned his claims to fairness, unmanageable in the North Wales context. The consequences for individuals who were the subject of criticism, too, were arguably more severe given the subject matter of the inquiry, so that an opportunity to test the evidence might well play a vital role in playing fair with witnesses.

Concluding comment

In this chapter we have tried to demonstrate the wider public inquiry context in which the North Wales Tribunal was situated. We now move on to consider the more general impact of inquiry processes on the childcare community.

Notes

1   The Jillings inquiry is discussed in further detail in Chapter 7. This inquiry hit many difficulties and as a result was never published and therefore failed to achieve its stated goals.

2   This inquiry was concerned with the lack of protection afforded by the relevant authorities to small investors.

3   Barker suggests that in the Arms to Iraq affair, chaired by Sir Richard Scott, the use of 'a series of virtually untrammelled written responses and wider comments is a more efficient process than the traditional routines of more adversial, advocacy-based methods' (Barker 1997, p.19).

CHAPTER 4

Inquiries into the Abuse of Children in the Community

Introduction

In the 1970s and 1980s child abuse was the subject of a series of inquiries, the vast majority of which were concerned with the physical abuse and neglect of children living in their own homes, usually already known in varying degrees to social workers because of previous concerns about parenting practices.

It is important to consider the issues raised by these inquiries before moving on to consider inquiries into residential abuse for the following reasons. First, both types of abuse have been dealt with under the same child protection procedures and inquiry processes. Second, by the time that focus came to bear on abuse in residential settings, social work and other professions involved in child protection had been opened up to public scrutiny for 15 years or more, and debates had been held and lessons learned about the benefits and dysfunctions of holding public inquiries. Third (as we shall see), the process of carrying out such inquiries was moving to a new stage by the beginning of the 1990s.

It is important, however, to acknowledge a key difference between the two forms of abuse, which means that there is need for care in making unqualified comparisons. In the case of abuse in the community, the abuser is usually the parent or carer, and so the focus of inquiries in these cases is largely on whether the health and welfare professionals involved could have by their actions prevented abuse or further abuse taking place. In the case of institutional abuse, the abusers are mainly residential social workers themselves, i.e. those entrusted with the direct care of children in the place of their parents. As will be seen, this leads to a number of different emphases and implications. Whereas the concern in abuse in the community cases is whether there has been some negligence on the part of individuals, the issues in residential abuse are ones of culpability and the possibility of corruption and cover-ups. Thus residential abuse inquiries are different in the sense that the agencies involved are on double trial. Their concerns are, first, why were children abused by the employees of the agency, and second, why did the agency not detect the abuse at an earlier stage and take appropriate action. In abuse in the community inquiries, only the second of these questions is appropriate.

Despite these differences, the structures and processes of the two types of inquiries are largely similar, which in our view justifies looking at the lessons to be gained from consideration of abuse in the community inquiries. In the following sections we provide a review of the way in which such inquiries have been conducted in the modern era, and we consider the impact that they have had on the development of child protection services.

Overview of the facts

In a recent study of public inquiries, we found that there were 57 public inquiries into the abuse of children in the community between 1945 and 1997 (Corby *et al.* 1998). Since that publication, we have identified one other from that period and two between 1997 and the present time.[1] Public inquiries are defined here as those whose findings are made public in the form of a report, and range from those with statutory powers to those acting purely in an advisory capacity. The list of inquiries reported on is not definitive: there are certainly more public inquiry reports in existence than we managed to trace. The fact that we and others (see Reder, Duncan and Gray 1993) have had difficulties in establishing a comprehensive record is due to the fact that there is no national collection of such reports readily available to the public or, indeed, to the professional community.

All but 3 of these 60 inquiries were concerned with physical abuse and neglect of children, the exceptions being Surrey (1977), Cleveland (Butler-Sloss 1988) and the Orkneys (Clyde 1992) which dealt with sexual abuse and ritual or organised abuse.

The use of public inquiries to investigate cases of child abuse in the community was rare until the early 1970s. Prior to 1973 we found only one such inquiry, that into the death of Dennis O'Neill, who was killed by his foster-father (Monckton 1945). Between 1973 and 1989 there were 45 such inquiries (an average of 2.6 per year) and between 1990 and 1999, there were 14 such inquiries (an average of 1.4 per year).

Forms of inquiry

There are three main types of public inquiries that have been used to investigate child abuse in the community cases. These are, first, inquiries that are ordered by a Secretary of State; second, those that are sponsored by the health and local authorities in whose area the abuse took place, using independent panels of investigators; and third, those carried out internally by health and local authorities, but nevertheless resulting in public reports. Statutory inquiries are relatively rare and figured more prominently in the 1970s and early 1980s when child abuse was emerging on to the policy scene. They have with time been replaced by the second and third forms of inquiry. Statutory inquiries have a range of powers not available to other forms of inquiry. These powers include the compellability of witnesses, the enforced production of documents, the taking of evidence on oath and the facility to pay legal and other costs to witnesses. There is a presumption that such proceedings will be held in public, though, if the Secretary of State gives no direction in this respect, those holding the inquiry may conduct the inquiry, or any part of it, in private. It should be noted that statutory inquiries may be conducted by a central government department or by local authorities at the behest of a central government department.[2]

Inquiries set up by local authorities and health authorities using independent panels are the type that have most often been used to investigate child abuse issues. Such inquiries do not have the powers of compellability of witnesses and production of documentation that are available to statutory inquiries. Nevertheless, in the absence of definitive government guidelines, many of them have employed formats similar to those of statutory inquiries. In particular they have adopted the quasi-adversarial approach favoured by such inquiries with lawyers as chairs of the panels, barristers acting on behalf of the inquiry and witnesses being legally represented. The Beckford (Brent 1985) and Carlile (Greenwich 1987) inquiries, both chaired by Louis Blom-Cooper QC, are examples of local inquiries which are closest in style, form and content to statutory inquiries. Other inquiries included in this category, more often those not chaired by lawyers, have adopted more informal styles of conducting their business (see, for instance, the Daniel Vergauwen (Hackney 1991) and Stephanie Fox (Wandsworth 1990) inquiry reports).

The third type of inquiry is that which is initiated locally but conducted by staff employed by the authorities which are subject to scrutiny. There is a strong element of internal review in such inquiries and they are conducted much less formally than most of the inquiries in the two categories already considered.

These inquiries are usually organised by Area Child Protection Committees (ACPCs) or their forerunners as part of their function to review problematic cases in their area. Much of the work that they carry out in this respect is not open to public scrutiny. However, some of their inquiries are made public as a result of localised pressure from relatives, communities, the media or judges presiding over the criminal trials of the abusers. Such inquiries draw information largely from written documentation – any interviewing of individuals usually being carried out more informally – and with less legal involvement than in the case of the other forms of inquiry considered.

Following the publication of the 1991 *Working Together* guidelines (DoH 1991a), which have recently been updated again (see DoH 2000a), clearer guidance is available for carrying out these internal reviews. More detailed consideration of these guidelines for what are now termed 'Part 8 Reviews' will be given below.

As can be seen, therefore, there is a continuum of inquiry types ranging from statutory inquiries ordered by a Secretary of State (with all the paraphernalia of a major inquisitorial process) right through to reviews carried out by the professionals themselves, resulting in reports being made available to the public. The differences between these types of inquiries are not as clear-cut as they might seem. Some of the locally initiated inquiries using independent panels have been very close in form and style to statutory inquiries whereas others have had more of the characteristics of internal reviews.

It should be noted that these forms of inquiry are those also used in residential abuse inquiries (see Chapter 5).

The process of establishing inquiries

Despite the large number of public inquiries into child abuse since the 1970s, an examination of the process whereby they are set up shows that a great deal of pressure has often been required in order to get inquiries established. For the most part, this pressure has come from families, relatives, local politicians, the media and communities. In modern society, there is clearly a considerable public need to know the facts when a child dies as a result of abuse. In the case of Darryn Clarke, a 3-year-old boy killed by his mother's partner in Liverpool (DHSS 1979), Darryn's extended family, who had been closely involved in his care before his mother had gone to live with her new partner, were instrumental, along with the local media, in securing an inquiry into the circumstances surrounding his death. The comments of the judge in the criminal trial of the mother and stepfather of Jasmine Beckford about the quality of social work intervention in that case was influential in the setting up of that inquiry (Brent 1985). Several public inquiries have followed on from other inquiries (often of a more internal nature) around which there are suspicions of cover-ups. This was true of the Paul Brown inquiry (DHSS 1980) and (as we shall see in following chapters), it has also been a feature of residential abuse inquiries such as Kincora (DHSS(NI) 1986) and the North Wales Tribunal of Inquiry (Waterhouse 2000).

As a rule of thumb, where there has already been an internal inquiry which is deemed unsatisfactory, the likelihood is that a more formal public inquiry will ensue, particularly if the concerns over the earlier inquiry are the subject of a public or media campaign. Whether this is a statutory inquiry or not depends on a range of factors, some of which are considered below. Whatever option is taken, the Department of Health is usually closely involved in the process. In non-statutory inquiries held by local authorities, DoH officials usually advise on matters such as panel members, terms of reference, etc.

Of the 17 abuse in the community inquiries held in the 1970s, 5 were Secretary of State-ordered inquiries, 7 local inquiries with independent panels and 5 of the internal inquiry type. The 1980s saw a shift in approach – of the 28 such inquiries which took place during this period, 4 were statutory inquiries, 12 were local inquiries with independent panels and 12 were internal review type inquiries. In the 1990s, almost all the inquiries were of the internal review type reflecting the introduction of Part 8 Reviews (see below).

Key findings of these reports

There is a remarkable similarity between the findings of many of the child abuse inquiry reports that are the subject of this chapter. The main concern expressed in most of the reports has been the lack of coordination between the various agencies involved in child protection work. In 1974 when the Maria Colwell inquiry (DHSS 1974) reported, this was perhaps understandable, as arrangements for inter-agency coordination were not well developed. This report did lead to the foundation of the key elements of our current child protection system, establishing the forerunner of present-day Area Child Protection Committees, interdisciplinary case conference arrangements and child protection registers. Nevertheless, there is a big difference between establishing a child protection system and using it effectively. Most of the reports up to the mid-1980s continued to point to a lack of interdisciplinary communication, a lack of properly trained and experienced frontline workers, inadequate supervision and too little focus on the needs of children as distinct from those of their parents and families as a whole. Thus, if one reads some important inquiries of that time, e.g. Jasmine Beckford (Brent 1985), Kimberley Carlile (Greenwich 1987) and Tyra Henry (Lambeth 1987), it is clear that child protection systems were well established, but problems with communication and a continuing lack of awareness on the part of child protection workers of the potential risks to children were in evidence. The Department of Health and Social Security was at pains to remedy this problem and in 1986 and 1988 produced new guidelines to achieve this shift (DHSS 1986, 1988).

The impact of inquiries into child abuse in the community became more complicated in the early 1990s as child protection concerns spread to sexual and ritual abuse of children. Inquiries in Cleveland (Butler-Sloss 1988) and the Orkneys (Clyde 1992) questioned the zealousness of social workers and other professionals. They queried the application of practices which had developed in relation to physical abuse and neglect to allegations of sexual abuse. Ironically social workers were viewed as being too child protectionist and not sufficiently sensitive to the needs and wishes of parents and carers. The findings of these inquiries led ultimately to a shift towards the more family sensitive approaches in the mid- to late 1990s outlined in Chapter 2. Nevertheless, other inquiries were demonstrating that lack of communication and failure to act more incisively and protectively in cases remain a continuing concern right up to the present time (see Bridge 1991, 1995, 1997, 1999).

Concerns about child abuse inquiries
Negative impact on individual social workers and the social work profession
Child abuse inquiry reports have by and large not been well received by child protection professionals, particularly social workers, and their impact has been seen as demoralising and dysfunctional by many commentators. Hallett (1989), drawing on reports published prior to 1988, asserted that they have assisted in the creation of poor public perceptions of social workers. There can be little doubt that individuals have been selected out from inquiry reports by the press for particular criticism; this was particularly a feature of the Colwell (DHSS 1974), Beckford (Brent 1985), Carlile (Greenwich 1987) and Henry (Lambeth 1987) cases.

There is clearly a tension between professionals' needs to operate without fear of unfair exposure to public scrutiny and a public need to understand why children who are known to, and some of whom are in the care of, public agencies are seriously and fatally abused. This has led to much debate over whether inquiries should be held in public and how findings should be disseminated. Prior to the Maria Colwell inquiry (DHSS 1974), the first major inquiry into child abuse in the community, social work with children and families was conducted largely in private. Suddenly, however, this work was exposed to public scrutiny, and social workers saw one of their colleagues being heavily criticised in the media for working in a way that was common to many of them at this time.

In particular, as further inquiries took place there was a growing view that reports failed to highlight factors such as inadequate systems and resources (see Hill 1990). However, the reality may be somewhat different. According to Munro (1996) who analysed 45 reports of inquiries held between 1973 and 1994, social work practitioners were not criticised in 42 per cent of them. Some inquiry reports have been particularly concerned about poor resources and difficult working conditions (see the Doreen Aston report: Lambeth, Lewisham and Southwark 1989; the Stephanie Fox report: Wandsworth 1990). Factors such as these, however, are less likely to be highlighted in the media.

It is also interesting to note that, in fact, only 8 of the 60 inquiries being considered here took place mostly in public: Colwell (DHSS 1974), Auckland (DHSS 1975), Clarke (DHSS 1979), Brown (DHSS 1980), Beckford (Brent 1985), Henry (Lambeth 1987), Cleveland (Butler-Sloss 1988) and Orkneys (Clyde 1992).

Conduct of inquiries

Linked to the debate about whether inquiries should be held in public, and whether and how reports should be published, is the issue of the way in which inquiries should be conducted. These matters were discussed in relation to inquiries in general in Chapter 3. As we have seen earlier in this chapter, inquiries into child abuse in the community have been conducted in a variety of ways. Social workers and other professionals have by and large felt alienated by the more formal adversarial approaches characteristic of statutory and some independent inquiries. They have felt on trial and, have therefore responded defensively rather than cooperatively in an effort to improve practice and ensure that such abuses are prevented in future. This view is clearly at variance with that of the legal profession, who see such procedures, despite the pain they create for participants, as the best means of producing the most reliable information.

Effects and effectiveness of inquiries

Another key issue is that relating to the effectiveness and impact of child abuse inquiries. The sheer number of inquiries held into child abuse together with the similarity of their recommendations (noted above) have suggested that they are not being effective. It has been argued that the long time-gap between the deaths of children and the publication of the inquiry reports may have contributed to this failure to respond adequately (see Hallett 1989). By the time the recommendations are available for consideration, the public shock and horror surrounding the tragedy have often subsided. The delays involved often owe much to the time taken to complete criminal trials of alleged abusers before which public inquiries cannot commence. When the length of time taken to set up and conduct the more formal and complex inquiries and to produce subsequent reports is also taken into account, it is not difficult to see how issues can appear to have lost their immediacy by the time they are ready to be aired.

Other commentators have pointed to inquiries having obvious dysfunctions, some of which have been referred to already. Walton (1993) argues that the child protection system in Britain has been distorted by its reliance on public investigations into cases that have gone wrong and that it lacks coherent and consistent goals and programmes as a result. The nature of public inquiries with their detailed attention to case events has also been seen to place too much focus on the shortcomings of individual practitioners and not enough on the context of practice, the shortage of resources and broader social issues (Hill 1990).

It has been argued that inquiries have the wisdom of hindsight, but that they cannot capture the complexities of decision-making at the time that events take place. They cannot, therefore, do full justice to the dilemmas faced by practitioners and can give a distorted picture of the reality of most child protection practice which may generally be of good professional standard (Hallett 1989). Another dysfunctional effect of inquiries, according to commentators, is that they have led to the adoption of bureaucratic procedural responses (Howe 1992) and defensive practices (Harris 1987). This trend (as noted above) has been particularly highlighted in Department of Health research set up in response to the concerns raised by the Cleveland inquiry (see DoH 1995) which found that families experienced child protection interventions as overintrusive and unhelpful and that their broader needs were often subsumed by professionals' concerns with seeking evidence of abuse.

Part 8 Reviews

Many of these matters had come to a head by the end of the 1980s, resulting in a shift to the use of internal review-type inquiries. This had been recommended in draft guidance issued for consultation by the DHSS (1986), was adopted in the *Working Together* guidelines published in 1988 (DHSS 1988) and revised in Part 8 of the 1991 *Working Together* guidelines (DoH 1991a).[3] In the case of child abuse deaths or child protection issues likely to attract major public concern, these guidelines recommended that each involved agency individually review its conduct and that the information derived from this process be used by the Area Child Protection Committee to produce composite reviews. The guidance requires that the Social Services Inspectorate (SSI) or the Welsh Office be notified immediately of such cases. Final reports are expected to be completed within two months of an incident occurring. Agencies within an area where such a review has been carried out are expected to implement any changes recommended by the review. However, there is no clear guidance as to whether review reports should be made public, and decisions on this issue are left to individual Area Child Protection Committees.

Reder and Duncan (1999) reported an average of 53 child death Part 8 Reviews between 1990 and 1995. At a Social Services Inspectorate seminar held in 1995 (SSI 1995) it was estimated that 60 such case reviews were being completed annually. What has been the impact of these reviews?

As regards reducing the degree of publicity surrounding child abuse, there can be little doubt as to the effectiveness of Part 8 Reviews in that, as has been seen, the number of inquiries has greatly reduced in the 1990s. In respect of physical abuse and neglect in the community it has been noted that the average number dropped by nearly a third. There has been no statutory inquiry during that time and no large independent inquiry of the type used in the Jasmine Beckford (Brent 1985) and Kimberley Carlile (Greenwich 1987) cases. Nearly all the public reports in the 1990s stem from original Part 8 Reviews where the matters have been seen as of pressing public concern.

There can be little doubt that the gaps between the abuse events and the reviews being completed have been reduced and the messages from individual cases have, therefore, been made more speedily available to the agencies involved.

In the case of reviews that have come into the public domain, it is notable that the process of inquiry has been more informal. In terms of reporting, names are not used. The Bridge Childcare Consultancy Service has conducted nearly half of the reports made public, and its style is to focus on communication issues and the working of systems rather than on the actions of individual workers.

However, the Part 8 Review system has several shortcomings. A key criticism is that the system of review is for the most part a private one, thus creating problems at two levels. First, the public's need to know more about the circumstances in which serious child abuse takes place is not satisfied by this means. Second, the need of professionals to learn from cases which go wrong is not met, as the findings of most reviews are referred back only to the agencies in the area where the child abuse took place. This has been made worse by the fact that there has been very little dissemination of information about the cases reviewed over the ten years or more since the new system was introduced. The Department of Health has provided no overview at all. Three research projects have been given access to the reviews (James 1994; Falkov 1996; Reder and Duncan 1999). James suggested that many of the concerns raised by earlier inquiries (particularly interprofessional communication problems) persist despite the perceived comprehensiveness of the 1991 guidelines. Falkov focused on the extent of psychiatric disorder among parents whose children were fatally abused. Reder and Duncan were concerned to build on previous research (based on earlier inquiry reports) about the link between family dynamics and processes and fatal child abuse (see Reder *et al.* 1993). It is notable that Reder and Duncan found that many of the reviews did not contain sufficient information on which to build a picture of the families. The focus of most reviews was on whether procedures had been followed or not, and the content and quality of them were variable.

In its attempt, therefore, to tackle some of the dysfunctions of the earlier public inquiry approach, the Department of Health seems to have created other problems. The current system is more profession-friendly than before, but it is less open to scrutiny and less accessible to professionals for learning purposes The newly published Department of Health guidelines (DoH 2000a) make only minor alterations to the review system. The main change is that there is a commitment to publish overview reports every two years.

Concluding comments

Inquiries into child abuse in the community have experienced a rise and a fall over a period of approximately 25 years mirroring in many respects the intensity of concerns about such abuse which was the subject of Chapter 2. The pattern of development was as follows. In the early stages of child abuse 'discovery', inquiries tended to be more of a statutory nature and to be concerned with the failings of systems and individuals. In this period, the philosophy and structure of the child protection system which persists to the present time was established. The problem did not go away, however; for as more cases came to public attention, the usefulness of child abuse inquiries came more into question. Professionals were becoming disillusioned and the same problems (mainly ones of poor communication) were coming up again and again, despite the newly established child protection system. At the same time, towards the end of the 1980s, there was a revision of thinking about the nature of child abuse in the community, and a growing concern that professionals were confusing deprivation with abuse which led to a new questioning of the system that child abuse inquiries had been instrumental in creating. Child sexual abuse (Cleveland) and ritual abuse concerns (Orkneys) proved to be the catalysts in this process, again through the medium of public inquiries. However, in contrast to the tenor of earlier inquiries, the concerns in these cases were why professionals had acted with such zeal, though again, particularly in Cleveland, interprofessional communication (or rather lack of it) figured largely. By the beginning of the 1990s, therefore, and since, inquiries into abuse of children in the community have ceased to exist in the old sense, to be replaced by a system of private reviews, a very small proportion of which are published as a result of the widespread public concern raised about them.

We shall now turn our attention to inquiries into abuse of children in residential care which dominated the 1990s.

Notes

1   Toni Dales and two in Caerphilly.

2   Child abuse inquiries before 1975 had relatively limited powers under Section 250 of the Local Government Act 1972. Powers of witness compellability and of enforcing the production of documents were laid down for such inquiries in Section 98(2) of the Children Act 1975 and reiterated in Section 81 of the Child Care Act 1980 and also in Section 81 of the Children Act 1989.

3   As noted earlier, these have now been superseded, though not greatly changed, by new guidelines published in 2000 (DoH 2000a).

CHAPTER 5

Institutional Abuse and Public Inquiries in the late 1980s and 1990s

Introduction

The aim of this chapter is to chart the rise in public concern about the abuse of children in residential institutions in Britain from the late 1980s onwards and the role played by public inquiries in the process.

In Chapter 2 some of the wider contextual factors in the development of concerns about institutional abuse in this era were charted. It was hypothesised that from the 1960s onwards there was an ever-increasing focus placed on children and their welfare needs, resulting from greater affluence and medical advances in the fields of birth control and treatment of children's diseases. The outcome of these developments was a heightened demand for risk elimination and for the need to protect children from various forms of harm, including child abuse within the family. It was also hypothesised that in the 1980s and 1990s there was a shift of focus away from intra-familial abuse on to abuse of children by strangers and by those caring for them outside their homes. In Chapter 4, we looked at the role of public inquiries in the development of concerns about intra-familial abuse. We now shift our attention to institutional abuse.

We noted in Chapter 1 that there was a lack of publicly expressed concern about abuse of children in residential care until the 1980s and 1990s. This can be attributed to a variety of factors in the case of physical abuse and neglect. First, residential care, certainly from the late eighteenth century onwards, was viewed as a last resort option for destitute children. There was always a concern that it should not be seen as a preferred option to family care. Second, for that very reason, conditions in residential care were not expected to be congenial, but to serve a deterrent function. Third, increasingly from the mid-nineteenth century, the residential school solution was used for young offenders; therefore discipline, training and control were the dominant characteristics of such establishments for well over a hundred years. In this type of climate, it is perhaps not hard to understand the rarity of public outcries about physical abuse and neglect.

When we turn to consider the issue of sexual abuse of children in residential care, the explanation for lack of expressions of concern about this form of abuse lies in its secretive nature and in the shame and stigma attached to being a victim of sexual assault until the late 1980s. As we saw in Chapter 2, sexual abuse remained a relatively hidden form of abuse generally in Britain until as late as the mid-1980s. Table 5.1 lists public inquiry reports into abuse of children in residential care between 1967 and 2000.

Table 5.1 Public inquiry reports into abuse of children in residential care 1967–2000

Number	Year	Type of abuse	Name	Concerns and allegations	Reference
1	1967	Physical	Court Lees Approved School	Excessive physical punishment of residents by staff members	Home Office (1967)
2	1985	Sexual	Leeways Children's Home	Sexual abuse of residents by the officer in charge	Lewisham, London Borough of (1985)
3	1986	Sexual	Kincora Working Boys' Hostel	Sexual abuse of residents by a staff member and existence of a paedophile ring	Department of Health and Social Security (Northern Ireland) (1985)
4	1988	Physical	Melanie Klein House for Girls	Excessive use of physical restraints	Social Services Inspectorate (1988).
5	1991	Physical and emotional	Pindown: community homes in Staffordshire County Council	Use of excessively punitive regimes	Staffordshire County Council (Levy, A. and Kahan, B.) (1991).
6	1991	Neglect	Grove Park Community Home, Southwark	Young people out of control and taking drugs	Social Services Inspectorate (1991a)
7	1991	Physical	St Charles Youth Treatment Centre	Use of drugs to restrain resident	Social Services Inspectorate (1991b)
8	1992	Physical	Ty Mawr Community Home	Concerns about incidents of self-harm and suicide by residents	Gwent County Council (1992)

9	1992	Physical	Scotforth House Residential School	Physical abuse of pupils with learning difficulties	Lancashire County Council (1992)
10	1993	Sexual	Castle Hill Residential School	Sexual abuse of pupils by the head of the school	Shropshire County Council (Brannan, C. Jones, R. and Murch, J.) (1992)
11	1993	Sexual and physical	Leicestershire: community homes	Sexual abuse of residents by head of home and other staff members	Leicestershire County Council (Kirkwood, A.) (1993)
12	1994	Physical	Oxendon House	Inappropriate restraint and therapy techniques used by staff on older children with emotional and behavioural problems	Bedfordshire County Council (Roycroft, B. and Witham, L.) (1994)
13	1995	Neglect	Islington: community homes	Concerns about risks to children from staff with previous child abuse convictions	Islington, London Borough of (White, I. and Hart, K.) (1995)
14	1995	Sexual	Meadowdale: community home	Sexual abuse of children with learning difficulties	Northumberland County Council (Kilgallon, W.) (1995)
15	1999	Neglect	Harrow: community home	Drug-related death of 13-year-old girl living in a children's home: concerns re failure to protect	Harrow ACPC (1999)
16	1999	Sexual	Lambeth: community home	Investigation into sexual abuse of a boy in care by a member of staff and the failure of the social services department to make an adequate response to it and its consequences	Lambeth, London Borough of (Barratt, J.) (1999)
17	1999	Sexual	Edinburgh: community homes	Sexual abuse of children by the heads of two homes in the Edinburgh area	Edinburgh, City of (Marshall, K., Jamieson, C. and Finlayson, A.) (1999)
18	2000	Sexual and physical	North Wales Tribunal of Inquiry: all residential homes and schools in Clwyd and Gwynedd	Sexual and physical abuse in a range of residential homes in Clwyd and Gwynedd	Waterhouse, R. (2000)

Court Lees 1967: an excess of punishment

The first main institutional abuse inquiry in the modern era was that into the excessive use of corporal punishment at Court Lees Approved School in Surrey in 1967 (Home Office 1967). Concerns were raised by a member of staff in a letter to the *Guardian* that beatings by the headmaster and the deputy headmaster at the school had resulted in severe bruising of a number of boys. There followed a Home Office inquiry conducted in private, which found that punishment rules had been broken. Boys were found to have been improperly caned, i.e. they were not wearing the required clothing when beaten, and they were beaten with a cane of above the weight limit laid down in the regulations. In addition there was a failure to record beatings on all occasions.

As a result of these findings and the refusal on the part of the management committee to dismiss the head and his deputy, the Secretary of State, Roy Jenkins, decided to close the school immediately, a decision which raised considerable opposition. This inquiry did not lead to any widespread review of punishment practices in approved schools; indeed there was no great public response of indignation.

Leeways and Kincora 1985 and 1986: sexual abuse allegations

In June 1985, following the conviction of Mr Cooper, Officer in Charge of Leeways Children's Home in Lewisham, for offences of indecency involving the taking of obscene photographs of children, an independent inquiry was established by Lewisham Social Services Committee to consider what had happened in this children's home and why it had not been detected earlier (Lewisham 1985). The inquiry found that the offences in question had taken place over a period of ten years and that, at least from 1978 onwards, Mr Cooper's immediate superiors were aware of unacceptable behaviour on his part that had dubious sexual connotations. The inquiry found that the welfare of children in Leeways Home came second to loyalty between staff members. Recommendations included the need to establish a safe complaints procedure for children, more careful recruitment procedures and better staff training.

In the following year, a report was published concerning the sexual abuse of residents in Kincora, a working boys' hostel in Belfast (DHSS(NI) 1986). There had been concerns expressed as early as 1980 about the possible existence of a paedophile ring being centred on this hostel involving highly placed public officials (including police officers) and businessmen. Three members of the staff of Kincora Hostel were prosecuted and convicted in 1981. The 1986 inquiry ordered by the Secretary of State for Northern Ireland followed an abortive inquiry in 1982, an internal DHSS inquiry in the same year, and a police inquiry which reported in 1983. The police inquiry had found no evidence of a paedophile ring involving highly placed persons, but failed to dispel public concern. The 1986 inquiry, headed by His Honour W.H. Hughes, was not required to look at these issues again, but to focus more closely on the working of systems that were meant to prevent abuse and to recommend improvements. The final report advocated more robust forms of home visiting by elected councillors, tougher monitoring by social work professionals and clearer complaints and investigations mechanisms designed to ensure protection for those making allegations pending their resolution. The rationale put forward by the inquiry panel for its recommendations on these matters was as follows:

> We sometimes had the impression in the course of the evidence that there was an ambivalence of attitude towards allegations. While they remained unsubstantiated they could be disregarded and even ignored: yet it was nobody's business to substantiate or discard them – an attitude at one irrational and self-defeating. The fact that such an attitude could prevail, and be regarded as proper, emphasises for us a need for a standard operating procedure which is quite unambiguous, is not discretionary but mandatory and which must always be followed. Such a procedure must indeed involve the closest cooperation with the police. (DHSS(NI) 1986, p.340)

In addition to those relating to investigations of complaints, recommendations were made about improving staff recruitment, gender mix, training, pay and management. The Hughes report is full of eminently sensible recommendations, many of which were echoed in reports later in the 1990s. However, they do not seem to have had much impact nationally. The impression gained from both this inquiry and that into Leeways is that the events in these two places were seen as isolated examples and not as indicative of the likelihood of more widespread abuse.

Melanie Klein House 1988: physical restraints

In 1988 the Social Services Inspectorate reported on the care of older girls in Melanie Klein House (SSI 1988), an establishment managed by Greenwich Social Services Department. The focus was on excessive use of physical restraint by staff to keep the residents under control. The general physical and material standards in the home came under criticism, as did the quality of staff, who were poorly qualified and trained for working with adolescent girls.

Growing realisation of the widespread nature of institutional abuse in the early 1990s

The early 1990s saw many concerns being raised about the treatment of children in care. Social Services Inspectorate reports were asked for in relation to Grove Park, Southwark, where residents were considered to be out of control, abusing drugs and alcohol, and frequently absconding, and at St Charles Youth Treatment Centre, where there were concerns about the use of drug treatment by staff to control the aggressive behaviour of a female resident (SSI 1991a, 1991b). Concerns were raised about the possible abuse of boy residents (including use of solitary confinement) in Ty Mawr in Abergavenny, Gwent, as a result of a number of incidents of suicide and self-harm. This home had a secure unit attached to it and, therefore, dealt with large numbers of young people with challenging behaviours. The inquiry, commissioned by Gwent, reporting in 1992, focused on the poor quality of staff, largely unqualified, inexperienced and inadequately trained for dealing with the type of young people that the home was supposed to cater for (Gwent County Council 1992).

Pindown 1991: excessively punitive regimes

It was the Pindown inquiry report in 1991, however, which really set the ball rolling in terms of more widespread concerns about the quality of care provided in residential homes for children (Staffordshire County Council 1991). Following a complaint made by a 15-year-old girl to a solicitor representing her in care proceedings, Staffordshire County Council set up an inquiry into a practice called Pindown that had been established in a small number of its homes by one of its area residential managers, Tony Latham. Pindown was a crude behaviourist regime aimed at dealing with problematic and challenging children in care. It consisted of taking children who were absconding or refusing to attend school to a poorly furnished room and confining them there, depriving them of daytime clothing and of any amusements such as television, not speaking to them and requiring them to do basic copying tasks as homework. This regime was not kept secret from management. Indeed it was formally established as a model for practice and, although some of the department's managers felt that it sailed close to the wind in terms of then existing Community Homes regulations, nevertheless it had departmental support. The regime was in existence for six years from 1983 to 1989, during which 132 children, some as young as 9 years old, experienced Pindown, some for weeks at a time.

The report of the inquiry, written by a leading children's lawyer, Allan Levy, and a prominent childcare expert, Barbara Kahan, was unequivocal in its judgement, that Pindown, despite its openness and despite there being no evidence of physical abuse, was indeed an emotionally abusive regime. It criticised Staffordshire Social Services Department for its parsimony in relation to childcare spending, the social services management for its acceptance of such practices, the recruitment and training standards among residential workers, and the poor complaints and monitoring procedures that existed within the department. There had been some additional concerns that children in the homes in question had been visited by relatives who were sex offenders. The report made recommendations to tighten procedures for notifying social services departments about a wider range of such offenders than before.

The repercussions from Pindown were immediate and considerable. Although those involved in setting up the regime were not prosecuted (indeed it would have been hard to prove that they had broken the law), Staffordshire County Council nevertheless compensated those children who had been subjected to the regime in out-of-court settlements. Another key development following Pindown was the distribution of a circular by the Department of Health to all English local authorities requiring them to check among their own children's homes for any elements of Pindown-type regimes (*The Times* 4 June 1991). It was clear, therefore, that there were suspicions that harsh and punitive treatment of children spread way beyond Staffordshire, and that the Pindown report's judgement and subsequent compensation claims had radically changed views about the acceptability of such approaches.

The trawl of local authority residential care establishments for children following Pindown revealed major concerns about standards of care in homes in Bradford and Sheffield. At the same time there were press reports about Pindown-type regimes in Scotland at the Brodie Youth Care Centre, Polmont, at Greybiggin School in Northumbria and at Kesteven House in Lincolnshire. As we have seen, there were also major concerns about the regime at Ty Mawr in South Wales.

These events added to the pressure on central government to review the quality of care for children generally and resulted in three reports in England (Utting 1991), Wales (SSI(Wales) 1991) and Scotland (Skinner 1992). The main thrust of these reports was to recognise that residential care for children had changed considerably over the previous ten years. The range of establishments had contracted, as had the number of residents, but crucially those that remained in care were those with the most pressing problems presenting the most difficult challenges to residential staff. Utting (1991), in particular, was adamant that, although residential care was coming to be seen even more as a last resort and that in some counties, such as Warwickshire, it had been dispensed with altogether, this placed the care system and children within it in a precarious position. A key result of the shrinkage was that more children were being placed in privately run accommodation, which was generally less well monitored than local authority establishments, and was often geographically remote from the homes of the children's birth parents. Utting emphasised the need for more residential care provision, not less, for better trained and more carefully recruited staff and for more emphasis to be placed on meeting the needs of children in care in accordance with the requirements of the recently implemented Children Act 1989.

Sexual abuse ⟵

By 1991, however, there were growing concerns about another even more disturbing form of abuse of children in care – sexual abuse. While such abuse had been a feature of two inquiries in 1985, they were largely considered to be isolated examples, and were attributed to the bad apple syndrome. In North Wales, following the conviction of Stephen Norris for indecent assaults on young boys at a children's home near Wrexham, and concerns about a number of other incidents that had arisen throughout the 1970s and 1980s, it was decided to conduct a major police investigation into all homes in Clwyd and Gwynedd. The details of this inquiry are dealt with more fully in the ensuing chapters. However, for the purposes of this chapter, it should be noted that this inquiry involved interviewing all those with complaints to make about their time in care over a decade and a half. The inquiry simply grew and grew. For instance, one complaint could lead to a whole series of investigations involving all children who had been in a home at a particular time, and all the children in other homes where the alleged abuser had previously and since been employed, and so on. The police inquiry lasted for two years and involved taking statements from over 3000 witnesses. This was probably the first such inquiry of its kind in the UK, but was soon to be followed by others, most notably in Lambeth and later in Merseyside and Cheshire. As we shall see, concerns about widespread sexual abuse have persisted relentlessly into the new millennium.

Also in 1991, Frank Beck, head of a children's home in Leicestershire, was convicted of a number of serious sexual and physical assaults on residents in his care. This conviction led to a series of responses. The Department of Health asked Norman Warner to examine the process of recruiting and training residential staff and to make recommendations for improvements, with particular emphasis on the need to protect children from sexual abusers. The Police Complaints Authority conducted an inquiry into the role of the police in responding to allegations of abuse in Leicestershire homes (Police Complaints Authority 1993) and Leicestershire County Council set up an inquiry chaired by Andrew Kirkwood QC. This reported in 1993 (Leicestershire 1993).

CASTLE HILL, SHROPSHIRE 1992

In 1992, while this inquiry was sitting, a report was published into the sexual abuse of children at Castle Hill, an independent special school in Shropshire (Shropshire 1992). The report was less an in-depth inquiry into the abuse that took place there, but was more concerned with developing a model of collaborative practice for the detection and investigation of abuse of this kind. However, the basic facts of what happened are as follows. Between 1987 and 1989, there were several complaints made by boys to the West Mercia Police about sexual abuse of them by the headmaster of the school, Ralph Morris, and other members of staff, but their allegations had little effect. A major weakness seems to have been that the boys making the allegations had been placed by different local authorities from across Britain, and this prevented one particular agency taking an overview of the situation. It seems that Morris was found out only when he abused a second boy from the same authority, Harrow Social Services Department.

There were various other factors that made it difficult to pinpoint Morris as an abuser. He was a charismatic leader of the school who was very much in control of the environment (see Jones 1994). It is clearly harder to challenge those at the top of the tree with allegations of this kind than those at the bottom; it was notable that Morris had misled his employers about his qualifications when appointed. Second, independent schools like Castle Hill were generally less well inspected and open to scrutiny than local authority establishments. Another key factor, by no means unique to Castle Hill, was that because they exhibited educational and behavioural problems, the pupils at this school were not regarded as boys who could be trusted to tell the truth. The report came up with many important recommendations, including the need to respond more thoughtfully to allegations and to support victims through the investigation and trial process. In addition, it pointed to the need for independent schools to be brought more fully under the purview of the authorities in which they are sited so that allegations of abuse can be seen in totality and responded to accordingly.

LEICESTERSHIRE 1993

The Leicestershire (1993) report showed, however, that charismatic leaders who use their influence and position of authority to conceal their abuse of children were not confined to the independent sector.

Frank Beck, when he was appointed in 1973, was a qualified residential worker who presented himself as experienced in working in a therapeutic environment. He introduced a crude form of regression therapy for dealing with problem behaviours which involved infantilising children of all ages. This form of 'treatment' was usually forced on children, and gave Beck the opportunity to sexually abuse a large number of them. Despite there being many complaints about Beck's activities from the children themselves and from others, including parents, foster parents, teachers, field social workers, students on placement and junior residential staff, they fell on deaf ears as far as Beck's managers were concerned. According to the inquiry report, a variety of interlinking factors enabled Beck's physical and sexual abuse of children to go undetected for so long. The first was weak management, which relied on heads of homes to run their own fiefdoms largely without interference as long as they were able to control them. This, combined with Beck's totally independent approach and his ability to contain difficult children much better than most of his peers, meant that he was virtually untouchable. Other factors contributing to this state of affairs were the lack of a proper complaints system, the low status attributed to children in care and the fact that Beck had so much influence in staff appointments, which allowed him to surround himself with vulnerable and unqualified workers whom he could either impress or intimidate.

A further contributory factor was the lack of response by the police to complaints. The Police Complaints Authority (1993) found that, in all, Leicestershire Police dealt with 29 complaints, few of which went any further than the initial contact. The inquiry considered that key factors in this inadequate response were that the children making the complaints had criminal convictions and that as a result most of the police officers dealing with them saw them as no more than juvenile delinquents who habitually told lies (Police Complaints Authority 1993).

The Kirkwood inquiry report (Leicestershire 1993) pointed to the need for improved management of residential care, better monitoring and visiting procedures, and a complete overhaul of the system for dealing with complaints.

The Warner (1992) report, which had been prompted by the conviction of Frank Beck, meanwhile provided detailed guidelines for the recruitment, selection and appointment of staff. Whether attention to these aspects would have prevented the appointment of the rare commodity of a qualified residential worker in 1973 is open to question. Certainly, in 2000, the reservations of Frank Beck's college tutor about his dogmatic views and approach would in all likelihood throw doubts on his suitability for the residential task. However, in reponse to the findings of both Utting (1991) and Warner (1992), the Department of Health took some steps to improve the pay and training of residential staff (but see Chapter 9) and commissioned a series of research programmes to gain greater knowledge of current practice in children's homes.

Continuing concerns about physical and sexual abuse up to 1995

Between late 1992 and 1995, police investigations into physical and sexual abuse of children in boarding schools and children's homes were becoming commonplace; examples in the press for this period include investigations into children being exposed to pimps and prostitutes in Islington homes, concerns about physical abuse of children with special needs at a residential school in Chepstow and in Scotforth House, Lancashire, a social worker in Sheffield being jailed for sexual abuse of boys in his care for a period of 13 years, and the commencement of a major police inquiry in Merseyside and Cheshire. In addition, there were concerns about the inability of some homes to contain children in their care. In January 1994, children were reported as being on the rampage at Oakhill House in Birmingham, prompting an inquiry by the Social Services Inspectorate. In December of the same year, a family support unit in Sheffield was closed after six months because the children were too violent to control.

OXENDON HOUSE 1994

In August 1994 an inquiry set up by Bedfordshire County Council reported on events that had taken place during the previous year at Oxendon House, a long-term residential home for 20 older children (Bedfordshire County Council 1994). Concerns had been raised by a newly appointed assistant director of social services about certain practices favoured by the long-established staff team there. These included the use of massage (neck-rubbing) to soothe residents who were experiencing emotional upsets, individual and anger counselling, physical restraints to control aggressive behaviour and playfighting. Following these concerns being raised, there were three allegations of abuse against staff (two sexual and one physical). The investigation of the director of social services led to the temporary closure of the home with traumatic consequences for some of the children. The report findings are curiously mixed. No evidence of actual abuse was found. The various practices which had been highlighted were seen to be faulty on two main grounds. First, the staff were not considered sufficiently qualified, particularly in regard to counselling, to offer these specialist forms of service. Second, the various physical contact practices were seen to be risky in that they exposed staff to potential abuse allegations. Third, while few children actually did make complaints, it was felt that they were not given a great deal of choice in the matter. The action of the director of social services to close the home was seen as regrettable but necessary in the light of the information that he had available to him at the time. Overall, the inquiry report is highly equivocal in relation to whether practices at Oxendon House were abusive or not. The main conclusion is that staff were well intentioned, but overzealous and ill equipped for the tasks that they undertook which in some cases had abusive consequences.

Summary

It is clear that by the middle of the 1990s there was already a wide range of types of abuse being recognised – physical and emotional abuse linked either to the regime of a home (as in Pindown) or to individual pathology (as in Leicestershire), sexual abuse by individual members of staff, and neglect or failure to provide adequate protection for children.[1]

The concerns being raised were about both historical and current abuse. Much of the physical abuse being exposed, particularly that relating to earlier periods, was indicative of a general lack of quality pervading residential childcare at the time it took place, and to some degree was a product of later definitions of what is abusive. More and more, however, particularly in recent times, such abuse could be seen as the result of misguided attempts, often by poorly qualified and trained staff, to tackle the problem of large numbers of children with deep-seated problems in a context of shrinking resources and limited managerial leadership.

In the case of sexual abuse, the constant stream of new revelations across the UK, even though much of it had allegedly taken place several years before, raised new questions about why it was apparently so prevalent. The bad apple theory seemed to be an inadequate explanation. More and more questions were being asked about paedophile rings and the targeting of children's homes by those wishing to abuse children sexually. These issues will be revisited after considering developments which took place between 1995 and 2000.

More and more revelations 1995–2000

Islington 1995

The year 1995 saw the publication of two more public inquiry reports into the abuse of children in residential homes. The concerns about care of children in Islington which had been raised in 1992 were dealt with in the first of these reports (Islington 1995). It had been alleged that staff had sexually assaulted children and teenagers in care, had encouraged children into prostitution and paedophile rings and had involved them in drug misuse. None of the allegations was found to be proven in the report, though it considered that it was possible that many of the allegations were true. The report was highly critical of staff practices in the homes, which were considered to be unprofessional and at the least to have placed children at risk. Council officials and managers were particularly criticised for not intervening in some of the practices because the staff involved were from ethnic minorities or gay, and they were afraid that they would not be supported in taking what might have been perceived to be discriminatory disciplinary action. In general terms, the management of Islington's social services was seen to be inadequate; it was considered to be insufficiently vigilant in both its recruitment practices and in its response to complaints about abuse.

Meadowdale 1995

At the opposite end of England, the Kilgallon inquiry reported into alleged abuse of disabled children in Meadowdale community home, Northumberland (Northumberland County Council 1995). The alleged abuse included sexual and physical assaults and neglect and dated from the early 1970s through to the late 1980s. The inquiry was satisfied that there had been widespread abuse. The standard of care provided was considered to be poor; there was no training provided for handling children with disabilities which the home specialised in from 1982 onwards; staffing levels were poor; monitoring was very limited, and the response to complaints was largely negative. It is notable that at its worst period, between 1972 and 1984, Meadowdale was run by a care officer described by residents and staff in the report 'as a bully who ruled with a firm hand' (Northumberland 1995, p.15).

Further concerns

There was no lack of other concerns at this time. The Kilgallon report put the spotlight on another children's home in Northumberland which was alleged to be running a regime akin to Pindown. In 1996, there were concerns raised about the physical abuse of children in a Scope-run home in Guiseley, Leeds, and in a privately run home in Kent. There were also concerns about the possible sexual abuse of children in Humberside, Cardiff and Buckinghamshire. In June 1996, Sir William Utting was asked to conduct a review of safeguards for all children living away from home; his 1991 review had focused on residential care for children provided by local authorities. This time his remit also included children in residential schools, in foster placements and in hospitals. Almost simultaneously it was announced that after a series of other inquiries, a Tribunal of Inquiry would be held into the abuse of children in homes in North Wales (see Chapter 6).

In 1997, allegations were made of brutality to children by Roman Catholic nuns in a home in Aberdeen (dating back 30 years). Allegations of sexual abuse dating back 20 years were raised by ex-residents of a National Children's Home establishment in Bristol. Further complaints about sexual and physical abuse of children in residential establishments were made in Dewsbury, Leicestershire, Northumberland, Lancashire, Sunderland, Glasgow and Halifax. The Utting children's safeguards review was also published in 1997. It found that there were grounds for concern about the protection of all children living away from home, and that children in foster care and residential schools were subject to less monitoring and official oversight than those in local authority residential care. It also stressed that abuse of children in residential homes remained a current problem exacerbated by the reduction in available places and the fact that children being accommodated in them were increasingly the most deprived and neglected of those being looked after away from home. In an article in *Community Care* in July 1998, is was stated that all but 5 of the 52 police forces in the UK had investigated allegations of abuse in care homes.

Edinburgh, Harrow and Lambeth 1999

The year 1999 saw the publication of three inquiry reports into institutional abuse, in Edinburgh, Harrow and Lambeth. The first of these dealt with the sexual abuse of large numbers of residents in two children's homes in Edinburgh by two staff members over a period of fourteen years. The inquiry drew attention to the fact that children had made complaints on numerous occasions, but nothing had been done until 1996, when finally an allegation was taken seriously resulting in the prosecution of the two abusers. The report is a conciliatory one in many respects and does not specifically allocate blame. However, it does make 135 recommendations with particular emphasis on facilitating the making of complaints, whistleblowing and listening to children.

The Harrow Area Child Protection Committee report was a Part 8 Review into the death of Aliyah Ismael, a summary of which was made available to the public because of the interest that the case had created. Aliyah, a 13-year-old girl who had been looked after by Harrow Social Services Department for approximately six months, died from an overdose of methadone. The report (Harrow ACPC 1999) showed that there had been considerable concern about Aliyah's behaviour throughout the period during which she had been looked after. She had been truanting from school, been involved in prostitution and had been treated for sexually transmitted diseases. Nevertheless, no action was taken to contain and control Aliyah until just before her death, when ironically a case was being prepared for a secure accommodation order under Section 25 of the Children Act 1989. The report concluded that there had been insufficient inter-agency sharing of information, that more attention should be paid to risk assessment in relation to older children who were challenging in their behaviours, and that child prostitution should be viewed more squarely as a child protection issue.

The Lambeth Independent Child Protection Inquiry (1999) looked into the circumstances of the abuse of a boy in their care by a member of staff who subsequently died from an HIV-related illness. The boy concerned had been abused while in Angell Road Residential Unit some time between 1989 and 1992 (when the alleged abuser died). He was then aged between 7 and 11 years. Although there had been considerable suspicion previously that he had been abused, he did not in fact make an allegation until 1996. Even then, the allegation was not properly investigated until 1998, when Merseyside Police became involved with Lambeth Social Services as part of the investigations that they were carrying out. The case raised considerable concerns about why the alleged abuse had not been investigated according to procedures, about why the boy involved had not been properly informed about the facts so that appropriate steps could have been taken to assess his state of health, and about why no checks had been made on other children who had been living in the same home when the alleged abuser had been employed there. The report concluded that Lambeth's systems of responding to abuse allegations and their residential care arrangements were woefully lacking in almost all respects.

'The year 2000'

The new millennium saw no reduction in concerns. The findings of the North Wales Tribunal of Inquiry (to be dealt with more fully in Chapter 8) were finally published in February 2000. The detailed accounts of abuse of children in care contained in this report, albeit dealing largely with abuse taking place in the 1970s and 1980s, make disquieting reading and have resulted in a rather panic-stricken focus on adoption as potential means of doing away with residential care altogether. Even more recently (28 February 2000) the *Guardian* reported that Avon and Somerset Police have opened up an inquiry into the alleged abuse of children over a 30-year period in assessment centres in Taunton and Bristol.

Impact of inquiry reports

These then are the main facts of the institutional abuse revelations since the mid-1980s. While we have tried to be as comprehensive as we can, it should be noted that there are no doubt even more cases reported on than discussed here, and we have not made reference to cases of sexual abuse in nurseries or in other organisations in the community.

The inquiry reports and other sources of information make sobering reading indeed. The impact of inquiry reports on residential care will be considered in more detail in Chapters 9 and 10. For now, however, it is worth summarising some of the main issues that they raise about the practice and management of residential care. For the most part, the inquiry reports we have considered have achieved the following:

- They have laid bare most of the available facts of the cases into which they have conducted their investigations, which is one of their key functions.

- They have paid attention to the contexts in which the abuses have taken place, in particular emphasising the impact of the increasing residualisation of residential care and its sizing down from the late 1970s onwards.

- They have within this context looked at the actions of individual practitioners and managers in an attempt to evaluate responsibility for the abuse at this level.

- They have made a series of recommendations for remedying the problems identified.

In summary, the inquiries have looked at a range of abuse types including sexual abuse, physical abuse, neglect and emotional abuse. In some cases, the treatment of children defined in reports as abusive was not necessarily seen as such by those alleged to have carried it out. This was particularly the case in relation to physical abuse, where much of the mistreatment in question was seen to be part of a controlling regime, as in Court Lees, Ty Mawr and Pindown; some of it was seen as an inevitable by-product of dealing with difficult older children, as in Greenwich and North Wales. However, this argument could not be used in the case of all alleged physical abuse. There are several examples of such abuse being used as an intimidatory form of control (North Wales and Leicestershire); it certainly could not be used in most of the cases of sexual abuse, which nearly all involved children being induced or forced into sexual acts without their consent by those in authority over them.

Almost all the reports have come to the conclusion that there has been little in the way of conspiracy in the abuse that has been investigated; this is probably also true of the police investigations. As pointed out above, in some cases abuse has been instigated by or tolerated by staff in homes as a means of controlling children, but more often, particularly in relation to more serious assaults, it has been carried out in isolation by certain individuals generally viewed as being bullies or authoritarian personalities. In the case of sexual abuse, none of the inquiries has found evidence that abusers were working together or passing children around via paedophile rings. There have been several cases where children have been abused by more than one person in the same home (Leicestershire, North Wales, Castle Hill), but the inquiries have found no connection between abusers in these cases.

None of the reports, however, has found it sufficient to blame individuals solely for the abuse investigated into. Far from it. As has been seen, there have been various reasons put forward, including some of the broader contextual factors referred to above, i.e. the low status of residential care and its increasing decline since the 1970s as a form of substitute care for children.

The main findings of inquiry reports have been as follows:

1. The existence of poor management of residential childcare by those with responsibility to provide oversight, direction and monitoring. A feature of many of the homes about which inquiry reports were written was the degree of autonomy given to heads of homes to organise and administer their establishments with the minimum of outside interference.

2. The lack of close inspection of homes by councillors and others with responsibilities in this sphere such as the Social Services Inspectorate in England and the Welsh Office in Wales.

3. Major deficiencies in the handling of complaints and the lack of clear procedures particularly prior to the implementation of the Children Act 1989 in October 1991. In particular, reports have pointed to the lack of opportunity to make complaints to persons outside of the homes.

4. Insensitivity towards the needs of children and a failure to listen to them. Several reports emphasise that more and more, as the overall resource shrinks, many children in residential care have major behavioural problems that bring them into conflict with staff. They also note that when such children complain they are often not listened to, and when they abscond, this behaviour is often seen as indicative of the problems they pose rather than as a possible response to abuse.

5. Poor standards of qualification among residential staff and insufficiently rigorous recruitment practices. Despite the fact that nearly all reports emphasise this as an issue, the level of qualification among residential childcare staff remains at around 15 per cent. Certainly until the 1990s, recruitment practices were relatively easy-going, influenced no doubt by the difficulties attached to attracting sufficient numbers to a low status occupation initially. Such practices could result in the appointment of individuals who were temperamentally unsuited to work with deprived children and, at the worst, those who had histories of actual or suspected child mistreatment.

These messages from inquiries are important ones from which much can be learned, even though the same issues are raised over and over again.

However, there are some criticisms to be made of the inquiry reports. First, they tend to focus heavily on factual information and not to theorise about the causes of abuse in institutions. To some degree this is understandable, but it does mean that there are key issues that receive less attention than they might. For instance, gender issues tend to be ignored. Commentators such as Berridge and Brodie (1996) have highlighted the fact that the development of macho cultures within homes can contribute to both physical and sexual abuse by both staff and peers. It is clear that male abusers are far more prevalent than female abusers, which has prompted some writers (see Pringle 1992) to suggest that the likelihood of institutional abuse would be greatly reduced if care homes were staffed by females only. While this may be a step too far for some, there seems to be sufficient evidence to suggest a need to address gender issues more closely in residential care.

A second concern is that inevitably inquiry reports focus on poor practice and that as a consequence, residential care as a whole is given a negative image, which can compound some of the problems that it is trying to tackle.

A third issue is that analysis of events with the benefit of hindsight can exaggerate the deficiencies of those faced with problems at the time they are happening. When we know that abuse has happened, it influences our interpretation of facts, behaviours, responses and decisions which took place without the outcomes being known. With hindsight, for instance, it is clear that in Leicestershire, Beck's regressive therapies were a cover for his abuse of children in his care. At the time, however, he was the head of the home and had gained some local reputation for being a skilled therapist. These 'factors' would have made it all the harder at the time to believe an allegation of abuse made against him.

A fourth issue relates to judging the past by today's standards. As we have seen, many, though not all, inquiries and investigations have been concerned with events that took place as much as 30 years ago. Attitudes to control and punishment, particularly in relation to older children, have changed considerably since that time. Corporal punishment in residential homes has been banned and there is greater awareness of the potential causes of children's challenging behaviour – particularly the part that the various forms of prior abuse may play in it. This has to be borne in mind when considering past events. Serious physical abuse and sexual abuse of children are less subject to changing interpretations over time. However, lack of awareness of sexual abuse until the 1990s or so may have contributed to the fact that it remained relatively undetected.

A final issue relates to the impact of abuse-focused findings on practice. In the case of abuse of children in the community, the outcome of public inquiry reports was (as we saw in Chapter 4) the development of defensive practices which resulted in families feeling scrutinised rather than supported (see DoH 1995). It is important that the same mistakes are not made in residential care as it develops more formal complaints procedures and protects whistleblowers from being discouraged from raising their concerns.

Concluding comments

This chapter has considered the rise of public concerns about institutional abuse of children since the mid-1980s with particular emphasis on the role of child protection inquiries in the process. The strengths and weaknesses of inquiry reports in relation to such abuse have been considered. We now switch our attention to the particular case of the North Wales Tribunal of Inquiry.

Note

1   A fourth form of abuse was also being highlighted in the literature, which could also come under the heading of neglect – that of failing to provide protection from abuse by other residents (see Thomas 1990).

CHAPTER 6

Events Leading up to the North Wales Tribunal of Inquiry into Child Abuse

Introduction

In this and the following two chapters we focus our attention on the specific case of the North Wales Tribunal of Inquiry, examining the events leading up to its establishment, the way in which its proceedings were conducted and its findings. The subject of this chapter is, therefore, a description and an analysis of the events that preceded and resulted in the inquiry. Material from previous chapters must be borne in mind when considering these details, most notably the following:

- the upsurge of concerns about the physical (and later sexual) abuse of children by their parents and carers beginning in the 1970s
- the particular emphasis on abuse of children in residential care throughout the 1990s
- changes in the nature of residential care from the 1970s onwards
- policies and politics in relation to the use of public inquiries in general and in relation to child abuse in particular.

Announcing the Tribunal of Inquiry

The North Wales Tribunal of Inquiry was announced by the Secretary of State for Wales, William Hague, in a statement to the House of Commons on 17 June 1996. The announcement followed a campaign which had started in 1986 and had led to the exposure of a series of alleged cases of physical and sexual abuse in children's homes in the two counties of Clwyd and Gwynedd. This campaign had aroused considerable suspicions regarding the way in which complaints and concerns were handled by those charged with responsibilities for residential care for children. In his speech to the House, the minister pledged that there would be no cover up and that he hoped that the appointment of the Tribunal would close a 'very sad chapter in the history of public childcare'.

Why North Wales? Why a Tribunal of Inquiry?

As has been pointed out in previous chapters, it is notable that at this time North Wales was not the only place where there was major concern about abuse of children in residential care. The police were conducting investigations in many parts of the UK and two public inquiry reports into the abuse of children (or exposure to abuse) in residential homes had been published the previous year – in Islington (1995) and Northumberland (1995). Indeed, such were the concerns about the spate of institutional abuse incidents during the first half of the 1990s that on the same day that the North Wales Tribunal of Inquiry was announced, Sir William Utting was asked to head a review of safeguards for all children cared for away from home.

In the light of these events it is interesting to speculate why it was felt that a major inquiry into events in North Wales was required, and why in particular it should take the form of a Tribunal of Inquiry, which (as we have seen) is the most formidable means of inquiry available to the state and which had never before been used to inquire into matters relating to child abuse.

The extent of concern about institutional abuse of children could have been a factor: it may have been felt that a detailed and authoritative investigation of the phenomenon in one area was what was needed to get to the bottom of the matter and to allay public and professional concern. However, the opposite could also be argued – that the general high level of concern and the existence of other recent inquiries and reviews lessened the need for an inquiry into this specific case. We shall return to these general questions towards the end of the chapter. For now, attention will be focused on the specific details of key events which took place in North Wales and on how these were shaped and framed in a way that led to a call for, and agreement to, the Tribunal of Inquiry.

The Secretary of State's announcement of the Tribunal in June 1996 was the culmination of a series of internal, independent and police inquiries and sustained pressure from agencies and individuals for a definitive and authoritative investigation of the state of childcare in North Wales. For a long time this was strenuously resisted but ultimately events converged in such a way as to make that pressure irresistible.

The organisational context

The 1970s: changes in social services, local government and residential care

The early 1970s was a time of considerable upheaval for local authority admin-istration in general, for the organisation of social services provision and for childcare services in particular. New local authorities were created in 1974 following the reorganisation of local government and it was at this time that the counties of Clwyd and Gwynedd were formed.

Just prior to this there had been a major reorganisation of the delivery of personal social services by local authorities. The Local Authority Social Services Act 1970 gave effect to the recommendations of the Seebohm Committee (Seebohm 1968) to establish unified social services departments to replace the previously existing health, welfare and children's departments. These new departments were required to organise the provision of the whole range of social services, one result of which was the diminution of specialisa-tion in the different areas of activity.

At about the same time, the Children and Young Persons Act 1969 was brought into effect. This Act aimed to regularise the increasingly blurred dis-tinction between the treatment of children who were deprived or neglected and those who came to the attention of the courts through their offending behaviour. The main aim of the Act was to bring fewer children before the courts and to provide more community-based interventions for young offenders. With regard to residential care (see also Chapter 1), the Act aimed to cut through the demarcation between differential treatment and regimes for offenders and non-offenders, and to meet the social, emotional and educa-tional needs of all children coming into care regardless of the route taken and the reasons for care being required. Children were to be accommodated in a range of settings provided by local authorities within a regional planning framework, including community homes and observation and assessment centres. Approved schools, which had been primarily geared to what were then perceived to be the needs of young offenders, were replaced by community homes with education on the premises, which were intended to satisfy the broader remit referred to above.

The two main local authority homes at the centre of the North Wales inquiries were created as a result of these changes. Ty'r Felin, in Bangor, was opened in 1974 as one of the new observation and assessment centres. Bryn Estyn, in Wrexham, metamorphosed overnight from an approved school, first established in 1942, to a community home which came to be administered by Clwyd County Council as part of the Welsh Regional Plan. It comprised an assessment facility, a remand home and long-term residential care for between 40 and 60 boys.

In both these homes, as was no doubt the case across the UK, residential staff had to come to terms with conditions and situations to which they were unused and for which they were often ill equipped as a result of a lack of training (and retraining). In homes like Bryn Estyn, for instance, many senior postholders had been employed in the previous harsher, more punitive era and they found it difficult to come to terms with more child-centred approaches. In effect, practice, training and the necessary resources were simply not in place to support the changes heralded in the Children and Young Persons Act 1969. This resulted in a confusion of aims and roles which was at the heart of many of the problems of residential childcare that emerged during this time.

Matters were made worse when cash limits were placed on local authorities for the first time as a result of the world oil crisis in 1975–6. As a consequence of this, prioritisation became the name of the game and in many areas children's residential care came low on the list of priorities. This was certainly the case as far as the North Wales authorities were concerned.

The 1980s: cut-backs in residential care for children – shuffling the pack

By the 1980s, there had been considerable reductions in the provision of residential services nationally and North Wales was no exception. Cuts in residential services were particularly harsh in Gwynedd, where great emphasis was placed on foster-care provision by the end of the 1980s. In Clwyd, Bryn Estyn, as was true of community homes with education on the premises throughout the UK, was closed in 1984. Its staff were dispersed to smaller community homes, and again they received little retraining and reorientation. The closure of community homes with education on the premises also meant that smaller homes were required to deal with more challenging residents than they had previously been used to. This led to major problems in relation to setting limits and dealing with issues of control and discipline.

Allegations in Gwynedd, 1986–91

It is in this context that the key events that led to the Tribunal took place. (A chronology of these events is in Appendix 2.) In 1986, Alison Taylor, who had previously worked at Ty'r Felin, the observation and assessment centre in Gwynedd referred to above, and was by this time officer in charge of another Gwynedd home, became concerned enough about the running of Ty'r Felin to approach a local county councillor with her complaints. Those complaints included allegations of assault, inappropriate conduct, and management deficiencies in the county's social services department.

As a result, a police investigation was conducted by the head of the Criminal Investigation Department (CID) for North Wales Police. On receiving the reports of the investigation, the Crown Prosecution Service (CPS) advised against any prosecutions. When further complaints were made by an ex-resident of the home at the centre of the incidents, the investigation was reopened in 1987. Again, reports were submitted to the CPS which, again, advised against prosecution of any individual.

In November 1987 Alison Taylor was suspended and dismissed from her post with the social services department. However, if Gwynedd County Council found her troublesome as an employee, it was to encounter even more problems with her as a dismissed former employee. She embarked upon a mission to expose what she saw as victimisation of herself as the arch whistle-blower in this affair, concealment of abuse and poor practice by the social services department, and the inadequate investigation of offences against children in care on the part of North Wales Police. She wrote prodigiously to officials and politicians, both locally and nationally, and contributed to various media projects which grew into a campaign to reopen the Gwynedd investigations.

Events in Clwyd

Despite the vigour of Alison Taylor's campaign, however, it is unlikely that her concerns about abuse in Gwynedd alone would have triggered a major inquiry. From the early 1990s, it was events in the neighbouring county of Clwyd that came to dominate the scene.

The Rutter and Norris cases

In April 1990, at a Deeside hostel for the homeless being run by a local housing association, a young female resident accused the warden, Fred Rutter, of sexual impropriety towards her. The 18-year-old resident complained to Clwyd Social Services Department and to North Wales Police. Rutter was suspended by his employers on 18 May 1990 and, though denying all allegations against him, resigned from his post in June that year. Other allegations followed and on 30 July 1991, Rutter was convicted of four counts of rape and two of indecent assault. He was sentenced to twelve years' imprisonment.

On 15 June 1990 a member of the care staff in Cartrefle community home for young people in Broughton, Clwyd, was informed by a male resident that the officer in charge, Stephen Norris, had sexually abused him. The boy had taken the opportunity to speak out about the abuse he had suffered while his alleged abuser was away on holiday. His complaint was quickly relayed to a social services department principal officer in charge of children's services and thence to senior management. The matter was referred to North Wales Police and a joint investigation under the terms of the Department of Health's *Working Together* guidelines (DoH 1988a) was initiated. On 5 October 1990, Norris was found guilty of indecent assaults on three boys and sentenced to three and a half years' imprisonment.

North Wales Police officers carried out investigations in both these cases and confined themselves only to the allegations made by residents of the homes in which the perpetrators were currently working. They did not broaden their inquiries to include, for instance, checking with residents in care establishments where Rutter and Norris had worked before. The police were later to be heavily criticised and treated with much suspicion for not doing so. However, it should be borne in mind that in 1990 the practice of pursuing networks of abuse was not yet an established one.

Cartrefle Panel of Inquiry

These incidents of abuse were seen as a blow to the credibility of Clwyd Social Services Department. At the conclusion of the criminal case involving Norris in October 1990, the director, Daniel Gledwyn Jones, established the Cartrefle Panel, with an independent chairperson, to inquire into the management of the abused children's cases, and the circumstances surrounding Norris's appointment and career of abuse. The department had approached the Welsh Office in the hope of persuading it to conduct an inspection or an inquiry, but was advised to go down the prescribed route of a Part 9 Review under the then existing *Working Together* guidelines (DHSS 1988). This type of review, however, had been largely designed for dealing with single cases of abuse of children by their parents and was not particularly appropriate for investigating residential abuse where several children were involved, and the staff and management of the homes were suspected of malpractice. The resulting inquiry was something of a compromise between such a review and a more formal wide-ranging investigation of the circumstances.

The final report, referred to throughout the Tribunal of Inquiry as the Banham report (though in fact John Banham conducted only that part of the review which dealt with social services management systems), was not delivered to Clwyd Social Services Committee until September 1992 and even then only in truncated form. Events had overtaken this report and a full-scale police investigation was by now under way (see next section). In the light of this and the possibility of further criminal prosecutions, the Crown Prosecution Service had advised against the whole report being made available for public scrutiny. Clwyd County Council's insurers, Municipal Mutual Insurance, also advised that the report should not be published, but for different reasons: the company was concerned that any admission of liability on the council's part would lead to a flood of compensation claims, not only from residents and ex-residents but also from staff and carers named in the report. The consequent non-publication of the full report added to the dissatisfaction and suspicion of those who wanted to pinpoint responsibility for the state of affairs which had allowed abuse to continue unchecked (see below).

North Wales Police Inquiry 1991–93
Political and managerial changes in Clwyd County Council

A significant change in approach to investigating concerns about abuse in children's homes in Wales had taken place in 1991. This was greatly influenced by (indeed it could be argued that it was a direct result of) significant changes in the political and managerial climate taking place at this time in Clwyd. The Labour party emerged from the 1989 local government elections with overall control of the county council for the first time. The approach of the Labour group in Clwyd was much more interventionist than that of any of the preceding administrations. As a result, the balance of power between chairs of committees and chief officers changed dramatically. According to the evidence to the Tribunal of Inquiry of a former Clwyd director of social services, members were not generally involved in determining operational policy other than considering and amending proposals presented by officers at Committee. The 1989 election, however,

> heralded a major cultural change in the role of the chair and senior members, which gained further impetus when Cllr Malcolm King became Chair of Social Services. (North Wales Tribunal of Inquiry. Unread Statements vii B pp.4970–4972)

While some senior officers found this difficult to deal with, others appreciated new forums which

> brought together the political and professional management of the Social Services Department, providing a political steer for officers on policy issues, enabled problems or dilemmas to be aired and kites to be flown away from the

glare of publicity and enabled feedback to be given to key members on the implementation of policy and operational issues. (North Wales Tribunal of Inquiry. Unread Statements vii B pp.4970–4972)

As a former employee of Clwyd County Council in the intermediate treatment field, Cllr King took a closer interest in children's services than any of his predecessors. His more proactive role was married with the new managerialism invading local government at this time when John Jevons was promoted to become director of social services in April 1991. With a background in management science and a belief in the power of effective systems and structures to deliver quality services, Jevons introduced a more open management style to the department. Unsurprisingly, this greater openness was soon to embroil him and his department in the long-running controversy surrounding allegations of child abuse in North Wales. Another significant change at the helm was the election of Cllr Dennis Parry as Leader of the Council in May 1991. Cllr Parry was also a member of the North Wales Police Authority and of the same interventionist persuasion as his colleague on the Social Services Committee.

Build-up of evidence, admissions, suspicions and queries

Prior to his elevation from deputy director, John Jevons had not held responsibility for any of the services provided for children, these being the preserve of a children's team, under the ultimate line management of the previous director, Gledwyn Jones. His first contact with Clwyd's childcare regime, as director, constituted not so much a baptism of fire as a steady stream of smoke coming from the children's homes in the county. In 1986 and 1987, David Gillison and Jackie Thomas had been convicted for sexual offences against young people in Chevet Hey Children's Home and then there were the convictions of Stephen Norris and Frederick Rutter (referred to above). Finally, during the Cartrefle investigation that followed the prosecution of Stephen Norris, other issues came to light, not least of which was the admission by another member of the staff in this home that she had been conducting a sexual relationship with one of the boys whom Norris had also been abusing. Factors such as these and the sheer number of convictions led Jevons to consider whether or not there was a linkage between these abuse incidents such as some form of paedophile ring or organised abuse.

A possible connecting link between many of the convicted and suspected offenders was that at some stage in their career, they had worked at Bryn Estyn Community Home (see above). The Banham report also made reference to connections between Cartrefle and Bryn Estyn – not surprisingly since, on the closure of Bryn Estyn in 1984, its staff were redeployed to other homes including Cartrefle. On 10 June 1991 Cllr Parry, the newly appointed Leader of the Council, met with Alison Taylor and received from her information about a number of allegations of abuse, mismanagement and police incompetence surrounding childcare in Gwynedd. Most of the allegations of abuse she relayed were second hand, she herself having witnessed only a few instances of physical ill-treatment. However, the person against whom most of her allegations were directed was also an ex-employee of Bryn Estyn.

Involving the police

This information was discussed with John Jevons and together with all the other material he had gathered it led him to feel that there was 'a very nasty smell coming from the direction of Bryn Estyn' (North Wales Tribunal of Inquiry Transcripts (NWTT) Day 152, p.22, 618). Although his initial concerns revolved around Bryn Estyn, he set out to map all the concerns and connections of which there was evidence. Action was taken to secure all management, homes, personnel and case files which might be relevant to a preliminary investigation. A small team with knowledge of the staff and the homes under suspicion was convened. As a result the authority collated information of all previous convictions of staff employed in residential homes from as far back as 1976. In addition to the recorded convictions, they unearthed several cases of allegations of sexual and physical abuse which were investigated by the police, but did not result in prosecutions. They also examined material from four internal inquiries into abuse incidents at children's homes which had been held between 1975 and 1990. On 17 July 1991 this information was presented to North Wales Police in a letter from Andrew Loveridge, the county council's secretary, along with an invitation to investigate the possibility of widespread abuse in Clwyd's children's homes. As a result the investigation into Bryn Estyn and other Clwyd homes began formally on 2 August 1991 under the direction of Detective Superintendent Peter Ackerley.

More from the Gwynedd connection

Meanwhile Alison Taylor was keeping up the pressure about her concerns: on 26 September 1991 she collaborated with Harlech Television's *Wales This Week* programme to expose the Gwynedd allegations. A number of former residents were interviewed and alleged physical abuse at Ty'r Felin. Among the allegations made by Ms Taylor were that the North Wales Police and the

Crown Prosecution Service had failed to initiate proceedings in the face of significant evidence of abuse. After the programme was broadcast, the director of social services in Gwynedd wrote to the chief constable asking him to investigate the allegations which had emerged. At the end of November that year, Alison Taylor produced her *Gwynedd County Council Analysis*, containing 75 separate allegations, many of which had not been referred to North Wales Police during the two investigations of 1986–87.

Ms Taylor was also gathering further information about abuse in Bryn Estyn. Her main sources of information were young people in care in Gwynedd who had spent time at Bryn Estyn, where she herself had been on placement as a student in 1982. She and Councillor Parry passed on a significant amount of this information to Dean Nelson, a freelance journalist writing for the *Independent on Sunday*. He was something of a veteran of child abuse exposés, having written extensively about abuse and poor practice at a South Wales home, Ty Mawr. Turning his eye to North Wales, he wrote an article, published on 1 December 1991, which implicated a retired police officer in allegations of a serious sexual nature at Bryn Estyn. These and other allegations against serving and former police officers added a new dimension to the atmosphere of distrust which permeated the political situation in North Wales. They also raised the spectre in the minds of those predisposed to such suspicions of Masonic influences being brought to bear. The possibility that serving or former police officers might have been implicated by such allegations caused Cllrs Parry and King to suggest that any further investigation should be undertaken by an outside force, but this (and any other form of external review suggested) was resisted by the chief constable. As a consequence, the allegations of partiality, or at least the appearance of partiality, persisted.

Merging the police inquiries

On 2 December the police decided to merge their Clwyd and Gwynedd inquiries into what was referred to throughout the Tribunal proceedings as the Major Inquiry. Detective Superintendent Ackerley remained in charge. The social services department management in Clwyd and Gwynedd cooperated fully with North Wales Police and an inquiry office was established to ensure that the 'Major Inquiry' team had free access to any reports, files and archives which would assist its investigation. As the scale of the allegations became clearer, Clwyd County Council decided to fund a Helpline operated by the NSPCC to offer support and counselling for witnesses and adult survivors of abuse.

However, despite all efforts by North Wales Police to demonstrate the professionalism of its response, speculation continued about its impartiality. In the light of this continuing criticism, they invited the Police Complaints Authority (PCA) to supervise the investigation of complaints against serving officers in January 1992. The PCA decided that this was not necessary. The Chief Constable himself, in a press release dated 4 September 1992, called for a full public inquiry into the North Wales affair. This was followed, a few days later, by a promise from Gwilym Jones, the Under-Secretary of State for Wales, that there would, indeed, be such an inquiry once the police investigations and any consequent legal proceedings had been completed.

There was, however, still no let-up in the pressure: the Chief Constable of North Wales, David Owen, was informally advised in October 1992 by Donald Elliott (Her Majesty's Inspector of Constabulary (HMIC) Wales) that it might be wise to draft in an outside force in the investigation of serving or former officers. This advice was rejected on the basis that, by this time, the investigation was well advanced. Seventeen people had been arrested in March 1992. Five of these – former and current care workers – had been charged with offences against young boys at Bryn Estyn. There was no argument, according to the Chief Constable, to justify involving an outside force and plenty of evidence that to do so at that stage might jeopardise a fruitful investigation. While it was recognised by the HMIC that this was, indeed, the case, it was the issue of public confidence rather than competence and integrity which had moved him to make his recommendation.

The promise of a public inquiry by the Welsh Office did little to quell local political discontent. John Marek, the Wrexham MP, and Cllr Malcolm King met with Earl Ferrers, a Home Office minister, to express their concern about the investigation. As a result, in February 1993, the Chief Constable of North Wales was further advised that an outside force should take over the investigation. The idea was rejected on the same grounds, but more strenuously since the inquiry was, by now, further advanced, reports were being sent to the CPS and prosecutions were imminent. In March 1993 files on the investigations into former and serving police officers were submitted to the CPS, which eventually advised against taking the matter forward. This decision was guaranteed to lead to renewed calls for the intervention of an outside force as well as an examination of the CPS's guidelines for deciding on the merit of prosecutions. The overall temperature had been further raised in June 1992 when a libel writ was issued by the former police officer who had been named as an alleged abuser in the *Independent on Sunday* article written by Dean Nelson.

Outcome of the investigation

In the face of all this pressure, the Chief Constable and his police authority remained resolute in their confidence in the integrity of the investigation and issued a press release to that effect in July 1993. On 13 August that year North Wales Police announced that the Major Inquiry had been completed and that all residual and fresh complaints would be passed to the relevant divisions. The opportunity was taken to repeat the chief constable's call for a public inquiry to examine thoroughly the conduct of all parties in fulfilling their respective political and professional responsibilities. By September 1993 the investigation had generated 3500 statements, 2500 witnesses and 6000 actions. The number of individuals against whom allegations were made and on whom reports were submitted to the CPS was 365. However, the number of individuals against whom the CPS advised prosecution was only 8, of whom 6 were eventually convicted. This 'poor' result ensured that the controversy, the doubts and the mistrust remained. It is notable that during the course of this police investigation, a number of abuse allegations emanated from Bryn Alyn children's homes, a privately run set of childcare establishments run by John Allen mainly in the Clwyd area. John Allen was the subject of several sexual abuse allegations and was one of the six convicted persons.

Jillings Inquiry

The persistence of suspicion

The outcome of the police investigation and the 'suppression' of the Cartrefle Panel of Inquiry report (as it was seen in certain quarters) ensured that the controversy would not die a death. In response it was decided that a further inquiry was needed and on 12 January 1994, the Social Services Committee in Clwyd approved the appointment of a Panel of Inquiry under the chairmanship of John Jillings, former director of social services for Derbyshire. The decision to opt for an independent inquiry was taken following discussions between the senior members and officers including the leaders of the two main parties on the council. A full public inquiry had (as we have seen) already been promised by Gwilym Jones, the minister of state with responsibility for social services at the Welsh Office, back in 1992. However, such an inquiry had to wait for the completion of any prosecutions arising out of the North Wales Police investigation. Clwyd members and officers were concerned that time was marching on: the legal processes were moving slowly and Clwyd County Council was due to be abolished and superseded by the new unitary authorities by April 1996.

Jillings' terms of reference

John Jevons, the director of the social services department, was particularly concerned that the council should hand over its responsibilities with a clean sheet and, in so doing, identify a way forward for childcare in the successor authorities. The terms of reference and recommendations for the panel were prepared by the director of social services and the county secretary and canvassed with the Welsh Office. These were essentially to ask the following three questions about abuse of children in Clwyd's care from 1974:

- What went wrong?

- Why did it happen?

- How could it have continued undetected for so long?

In pursuing these terms of reference, the panel was to pay particular attention to social services' staff recruitment, training and supervision; complaints procedures; the role of other agencies; foster parent procedures; and procedures adopted since the conviction of Stephen Norris. The period to be covered was from 1974 to the time of the completion of the panel's work. According to the ground rules laid down by the director and the county secretary, the report was to be delivered to them as officers and submitted to the Policy, Finance and Resources Committee of the council by October 1994. The panel had no power to compel cooperation from staff and other witnesses nor could it demand that other agencies provide information or documents to inform its work. On the county council's part, instructions were issued to staff to cooperate with the panel. The message which went out was that they were expected to cooperate; any evidence of criminal conduct would be referred to North Wales Police for investigation; and staff who knew of inappropriate conduct but failed to report it at the time would not be subject to disciplinary action. This was intended to encourage openness from staff who were innocent of any offence but may have turned a blind eye to concerns about colleagues.

Insurers' concerns

The solicitors to the council's insurers had been in constant contact with the local authority since the appearance of the Cartrefle Panel and its report. The public statements of the chair of the Social Services Committee that were reported in the national and local press had been a cause for concern for some time. Reported in the *Observer* newspaper in September 1992 as having admitted to 'the biggest failure to protect children in the history of Britain', Cllr King was clearly regarded as a loose cannon. The insurers advised the county council of its duties under the general conditions of the policy of insurance: to act in the utmost good faith with respect to the company and to say nothing which would prejudice its interests. Cllr King's conduct was perceived as so prejudicial to their interests that it was suggested that, if he wished to continue making such statements, he should remove himself from any position in which he might be seen to be speaking on behalf of the council – in other words he should relinquish the chair of the Social Services Committee.

The insurers' concerns surfaced once more on 24 February 1994 when their solicitors wrote to the county secretary expressing 'grave concern' at the council's decision to conduct an internal inquiry and at the terms of reference issued to the panel. Their concern was based on the timing of the inquiry and the possibility of building up a head of steam around the allegations alongside ongoing prosecutions and a libel action which might encourage a rash of claims from ex-residents. They took the view that

> every inquiry is a further dress rehearsal for claimants and a further incentive to the bandwagon syndrome, we do not see why it is necessary to have such a wide inquiry. (Letter from the insurers' solicitor to the county secretary, 24 February 1994)

The insurers were also concerned about the possibility of resurrecting activity on the part of particular complainants and referred to the need

> to avoid stirring up claimants, particularly as two of the ringleaders have given up. It would be unfortunate if they were encouraged to start again because of contact with the inquiry panel.

The Jillings inquiry forged ahead regardless. However, it raised even more concerns with the insurers in March 1994, when John Jillings made it known that he intended to advertise the existence of the inquiry and to encourage witnesses (including victims of abuse) to come forward with evidence. The local authority, having determined that the inquiry should be truly independent, took a back seat throughout its duration.

Delay and 'suppression'

Though it was planned that the panel should complete its work by October 1994 at the latest, it in fact carried out its investigations between March 1994 and December 1995 and the report was not actually delivered until early 1996, after the director had taken his leave of Clwyd County Council and close to the date at which Clwyd County Council would cease to exist. To the exasperation of those most closely involved, the panel had sought several extensions of time. The Welsh Office was particularly concerned that the report should be considered alongside the advice commissioned earlier in the year by the Secretary of State from a leading barrister, Nicola Davies QC. She had been appointed to undertake 'an examination of relevant papers held by the various agencies concerned' and to advise 'whether an inquiry is required' and, 'if so, the form it should take and the issues to be addressed' (Davies 1995 appendix).

Frustrated in this plan, the Secretary of State went on without the 'benefit' of the Jillings report; the Davies report was submitted to the House of Commons on 11 December 1995. The Davies report was in fact only a summary. Miss Davies reported that 'to publish the report would be to breach the trust which the various agencies placed in me when disclosing relevant documents. Further, much of the information contained in the report is sensitive and confidential and publication would prejudice the interests of any children involved' (Davies 1995, letter to the Secretary of State). Although she stated that 'the events prior to 1989 were serious' (para. 11) and that she had only 'limited means' to 'test the strength of the allegations in the police documents other than those admitted or proved in the course of the prosecutions' (para. 5), she recommended against a public inquiry because

> the criminal aspect has been investigated by the police. Another type of inquiry would be into the systems and procedures which existed and permitted the events to occur. Yet such events are a minimum of six years old; the systems and procedures have now been revised: and an inquiry into them would in effect be one of historical interest. (para. 11)

Her proposal was for an examination of the policy, practice and procedures relating to child care in Clwyd and Gwynedd to ensure that arrangements put in place by the Children Act 1989 were working to safeguard the welfare of children in North Wales. This was duly acted upon and a report was commissioned to be carried out by Adrianne Jones, former director of Birmingham Social Services Department. However this move was widely interpreted by critics of the government and the Welsh Office as back-pedalling on its promise, three years earlier, to hold a full public inquiry. When the Jillings report was actually delivered to the county secretary and other senior officers on 22 February 1996, they were dismayed at 'the number of inaccuracies contained therein and the style and content of the report' (NWTT Day 153, p.28335). The impact of the report's alleged deficiencies was such that the county secretary, armed with comments from the Social Services Department, consulted with North Wales Police and the insurers, and sought legal advice. He was told that there were 'insurmountable legal hurdles to publication' (NWTT Day 170, p.25167).

Although still committed to the principle of publication, Clwyd County Council found that its options were rapidly closing down. The council was due to be dissolved on 31 March. The problems with the report revolved around issues of insurance, defamation and, to a lesser extent, interference with public justice. Jillings was said to have exceeded his terms of reference so that any possibility of claiming qualified privilege for a public debate on the report (already problematic) was further undermined. The council's legal advisers, having considered the special circumstances of a statutory authority with responsibility to balance the public interest in child protection against its duty to its insurers, considered that the prospects of successfully arguing this point were limited.

As a result, it was decided that the report should be circulated only within the council and among other agencies such as the police, Crown Prosecution Service and the insurers for the purpose of checking for factual errors and making comments. All recipients of copies of the report were asked to give a formal undertaking that they would not publish its contents and that they would return it on demand. Many apparently found it too hot to handle and returned it without any perusal of its contents. Subsequently, as a result of further legal advice, the county sought to retrieve all copies of the Jillings report which had been distributed in order to avoid any possibility of a claim of breach of contract by the insurers.

The report was finally presented to the council on 26 March 1996, but under the terms of the legal advice obtained by the council and the threat of the insurers to withdraw insurance cover, any discussion of the report was precluded. The council resolved to note the report and to ask the Secretary of State for Wales to consider it alongside the report recommended by Nicola Davies into policy, practice and procedural issues in relation to childcare in Clwyd and Gwynedd, which had been undertaken by Adrianne Jones, ex-Social Services Director of Birmingham (Jones 1996). The fact that the Jillings report was not published added further fuel to the beliefs of those who suspected that the truth of what was happening in children's homes in North Wales was being suppressed in order to protect officials and other individuals. These suspicions were also inflamed by some of the claims in the report that were later to be quoted in the press (see p.113).

Further implicating events

During the course of the Jillings panel's deliberations, there was a steady stream of sensational publicity surrounding the North Wales allegations:

1. The trials of two former Bryn Estyn staff were held in June and November 1994. The June trial, in particular, resulted in details of allegations of sexual abuse being widely reported in the press and the conviction of Peter Howarth, former deputy officer in charge, on counts of indecent assault and buggery.

2. The libel trial (previously referred to) involved allegations of a sexual nature against a former police officer, made by Harlech Television, two broadsheet newspapers and *Private Eye* magazine. This ended in December 1994 with a verdict in favour of the plaintiff.

3. The trial took place in January 1995 of another former Bryn Estyn employee, who was acquitted of charges ranging from physical assaults to buggery.

4. The trial and conviction of John Allen, the ex-director of the Bryn Alyn Community, a network of private children's homes in North Wales and surrounding areas, took place at Chester Crown Court in February 1995 on counts of indecent assault against six ex-residents.

5. Other less sensational trials and convictions were reported in the local and national press, including the conviction, in June 1995, of a foster carer and his son of offences of physical assault and child cruelty.

By the time the Jillings report was finally delivered, then, child abuse in North Wales had hardly been off the public agenda.

Press reporting of Jillings' findings

Of the national printed press, only the *Independent* newspaper had covered the abuse allegations consistently. Bruised from unsuccessfully defending the libel action taken against it by the former North Wales police officer, the paper nevertheless continued to take an interest in the issue. On 10 March 1996, Cllr Malcolm King, who by then had had access to the Jillings report, gave an interview to Roger Dobson in which he was quoted as saying:

The evidence emerging is that children's homes were a gulag archipelago stretching across Britain – wonderful places for paedophiles but, for the children who suffered, places of unending nightmares.

On 28 March Labour's Health spokesperson in Wales asked William Hague, the Secretary of State, whether he was proposing to hold a judicial inquiry into the affair. At that stage, the Welsh Secretary said that he had no intention of setting up such an inquiry. Thereafter, as details of the contents of the Jillings report started to leak through, the *Independent* conducted a campaign through its columns under the heading, 'Victims of the Abusers', to press for a public inquiry. The non-publication of the Jillings report by Clwyd and, subsequently, by the successor authorities, provided extra ammunition for the campaign. Throughout April and May 1996, articles appeared in the *Independent* and other newspapers with verbatim passages from the Jillings report. Among the published statements were the following:

extensive and widespread abuse [had] occurred within Clwyd residential establishments for children and young people

an internal inquiry could not hope to address the wider concerns such as the existence of a paedophile network or the involvement of prominent people

time and again the response...was too little and too late

criticisms apply not only to the county council but also to the Welsh Office, North Wales Police and constituent agencies

there has been a conflict of interest between safeguarding professional positions versus the safety of children and young people. The interests of children have almost invariably been sacrificed

at least three current employees of Clwyd SSD were interviewed as part of the police investigation. To our knowledge none of them has been disciplined

at least 12 young men who were ex-residents, died around the time of the investigation and prosecution of the abuse cases. Nine of these died after the charging of their abusers

on the whole, interviews and statements which we read gave a clear indication that the residential care experience for a significant number of young people was little short of a living nightmare

there appears to be no mechanism to ensure that independent investigations are conducted of allegations made against...police officers and that the police authority handling of investigations can in some circumstances avoid public scrutiny.

Clwyd was described as being 'very good at reviewing itself but less good at learning lessons'.

The internal inquiries pointed to 'a chaotic state of overall management by Clwyd Social Services of its residential childcare provision' and to a ' lack of rigour in the matter of personnel policy and procedure'.

Need for a further inquiry

Mounting pressure

The Jillings Panel felt that, despite the duration of the inquiry, there were still major gaps in their knowledge, largely because of the lack of cooperation of certain agencies and individuals. In the summary at the start of its report it expressed the view that an internal social services inquiry such as that which it carried out, could not hope to successfully address the wider issues of concern that were identified during the course of the investigations because it had neither the resources nor the authority to do so. What the Jillings report did do, however, was to raise further suspicions. For instance, while it did not seek, or uncover, any evidence concerning abuse by public figures, or of the existence of a paedophile ring, it did feel that these issues needed further exploration because of the degree of concern and disquiet felt in a number of quarters (from ex-children's homes residents themselves through to government ministers) and because of the wider allegations being made by the media. The presence of views such as these in the Jillings report led to a clear sense of unfinished business that only an inquiry with powers to compel the attendance of witnesses and the submission of documents could resolve. For these and other reasons the major recommendation of the report was that a public judicial inquiry should be initiated by the Secretary of State under the arrangements set out in Section 250 of the Local Government Act 1972. The Secretary of State came under pressure to find a way of ensuring that Jillings' findings and recommendations were placed in the public domain. Meanwhile Mr Hague preferred to blame the ineptitude of the county council for commissioning the inquiry in such a way that its findings could never be published. Attempts were allegedly made by the Welsh Office to get the successor authorities to cooperate with Jillings to produce a publishable version of the report, but this did not prove possible.

In mid-May, Hague wrote to the Prime Minister to call for a 'summit' on the issue of 'coordinated national action by the Government to stamp out sexual and physical abuse in children's homes'. He referred in his letter to the need to be seen to be doing something in view of the strong public reaction to the issue and the campaign conducted by the *Independent* newspaper. On 13 June, the Prime Minister gave notice of a cabinet decision to set up two inquiries: one – a Tribunal of Inquiry – in relation to the North Wales abuse and another national review by Sir William Utting of safeguards for children in care. As we have seen, the announcement of the Tribunal of Inquiry, its terms of reference and the appointment of Sir Ronald Waterhouse, a retired High Court judge, as chairman, was made by the Secretary of State for Wales on 17 June 1996. The change of heart was attributed to the findings of Adrianne Jones' examination of policy, practice and procedures in childcare in North Wales, received on the same day (Jones 1996). Close analysis of this report suggests that it was not the true catalyst at all. In reality the government had succumbed to pressures exerted by local politicians and campaigners in a climate where abuse of children in residential care was perceived as widespread and unacceptable.

Functions of a Tribunal of Inquiry

As we noted in Chapter 3, the function of any Tribunal of Inquiry set up under the 1921 Act is statutorily defined as:

> for enquiring into a definite matter prescribed in the Resolution [by both Houses of Parliament] as of urgent public importance. ([11 Geo. 5] Tribunal of Inquiry (Evidence) Act 1921 [Ch. 7] Para. 1)

The 'definite matter[s] … of urgent public importance' are often not only the substantive events complained of, but also the manner in which public agents and bodies may have responded to them. Such was clearly a key objective of the North Wales Tribunal of Inquiry where, whether real or imagined, the public perception after many years of rumour and speculation, was that all was not well with residential childcare services in Clwyd and Gwynedd and that those responsible for the service were concealing the fact.

Terms of reference

The terms of reference of the Tribunal set out by the Secretary of State reflected these concerns. They were as follows:

- to inquire into the abuse of children in care in the former county council areas of Gwynedd and Clwyd since 1974;

- to examine whether the agencies and authorities responsible for such care, through the placement of the children or through the regulation or management of the facilities could have prevented the abuse or detected its occurrence at an earlier stage;

- to examine the response of the relevant authorities and agencies to allegations and complaints of abuse made either by children in care, children formerly in care or any other persons, excluding scrutiny of decisions whether to prosecute named individuals;

- in the light of this examination, to consider whether the relevant caring and investigative agencies discharged their functions appropriately and, in the case of the caring agencies, whether they are doing so now;

- to report its findings and to make recommendations to the Secretary of State.

Analysing the events

In what follows, an attempt will be made to evaluate whether the process by which the North Wales Tribunal of Inquiry was established was similar (or not) to the way in which preceding inquiries, both generally (see Chapter 3) and particularly in relation to child abuse, were set up.

Inquiries as a catalyst of public policy

In some cases, an inquiry may be readily established by central government where it is felt that it can contribute to the development of public policy in a way which that government supports. One might conclude that the Bloody Sunday Tribunal of Inquiry served this sort of function in relation to the development of the peace process in Northern Ireland. In the specific case of child abuse, Parton (1979) argues that the wish of the then Conservative government to place greater service focus on dysfunctional families was a crucial factor in the decision to set up the Maria Colwell inquiry (DHSS 1974), which was influential in the formation of the current child protection system. In these cases, it can be argued that public inquiries are being used by central government as a tool for implementing policy change.

Inquiries as concessions to pressure

In other cases, however, public inquiries are not so readily entered into. Indeed they are generally conceded by authorities in the light of considerable pressure from a range of sources, including extended families and local communities (often with the support of the local media). The Darryn Clarke inquiry (DHSS

1979) is a good example of this. Another key catalyst is the comments of the judiciary after the trials and convictions of abusing parents or carers – this was particularly evident in the case of Jasmine Beckford (Brent 1985). The role of the press, local and national, is another key issue. Aldridge (1994) provides a thoughtful analysis of how and why some cases gain more coverage than others and, therefore, have influence on the pressure placed on authorities to undertake inquiries. A great deal depends on timing (in relation to competing news items), the degree of human interest and whether there is a particular angle to the story, e.g. a racial dimension. While it would be naive to believe that press reporting *per se* was the cause of an inquiry being held, the role of the press in the process should not be underestimated.

Inquiries to unravel cover-ups

Another key issue in relation to the establishment of public inquiries is suspicion of secrecy, cover-up and misconduct. Frequently, such inquiries have been preceded by other inquiries which some party or other has not considered to be sufficiently thorough. This was the case in relation to the Paul Brown (DHSS 1980) inquiry where it was considered that relevant documentation had mysteriously gone missing. In cases such as these, more informal inquiries are followed by more formal ones with greater powers to compel key personnel to give evidence.

Inquiries into issues of public concern

Another factor is the focus of concern that may prevail at different times. As we saw in Chapter 4, in the case of abuse of children in the community, a point was reached at the end of the 1980s where central government reached the conclusion that inquiries were becoming less and less useful in terms of the development of public policy because they were raising the same problems and issues over and over again. In addition there were concerns that the publicity surrounding such inquiries was undermining credibility in the professions involved (particularly social work). As a result, in the 1990s following the publication of the *Working Together* guidelines (DoH 1991a), Area Child Protection Committees were advised to carry out Part 8 Reviews in cases where children had been fatally abused or abused with serious physical and psychological consequences. Such reviews are not generally made public, but are intended to be used by child protection professionals in the areas concerned to monitor existing practices and to introduce new ones. In some cases which have aroused particular concerns, the reviews are produced for public scrutiny (see Bridge 1991, 1995; Gloucestershire ACPC 1995; Nottinghamshire ACPC 1996).

However (as we saw in Chapter 5), concerns about abuse of children in residential care are a relatively new phenomenon. The 1990s saw a major shift of focus on to institutional abuse and for many the extent of the problem has been shocking. The reasons why this is the case have already been addressed. Here, it is important to note that this is an issue where in the current climate something must be seen to be done.

Factors impinging on the North Wales Tribunal of Inquiry

It will be clear that three of the factors discussed above are directly relevant to the setting up of the North Wales Tribunal of Inquiry. The most obvious of these is that relating to pressure. There can be little doubt that the efforts of Alison Taylor and Councillors King and Parry were, in the long run, highly effective in creating a level of pressure that ultimately could not be denied. Alison Taylor in particular hounded politicians of all hues in order to ensure that action was taken. The media played an important part in the process as well, both televison and the press ensuring that issues were given ample coverage. The role of the *Independent* newspapers was central. Reporters employed by them were dogged in their persistence despite being at the wrong end of an expensive libel suit.

A second factor was that relating to a cover-up. The concerns of those pressing the case were as much about the fact that those with managerial responsibility for the care of children and investigation of complaints seemed to have been at the least negligent and at the most conspiring to keep the lid on too many suspicious events, as they were about the incidents of abuse themselves. Clwyd Social Services Department in particular had set up several internal inquiries over a number of years which had been critical of their practices, but they ensured that these findings were not widely disseminated and they rarely acted upon them. Not entirely through their own fault, the two inquiries that they commissioned in the 1990s were also not made public, thus increasing suspicions of stealth and cover up. Similarly, the North Wales Police were thought to have something to hide because of the alleged involvement of some of their own officers in the abuse being investigated.

A third factor was the context. Concerns about abuse of children in residential care were beginning to impact on the public consciousness from the 1990s onwards. The broad-based inquiry conducted by North Wales Police in 1992 and 1993 was the first of its kind, and resulted in a large number of complaints despite the low number of prosecutions. At that time when abuse was still thought to be a relatively isolated event in residential care, the sheer extent of the perceived problems in Clwyd and Gwynedd was seen to be atypical and an indicator of a particularly pathological set of regimes which, given the atypicality, were probably interlinked and probably indicated paedophile rings and widespread exposure of children to organised abuse.

The missing factor

The factor that was missing was the government wishing to use the North Wales Tribunal as a means of influencing public policy. Although as pointed out above, North Wales was probably the first area where widespread concerns about institutional abuse were raised, by the time the inquiry was established in 1996 (as we saw in Chapter 5) much had already been done in response to tackling the problem. By the time of the publication of the inquiry report in 2000, even more developments had taken place in relation to recruitment and training (Warner 1992), conditions of service (Howe, Lady E. 1992), management (Utting 1991, 1997), inspection (DoH 1998c) and research (DoH 1998a). There were, therefore, considerable policy and practice changes taking place in residential care of children before the North Wales Tribunal reported. As a result, it is unlikely that the recommendations of the Tribunal will have any great impact on policy and practice. This is partly as a result of the long period of gestation before the Tribunal was set up – ten years after complaints were first made by Alison Taylor. It is also as a result of the time taken from the commencement of the Tribunal to the time of the publication of its report – three and a half years, which in turn is due to the range and complexity of the issues inquired into and the fact that they took place over such a long period of time.

Concluding comments

Although the process of establishing the Tribunal of Inquiry has much in common with that of previous inquiries, it has these unique features which call into question its likely impact on policy and practice. Again this is a not entirely new criticism made of inquiries: both Hill (1990) and Hallett (1989) make the point that other inquiries have had lessened impact because of the time-gap between the events being inquired into and the subsequent publication of the inquiry report. The issue here is that the North Wales Tribunal is probably an extreme example of this. The essential features of the establishment of the North Wales Tribunal are that it was a response to pressure from those that felt that matters of concern were being covered up by the authorities possibly because they, or their officials, were party to the activities under investigation. In this sense, the main purpose of the inquiry was to satisfy a public need to know the truth.

CHAPTER 7

North Wales Tribunal of Inquiry

Issues of Process

Introduction

In this chapter we examine the way in which the North Wales Tribunal conducted its inquiry into the concerns outlined in Chapter 6.

It is important to examine the process by which an inquiry comes to its con-clusions and findings because awareness of the means by which information is collected and interpreted enables one to evaluate it more comprehensively and to attach more appropriate weight to its recommendations.

This is particularly important with regard to an inquiry as complex and contested as that conducted by the North Wales Tribunal. At one end of the spectrum, it was being argued that there was wholesale organised abuse of young people in care and gross mismanagement of residential care services. At the other, it was being argued that abuse had been committed by individual care workers, unknown to the rest of the staff, and that the extent of abuse was being grossly exaggerated by ex-residents of doubtful character wishing to profit from compensation claims.

It was in a climate such as this that the North Wales Tribunal of Inquiry had to gather, sift through and make judgements about the information placed before it. As noted in Chapter 6, in its terms of reference, the inquiry had to consider material from all the children's homes which functioned in Clwyd and Gwynedd over a period of 22 years. Thus the task was a formidable one even without the intense disagreement between various contesting parties.

It is unlikely, therefore, that the inquiry's findings will be accepted as a satis-factory outcome by all concerned. Hence the importance of careful consider-ation of the process in order to make an informed and balanced judgement on the importance of the findings.

In what follows, we look at four aspects of the inquiry process. Initially, we consider the preliminary preparation stage in which the personnel were recruited and agreements reached about the strategy for the Tribunal's work, the forms of procedure and the practicalities of the process, including venue and timing.

Then, in turn, we look at three key aspects of the administration and management of the Tribunal which, we argue, had an important influence on the outcomes.

The first to be considered is the general overall direction of the Tribunal as a public event – what we term the 'stage management' of the proceedings, the goal of which was to ensure its smooth running and a sense of fairness to the parties concerned.

Second, and linked to this, we shall look at the issue of the publicness of the Tribunal. It will be seen that it is of key importance to the workings of a Tribunal such as this that its proceedings be open to public scrutiny, i.e. that it should have an audience. Nevertheless there are tensions created by this emphasis on publicness which can have an impact on the search for the truth or the facts. We shall look at how the North Wales Tribunal handled this key issue and the impact of its decisions in this respect.

Third, there is the issue of the style in which the Tribunal carried out the proceedings. As will be seen, Tribunals of Inquiry have only limited rules dealing with the way in which they should be conducted. They are essentially inquisitions, i.e. methods of ascertaining the truth and, in theory, therefore, can be conducted in any way they wish. In practice, the major actors are, however, professional lawyers and therefore the conduct of inquiries is to a large degree determined by this fact. Lawyers are schooled to operate in an adversarial manner: this is the style that pervades the whole of our judicial system in that disputes are settled and judgements reached by two sides arguing the case before a judge (aided in some cases by a jury) who decides which of the two has put forward the most compelling case. It should be no surprise, therefore, that this form of adversarial interaction is the method and style adopted in major inquiries. As we shall see, this approach was most evident in the North Wales Tribunal and an understanding of its impact on the process and outcome is particularly important.

It will be noted that the language of the theatre is frequently used in the previous paragraph. This is no coincidence. The terms 'stage management', 'audience' and 'actors' are used intentionally to emphasise that one of the main functions of Tribunals of Inquiry (and the North Wales one is no exception) is to satisfy the public on issues of key concern. Justice, above all, has to be seen to be done. Tribunals, in this sense, are public performances which need to be presented before an audience. The key issue for those evaluating the performance is to consider what impact these requirements have on the production of the truth.

Preliminary process

The setting up of a Tribunal of Inquiry and the rationale for adopting its particular format are topics that are not much discussed either within the body of final reports or among writers and commentators. Yet they are likely to have a key impact both on the type of inquiry that ensues and in turn on the findings that are made. In this section, we look at issues relating to costs, personnel, the venue and the rationale behind the chosen methods of securing the appropriate information. To pursue the theatrical analogy, these are equivalent to the production budget, the director and cast, the theatre itself and the stage and acting directions. The only predetermined factors were the play itself (the terms of reference of the Tribunal) and some minimal house rules, as laid down by the Tribunal of Inquiry Act 1921 and the Salmon Committee report recommendations (Salmon 1966) (see Chapter 3).

Costs

The Welsh Office initially allocated £10 million to the North Wales Tribunal as running costs; it was obvious, therefore, from the start that a long process was anticipated. In fact the final cost to the Welsh Office was estimated as being £12.8 million – a budget overspend of the kind more associated with the cinema than the theatre! A great deal of this expenditure went on legal fees. Although not a statutory right under the 1921 Act, the Welsh Secretary indicated in advance that he would authorise the payment of costs from public funds for those who would otherwise be unrepresented through lack of means and whose interests would be prejudiced thereby. In our estimation, on any one day, a possible 10 Queen's Counsel, 24 junior counsel and 3 solicitors or advocates could appear before the Tribunal according to the relevance of that particular day's proceedings to the interests of their clients. Of these, 8 Queen's Counsel and 21 juniors and solicitor advocates were regular attenders throughout the 209 days during which the Tribunal sat. Add to this the attendance of instructing solicitors with whichever clients were to give evidence on any particular day and the sheer physical presence of legal representation begins to become apparent. It should also be noted, however, that many of the major parties were bearing their own costs – the police, health agencies, successor authorities and Municipal Mutual Insurance. Thus the money contributed by the Welsh Office does not represent the full cost of holding the Tribunal or, indeed, the full amount falling to the public sector.

Despite the overspend, it has to be acknowledged that there was constant reference to the budget throughout the Tribunal's hearings and that the need to keep within budget was a factor which influenced procedures to some degree.

Personnel

Sir Ronald Waterhouse, a retired High Court judge, lately of the Queen's Bench Division, but with experience in the Family Division, was appointed to chair the Tribunal. The mechanisms by which Tribunal chairpersons are appointed are to say the least opaque. The best way to describe the process is to say that soundings are taken and a candidate emerges. Without being too cynical, one factor in Sir Ronald's favour was that his being retired meant less disruption to the administration of justice generally. Perhaps more to the point were the facts that he originated from North Wales, had spent much of his working life on the Wales and Chester circuit, and was familiar with the geography and, to some extent, the politics of the area. Thus he had the required expertise and the sort of local knowledge that would enable him to gain an early grasp of the context. His familiarity with the area might have been seen as a disadvantage because of all the speculation and concerns preceding the Tribunal about the perceived incestuous nature of institutions and their personnel in North Wales. It is, perhaps, some measure of the stature of the chairman that in these circumstances his appointment was widely greeted as a positive choice.

The chairman was assisted in his task by Mr Morris Le Fleming, former Chief Executive of Hertfordshire, who had been a panel member of the Leicestershire child abuse inquiry, and Ms Margaret Clough, a former senior official of the Social Services Inspectorate with expertise in children's services. Since the investigations conducted by North Wales Police had been the focus of some criticism and speculation, an adviser on police-related matters was also appointed. Sir Ronald Hadfield, former Chief Constable of the West Midlands Police, fulfilled this role.

As stated above, lawyers were predominant among the remaining cast members. Those participating in the tribunal fell into different categories:

1. Counsel to the Tribunal and his team, who were appointed by the Attorney-General and instructed by the Treasury solicitor. Their task was effectively to conduct the inquiry on behalf of the

Tribunal panel, to present the issues and know facts and to conduct questioning or cross-examination.

2. Counsel for the complainants and their team. In total there were 139 complainants. The original intention had been to provide a single team of barristers to represent them all, but a split developed within the survivors' organisation, NORWAS (North Wales Abuse Survivors), in the run up to the Tribunal and the resulting two groups were represented separately.

3. Counsel for the Salmon Letter recipients (SLRs), which included those already convicted for offences, those in the frontline accused of varying degrees of abuse to children, and those in lower, middle or higher management within the local authorities who were accused of operating and presiding over systems which allowed the abuse to go unchecked. Also included among the SLRs was anyone else outside the two local authority social services departments considered to have been involved in the abuse or the investigation of it. The SLRs, therefore, were a disparate group of people, including managers and care staff from both the statutory sector and Bryn Alyn, the independent care group, agency foster carers, teachers, former and serving police officers, and people in the gay communities around North Wales and Chester who were alleged to have had contact with young people from care. The range of SLRs, and the potential conflicts among them, resulted in a greater degree of separate representation than was true in the case of the complainants, despite significant and successful efforts at rationalisation.

4. Counsel for the successor local authorities (those authorities which had taken over local government responsibilities in the wake of the 1996 reorganisation). These new successor authorities effectively 'disowned' the acts and omissions of their predecessors, choosing instead to act as servants to the Tribunal by feeding the Treasury team with relevant information culled from 22 years' worth of files and documents. They carved a niche for themselves as honest brokers interested only in the emergence of the truth and the improvement of policies and systems.

5. Counsel for a variety of other parties including the North Wales Police, the quality of whose investigations had been questioned;

the Welsh Office, the quality of whose inspections and monitoring exercises had been called into question; the local authority insurers, Municipal Mutual Insurance, whose role in providing advice about the publication of previous inquiry reports had been heavily criticised; and the relevant heath authorities and trusts whose employees such as psychiatrists and psychologists had been involved with the complainants while in residential care. Key individuals such as Alison Taylor, 'the whistleblower', and Councillors Parry and King, who had pushed for an inquiry to take place, were also separately represented, as was the children's rights organisation, Voices from Care.

One consequence of this array of legal representatives was that there were many voices competing in the Tribunal working to ensure that the individuals and organisations that they represented got a fair deal. This resulted in much debate over the process and (as will be seen in the section on the use of adversarial methods) gruelling cross-examination for those giving evidence, which seemed particularly hard to bear for many of those making complaints of having been abused.

Finally, it should be noted that the Tribunal was, by virtue of the dominance of the legal profession, conducted in the form of a trial or series of trials, an issue which will be explored later in the chapter. As we saw in Chapter 3, this is the norm for such forms of inquiry and is almost inevitable, given the fact that Tribunals are usually dealing with disputed and contested matters (as indeed this one was) of the kind that are usually determined in legal settings and by legal rules. Nevertheless, the limited use of non-legal expertise was notable. Only towards the end of the Tribunal, and then for two days only, were the views of experts sought. The non-legal panel members presumably had some role in providing expertise in their particular fields, but with the exception of Sir Ronald Hadfield, who made a conspicuous contribution to putting the actions of the police in context, this was not very much in evidence.

Administration

So far the focus has been on the on-stage actors in the Tribunal. Shifting our attention to the backstage, it should be noted that the administrative structure required to sustain such an inquiry was also significant. Its work was overseen by a triumvirate of the Treasury solicitor, the clerk to the Tribunal and the chief administrative officer. In addition to the Treasury solicitor there were four other solicitors, seven assistants, an administrative team servicing the Tribunal and an investigative team of retired police officers employed to trace and interview witnesses. A press officer was appointed to act as a conduit for all press inquiries and advice and to act as an early warning system for any difficulties in terms of the public presentation of the Tribunal's work. Finally and significantly, given the nature of the inquiry's work, the Bridge Childcare Consultancy Service was contracted to provide witness care and counselling services. How all these and the other personnel were organised to get the show on the road is the subject of the next section of this chapter.

Venue

It was decided to hold the Tribunal proceedings in the recently completed Flintshire County Council offices and chambers in Ewloe, which is a small village about 15 miles west of Chester and 20 miles north of Wrexham. The buildings were ideal for holding the Tribunal and were clearly chosen for this reason. No doubt cost also played a part in the choice. However, geographically, Ewloe was rather isolated and access by public transport was very limited. This undoubtedly had an effect on the audience, an issue that will be dealt with in more detail under the section on publicness.

Stage managing the proceedings

This section looks at how the process was managed. The notion of stage management was brought home to us following an interview with one of the Treasury counsel team, who made it clear that the main perceived initial difficulty was that of gaining sufficient trust with the complainants to encourage them to come forward to be witnesses. Put bluntly, without achieving this, the show could not go on. Without complainants, there was no possibility that the Tribunal could carry out its remit, which was to satisfy the general public that everything possible had been done to ensure that all available knowledge and information was out in the open. The history of alleged cover-ups and the general climate of suspicion made this a sine qua non. This need, therefore, was a driving force behind much of the early pre-hearing work and was also much in evidence during the hearings themselves. However, there was also a major counter-factor to be taken into consideration, namely that, despite the importance attached to encouraging witnesses to come forward, there was a need to safeguard against false allegations being made. As will be seen in the remainder of this section, these tensions and contradictions had considerable influence on the preliminary stages of the process.

Seeking out complainants

In its quest to target witnesses to make statements, the Tribunal decided to start with the former children's homes' residents who had been interviewed by North Wales Police during its major investigation. This investigation had, by December 1996, shortly before the Tribunal was to open its doors to the public, taken 3860 statements from 2719 witnesses. Of this last figure, 1700 were former residents of North Wales homes. About 500 of these alleged that they had suffered either physical or sexual abuse while in care and, of these, 156 were alleging sexual abuse. The Tribunal decided to reinterview all these complainants, using the investigative team of former police officers referred to in the preceding section. In addition, the team selected a random 600 ex-residents from 12,000 files of children who had been in care in Gwynedd and Clwyd during the 22 years between 1974 and 1996, and attempted to trace and take statements from them in order to test the thoroughness of the police trawl. In fact only 10 per cent were traced and, as the number of positive responses was very low, the exercise was eventually abandoned as unproductive. In addition to those interviewed by the police and the random selection from case files by the Tribunal, publicity generated by the parliamentary announcement and by the Tribunal itself yielded between 130 and 140 additional witnesses.

Thus there can be little doubt about the thoroughness of the process – how sensitive it was is another matter. We did not interview witnesses about the impact of the investigative process, but during the course of their giving evidence, many complainants spoke of the difficulties they experienced of being approached on more than one occasion to talk about painful matters which they had long since tried to bury. To some degree, any attempt to unearth humiliating experiences (which seemed to be particularly true in cases where sexual abuse had been carried out) would have been difficult. However, the wisdom of appointing former police officers to carry out such interviews is questionable. It was clear from witness statements that many had previously had their own brushes with the law and were initially distrustful of communicating with police-related personnel.

Another concern expressed by some of the counsel for the complainants was that by using statements to the police about alleged offences as a starting point, and then reviewing those statements at a later date, the whole process became centred around incidents of abuse and the extent to which these were criminal acts or not. Important though such information was, it gave complainants little opportunity to provide the Tribunal with a broader picture of life in local authority care in the two counties between the relevant dates. As will be seen, such an approach also led to a rather narrow focus in the cross-examination of witnesses later on during the hearings, where a great deal of time was spent in establishing or eliminating contradictions in the various statements made to either the police or the Tribunal investigation team.

Supporting complainants

The Bridge Childcare Consultancy Service was commissioned to provide advice, support and counselling for all witnesses apart from those managers who were giving evidence in the later phases about possible system failures. In fact, however, the service was used mainly by complainants. Much of the help offered consisted of giving witnesses a preview of what to expect, familiarising them with the geography and procedures of the Tribunal and providing support on the day of their giving evidence. The Bridge workers were also contracted to provide more in-depth support to those who were deeply affected by the process of having to recall and relate intimate and emotional experiences in a court-type setting.

This 'counselling' service, as it was referred to throughout the Tribunal, was itself the subject of criticism by some of the more prominent complainants. They were aggrieved because they wished to take on a support and counselling function themselves, arguing that self-help was a more effective way of doing this. They accused the Tribunal of interfering with the progress they were making with pre-existing counselling and of refusing to bear the cost of that. It was clear from the debates in the preliminary hearings that the Tribunal did wish to curtail their activities and that it was determined to confine counselling support to the Bridge Consultancy team as far as possible in order to limit opportunities for collusion between witnesses and to ward off the likelihood of complaints from those representing alleged abusers that such collusion was indeed taking place.

The situation was not helped by the fact that there were teething troubles in setting up the Bridge counselling service which delayed the establishment of a physical presence in an accessible base until early in 1997. The Tribunal was thus accused of forcing some witnesses to endure the stress of making their statements before the service was available to pick up the consequences.

Dealing with those complained against

From the statements of ex-residents and others emerging from the police trawl, a raft of allegations was collated and used as the basis of the Salmon Letters which were issued. These notified individuals of the accusations which they had to answer. They were given information about their rights to legal representation and notification about where to seek this. As with the complainants, those complained against had developed support groups, the most prominent of which was that set up for former members of staff at Bryn Estyn. The Tribunal team were equally concerned about the potential for collusion among members of this group as they were about the complainants' groups, possibly more so. Certainly in the course of the hearings, counsel for the Tribunal cast much doubt on the credibility of witnesses who were prominent in the Bryn Estyn Support Group.

It was decided early on that any complaint made, however apparently trivial, would be followed up. Initially this caused much concern among counsel for those complained against. There seemed to have been some expectation on their part that only the more serious allegations would have been pursued in such detail. Indeed several of these barristers interviewed at the end of the Tribunal hearings expressed the view that in its efforts to encourage complainants to speak out, the Tribunal had loaded the dice against the Salmon Letter recipients. They felt that many of their clients had been unnecessarily exposed to distress and the sort of experience that their alleged misdemeanours would not have warranted even if they had been true. A sense of indignation, whether manufactured or truly felt, pervaded these barristers' representations on behalf of their clients. Arguably, they had a considerable influence on the issues of publicity and on the adoption of adversarial techniques which are considered in the remaining sections of this chapter. It should be noted that the initial Salmon Letters and the responses made were not the end of the story as far as their recipients were concerned. As the Tribunal progressed, further allegations came to light and further Salmon Letters were issued. Discrepancies in oral evidence raised even more questions to be answered by further letters, and the responses themselves were examined for their adequacy, and so on.

Handling written information

In this final subsection on the stage management of the Tribunal we look at the more mundane backstage work, namely the collection, analysis and presentation for the Tribunal's use of all the available relevant written documentation about the 89 residential establishments under scrutiny and their staff and residents. This work required the processing and filleting of thousands of case files, personnel files, day-to-day records, departmental memoranda and policy decisions, inspection reports, and a wide range of other written material situated in the two main social services departments, the voluntary and independent agencies, the Welsh Office and the police, health and education authorities serving the North Wales region. By any standards, the volume of material which had to be processed by the Tribunal and its parties and legal representatives was enormous. Information technology was employed to assist in the task of processing and tracking this information. It was made available to the panel team of the Tribunal and the various counsel via computer screens throughout the course of the hearings. The scanning of documents into the Tribunal's database also allowed material referred to in examination to be readily displayed on computer screens for the assistance of witnesses and legal representatives.

It is also worth noting here that the Tribunal produced a daily transcript of proceedings that was available to all parties and also to the public at a cost.

The issue of publicness

Presumption of openness

As stressed at the beginning of this chapter, a key function of Tribunals of Inquiry is to satisfy the public that a thorough and fair effort has been made to sort out disputed facts and to uncover any concealments. This purpose is expressly stated in the Tribunals and Inquiries (Evidence) Act 1921 as that of 'inquiring into a definite matter...of urgent public importance'. The Act further states that a tribunal established in pursuance of this purpose

> shall not refuse to allow the public or any portion of the public to be present at any of [its] proceedings...unless in the opinion of the tribunal it is in the public interest expedient to do so for reasons connected with the subject matter of the inquiry or the nature of the evidence to be given. (Para. 2(a))

The Salmon report endorses this feature of the Act:

> When there is a crisis of public confidence about the alleged misconduct of people in high places, the public naturally distrusts any investigation carried out behind closed doors. (Salmon 1966, para. 116)

The public aspect of any inquiry of this sort is, therefore, crucial.

The North Wales Tribunal hearings, in line with the intentions of the Act and of Parliament, were indeed held in public. In practice, however, attendance by the genuine 'public' was limited, and it has already been argued that to some degree this was a result of the choice of a relatively isolated venue for the proceedings. The 'audience' in the public gallery only rarely reached double figures. Regular attenders included a small number of complainants who had campaigned for the inquiry and members of the Bryn Estyn Support Group for residential workers, but they were parties rather than the interested public. A small number of journalists who had followed the North Wales events from the early days also kept in regular contact with the Tribunal. Otherwise the public seats were taken up by people attending to give evidence, by one of the three of us, and occasionally by a few interested professionals. The interest of the wider press was limited to the landmark dates when some of the main protagonists were giving evidence or major submissions were being delivered. Their lack of consistent involvement may in part be attributed to the events described in the following section.

For the protection of witnesses

Holding hearings in public is one thing; national reporting of the proceedings with use of names is another. The view of the Salmon report was that the contemporaneous reporting of such hearings is in the interests of the innocent party who is the subject of allegations since it allows him or her the opportunity to 'destroy...the evidence against them in the full light of publicity' (Salmon 1966, para. 119). It also ensures that as wide a section of the public as possible is made aware of the evidence and the work of the Tribunal in getting at the truth. Such a view showed touching faith in the fairness of the press and its willingness to be just to all parties involved in such an inquiry. However, later in his report, Salmon conceded that the Tribunal should have a discretion to exclude the press and public in certain circumstances as outlined in the Act, i.e. where there might be security risks. He also recognised that 'it is impossible to foresee the multifarious contingencies which may arise before a Tribunal of Inquiry' (Salmon 1966, para. 122) and suggested that such discretion could be applied more widely to further the interests of justice and humanity. His final advice on the matter was that such discretion should be used only rarely.

When the setting up of the North Wales Tribunal of Inquiry was debated in Parliament, the issue of its publicness was the subject of much discussion. In response to a demand for assurances from his Opposition counterpart that there would be 'no unnecessary in camera sessions and that there [would] be full publication of the report and all supporting documents' (*Hansard* 17 June 1996), Mr Hague confirmed that the inquiry would comply with the terms of the 1921 Act. Concern was expressed by some of the MPs who had had personal contact with complainants through their constituency work at the potential vulnerability to publicity of witnesses who had been or were alleging abuse. Alex Carlile, MP for Montgomery at the time, and himself a leading barrister, asked the Secretary of State to confirm that

> it will be possible for witnesses…many of whom are now adults leading ordinary lives, many of them married with children, to have anonymity in terms of public identification.

Rod Richards (Clwyd NW) and David Hanson (Delyn) joined in the calls for protection of the interests of vulnerable witnesses from the damaging effects of sensational press coverage. The Secretary of State undertook to discuss the matter with the inquiry chairman, whose judgement and decision would ultimately be made in pursuance of the terms of reference of the Tribunal.

In the course of his opening statement to the Tribunal, Sir Ronald Waterhouse, the chairman of the Tribunal, made the following rulings about the public nature of the inquiry:

1. Although the hearings would be held in public, in keeping with the spirit of the Act, anonymity would be offered to those complainants who wished it.

2. Applications would be considered about the way in which any complainant witness would wish to be heard, i.e. they could be given the opportunity to be interviewed behind a screen shielding them from the public.

3. Those who were the subject of allegations would also receive anonymity, being referred to throughout the proceedings by a number or letters.

4. There would be an expectation that the media respect Tribunal rulings and statutory provisions regarding anonymity of witnesses as they would those relating to civil or criminal proceedings and, where they defaulted from this, proceedings for contempt would be initiated.

5. Only those who had been convicted of abuse or those who were the subject of criticism about the way in which they fulfilled their public duties could be named with impunity.

6. Witnesses wishing to waive their anonymity would require the consent of the Tribunal to do so.

Spoiling the media's party

These 'rulings' incurred the indignation of parts of the press and broadcast media and were the subject of an application to the Tribunal by the BBC, the *Western Mail* and the *Liverpool Daily Post* and *Echo* newspapers. After lengthy argument over two days, the chairman gave his response. He maintained the right of the Tribunal to determine how it would conduct its hearings and to report any infringement of its 'rulings' on press reporting to the High Court as prima facie evidence of a contempt. If such an eventuality arose, the press would have to take its chances with the High Court. The Tribunal's purpose was to get at the truth. In order to do this it required that as many witnesses as possible should feel able to come forward without fear of embarrassment or vilification. The call was still out for potential witnesses. Any diminution of witness care and protection could deter their cooperation and present a

> substantial risk that the course of justice and the proceedings of the tribunal would be seriously impeded and prejudiced if there was to be general publication of the identity of the abusers and persons against whom allegations of abuse were made. (NWTT Day 12, page 1659)

However, while alleged victims, abusers and certain third parties were protected by the chairman's intimations, he made it clear that those giving evidence in future phases, concerning the administrative and policy contexts of childcare in North Wales, would not benefit from anonymity.

Objections from the Salmon Letter recipients

While anonymity in the contemporaneous press reporting of the Tribunal was secured for certain parties, individuals could not be guaranteed the same concession in the Tribunal's own report. Counsel for the Salmon Letter recipients – both alleged abusers and managers whose competence and conduct were in question – had sought early indications about the 'naming of names' in its final report. Part of their argument was that, in its effort to place former residents at the heart of the Tribunal's work, its counsel had adduced evidence of large numbers of very minor incidents which in their view were indicative of childcare practices of their time rather than of abuse. As such, it would be unfair to name as culpable in the final report people who were simply doing a job according to prevailing standards of care and who could not truly be regarded as abusers. Such individuals, some of whom were still employed in social services departments, could be tainted with 'guilt by association' merely by virtue of giving evidence to the Tribunal. Similar cases were put on behalf of middle managers who, it was argued, had been constrained by ever-increasing responsibilities and ever-decreasing resources.

The Tribunal, however, rejected these arguments on the grounds that its key function was to demonstrate publicly the facts of the matter.

Finding the balance

As can be seen from the foregoing, the Tribunal was under a variety of pressures that dictated to some extent the course it took in the public–private debate. It was keen to encourage complainants to come forward and to protect them as far as possible, and it was sympathetic to the view that, during the course of its hearings, many of the Salmon Letter recipients should remain anonymous. However, where it was felt that publicity would not be unduly harmful (in the case of those already convicted and managers of services and high ranking officials from involved agencies), it placed no embargo on the press and media. It was also determined that the names of SLRs should be used in the final report regardless of the seriousness of the issues under question.

There was a very fine line to be drawn between providing reasonable protection for witnesses during the hearings and making oneself vulnerable to accusations of operating with stealth and secrecy, as had happened with other inquiries into the events in North Wales. An article by the *Guardian* journalist, Nick Davies, on 16 October 1997 made just such an accusation. In it he listed the most sensational of the allegations made to the Tribunal by a small number of complainants, who sought to establish that a paedophile ring was operating in North Wales, comprising members of 'the great and the good' as well as individuals from the Chester and Wrexham gay communities. This ring, it was alleged, was preying on young men in the care of North Wales authorities and, by his action in granting anonymity to those not convicted of any offence, the chairman was continuing to protect the perpetrators. The article went on to quote the chairman as arguing that 'his ruling will encourage alleged paedophiles to come forward and give honest evidence without fear of retribution'. In fact this was a travesty of the rationale offered by Sir Ronald Waterhouse for his decisions about anonymity. In response to the criticisms in the *Guardian* article, at the Tribunal hearing on the following day, the chairman reiterated his intention to ensure that any fresh allegations relating to paedophile activity would be passed to the police. In addition it was confirmed that the anonymity ruling applied only to the duration of the Tribunal so that information contained in the public transcripts of the inquiry could be published thereafter subject to the laws of libel or any order of a court.

Despite assurances such as these, the press and broadcast media continued to convey an impression of secrecy and cover-up right to the end of the Tribunal's work. A Channel 4 News reporter, Tania Sillem, declared on 17 February 1998 that:

> Although this Tribunal has been sitting for more than a year, special restrictions mean the media hasn't been able to report most of the proceedings.

In fact only a very few, brief, in camera sessions had been held, mostly to discuss applications from counsel. There had been no bar on reporting the remainder of the 'proceedings'. The 'special restrictions' referred to concerned only the anonymity ruling regarding contemporaneous reporting.

The overall impression gained is that the Tribunal managed the public–private issues sensitively and strategically, and that the press and media response was one of considerable pique through having been deprived of what it considered to be a wealth of newsworthy stories.

Adversarial or inquisitorial?

It was frequently stated throughout the Tribunal that it was an inquisition not an adversarial trial. In his opening address to the Tribunal, Sir Ronald Waterhouse stated that the Tribunal would not conduct a series of criminal trials or prosecutions and that its procedure would be essentially inquisitorial rather than adversarial, while allowing anyone who was the subject of an allegation an adequate opportunity to answer it.

Meaning of the terms

The distinction between inquisitorial and adversarial modes of procedure seems to be a very fine one indeed. The understanding of the term 'adversarial' among the Tribunal participants seemed to be that which pertains in normal court procedure, whereby two sides of the case are put according to laid down rules and the judge acts as an umpire as to whether evidence is admissible and then finally decides on the outcome. The definition of 'inquisitorial' used at the Tribunal seemed to be anything that deviated from this process. In theory the Tribunal was not a court in that there was no defence and prosecution. The chair, Sir Ronald Waterhouse, and his panel members were inquiring into the events in question. They employed counsel to undertake the ground work on their behalf. Using the definitions outlined above, the process could not, therefore, logically be adversarial; it had to be inquisitorial. In practice, as will be seen, the conduct of the Tribunal to any lay person seemed to be carried out in a highly adversarial fashion. In the following section we look at the procedure adopted for gathering the views of witnesses to the Tribunal.

Conducting the examination of witnesses

With regard to complainants, the procedure followed by the Tribunal was this: the Tribunal team, having gathered its evidence, presented complainant witnesses before the Tribunal and went through their statements with them. These statements usually included an allegation against one or more residential care workers. Barristers acting for the complainants then asked additional questions of their clients if they felt it was necessary. Barristers acting on behalf of those persons alleged to have carried out the abuse were then given the opportunity to ask questions of the complainants, and, if the allegations of abuse involved several parties, this could entail being questioned by several barristers. If the evidence from the complainants had implications for the police or any other represented agency then their representatives also asked questions. Finally, the counsel for the Tribunal returned and asked any further questions which he felt were needed given what had preceded. Strict rules of evidence were not adhered to, and the chairman of the Tribunal frequently intervened to clarify matters or pursue issues that had not been sufficiently drawn out for him by the different counsel.

The process for Salmon Letter recipients was as above, but in reverse. Their barristers took them through their evidence and then they were asked questions by the counsel for the Tribunal and barristers for the complainants. If they made statements that implicated any other witness, then they were normally questioned by that person's or agency's representative.

Essentially an adversarial structure and style was being used to gather evidence (or carry out the inquisition). Clearly this was thought to be the fairest and most effective way of proceeding. It was also the style to which barristers were most accustomed. The evidence of both complainants and Salmon Letter recipients was to be tested by adversarial methods in order to measure its validity. Thus if, during questioning, inconsistencies or contradictions arose, this could obviously be taken into account by the Tribunal panel in weighing up the evidence. Looked at in this light, the debate as to whether inquiries are adversarial or inquisitorial mechanisms seems somewhat redundant. It is clear that the methods are closely interlinked and that this is a result of the dominant role played by the legal profession in carrying out such inquiries. This is not meant as a criticism, but more as an explanation of the conduct of inquiries such as this one. Whether or not there are better methods of establishing truth in matters of this kind will be considered in the concluding chapter.

What is clear, however, was that the Tribunal had the appearance and the substance of an adversarial contest. Despite the constant attempts of the Tribunal chairman and occasionally some of the barristers to defuse some of the tensions that arose by reminding their colleagues that this was an inquiry not a trial, the adversarial atmosphere prevailed. Our interviews with various barristers supported this view. Those acting on behalf of the Salmon Letter recipients felt that counsel for the Tribunal were responsible for the conflictual nature of the proceedings. They felt that the dice were loaded in favour of the complainants, that they were given preferential treatment because they were generally seen as injured parties needing to be encouraged to come forward to give evidence. By contrast they felt that their clients were dealt with rather aggressively and immediately put on the defensive. Their response was to some degree to fight back and defend their clients and to work even harder to discredit some of the complainants. These accounts of what had happened confirmed the impression gained from observing the Tribunal's proceedings, namely that they were clearly adversarial in nature.

In the remainder of this section we consider the impact of this type of approach on the two main sets of witnesses – those making complaints and those complained against.

Trials of the complainants

Much of the evidence that was given by many of the complainants was painful and difficult to relate. Some of these complainants had already given the same evidence at the prosecutions of their abusers in previous court proceedings. According to the barristers acting on their behalf, the Tribunal experience was often considered by such witnesses to be far more arduous and harrowing than anything they had experienced in court. It was not only the retelling of their stories but also the adversarial nature of the cross-examination by a long queue of counsel which accounted for this. Much store has been set by campaigners on behalf of the survivors on the beneficial, cathartic effect of relating traumatic events. One cannot help but think that such claims are overplayed. The impression given by a number of witnesses was that they had given their story once too often and were keen to get on with their lives. The following exchange highlights the pains of the cross-examination experienced by one complainant:

Counsel: …Have you found it a distressing experience giving evidence to this Tribunal?

Witness: Giving evidence in this trial [sic] was worse, much worse than giving evidence in the Crown Court trial.

Chairman: … You said you found it much worse giving evidence to the Tribunal than doing so before the Crown Court … Could you just explain why it has been more terrible?

Witness: I don't think the Crown Court went into this much detail.

This type of experience was not untypical. It was particularly distressing for complainants to come forward to give their evidence and to have it torn apart in forensic detail by 'opposing' counsel. All the classical strategies of cross-examination were used to discredit their accounts. First, any inconsistencies between the various statements that had been made to the police and the Tribunal team prior to the hearing were brought to the fore. Second, considerable attention was paid to the details of the alleged abuse, which in the case of sexual abuse was acutely embarrassing for many of those giving their accounts. Third, some witnesses who were seen to be particularly aggressive were deliberately goaded with a view to demonstrating that their angry responses were evidence of their volatility and, therefore, unreliability. In the case of one of the complainants who had played a leading role in demanding that a Tribunal of Inquiry take place, such goading resulted in his physically attacking one of the barristers. His reaction was unique, but displays of verbal aggression in response to this type of questioning were not uncommon. Another line of attack by the barristers was to try to discredit the complainants on the grounds that they had criminal records involving deceit and violence, or that they themselves had abused other boys while in care. Yet another was to suggest that they were distorting the facts because they were making compensation claims. The barristers also used a range of verbal techniques to discredit the evidence given by complainants such as referring to their accounts as 'stories' (i.e. lies) and by suddenly bringing questioning to an end, usually at a point where the complainant was floundering a little: 'Thank you, Mr X, that will be all.' Not all the witnesses were treated with equal harshness. Those who seemed to be more emotionally distressed by the proceedings were treated with more care. To be cynical, it could be argued that to have pursued witnesses like these more vigorously might well have undermined the goals that the barristers were seeking to achieve.

For many in the counselling, psychiatric and social work professions, this type of treatment of individuals coming forward to talk about their abusive experiences seems both unacceptable and unproductive. They believe that it is important to talk about experiences in order to exorcise their effects on the personality, and that therefore individuals giving accounts of their abuse should be treated with care and great respect for their feelings (Miller 1985). Of course, their goal is one of therapy, whereas that of lawyers is to establish the facts. The barristers at the Tribunal were, therefore, doing their jobs as they saw fit. The chairman of the Tribunal could have intervened to protect witnesses had he so wished (and this he did do on occasions). However, the fact that he did not do so more often was probably because he needed to make a judgement about the evidence given under the rigours of adversarial cross-examination.

Trials of those complained against

Those complained against were also at the receiving end of rigorous questioning and cross-examination. The opening statement of the counsel to the Tribunal made it very clear that he was of the view that widespread abuse had taken place in children's homes in Clwyd and Gwynedd over the period in question. He expressed a determination to get to the bottom of this throughout the course of the Tribunal's hearings. Some of the barristers for the Salmon Letter recipients felt that this statement was tantamount to a presumption of guilt on the part of those of their clients who had not previously been convicted of any crime.

Their views were to some degree borne out by the tenor of much of the cross-examination of residential staff and managers. Certainly, many of these individuals were immediately placed on the defensive, and it was clear from much of their testimony that they were at great pains to avoid saying anything that would incriminate either themselves or their colleagues. This led to expressions of frustration on several occasions by the chairman of the Tribunal, who kept reminding such witnesses that they should answer the questions truthfully without thinking too much about how their answers might be construed or interpreted.

It could be argued in this respect that the adoption of an adversarial style to a large degree inhibited the discovery of the true facts.

We realise that this section has been very critical about the mode of operation of the Tribunal without offering a constructive alternative at this stage. To some degree this will be remedied in Chapter 10, when some proposals are made for the future of inquiries into institutional abuse.

Concluding comments

This chapter has been concerned with the influence of the process adopted by the Tribunal on the collection of information that has formed the basis of the report itself. This has been done in the belief that understanding the process allows one to weigh up and evaluate the strengths and weaknesses of the Tribunal's findings and recommendations. Another aim has been to provide a detailed critique which could have some influence on any future inquiries into issues such as those dealt with here.

We have shown how preliminary decisions made about personnel, costs and venue can have an important impact on the Tribunal's conduct, and how decisions taken early on in the process about how to gather and collate information can influence the direction the Tribunal takes. We have also examined some key issues in relation to the way in which the Tribunal's hearings were carried out, particularly the public–private debate and that relating to the adversarial and inquisitorial modes of inquiry. In both of these issues we have seen that it is not a question of either one or the other, but that there is an interplay between both. In our view, the Tribunal handled the public–private issues sensibly and well. In relation to the adversarial–inquisitorial continuum, we consider that the adversarial mode was dominant for a variety of reasons and we have pointed out some of the dysfunctions of this emphasis.

CHAPTER 8

North Wales Tribunal of Inquiry

Outcomes

Introduction

On 12 March 1998, the North Wales Tribunal of Inquiry heard its final submission. The hearings had been expected to last until the end of 1997 (*Hansard*: written answers 24 July 1996) so that the overrun was about three months. As we pointed out in Chapter 7, the cost also overran by about 30 per cent. The Tribunal had sat for a total of 201 days. It received evidence from 575 witnesses, of whom 264 attended to give oral testimony. Of those giving evidence, 259 were complainants, of whom 129 gave their testimony in person. In addition (as we saw in Chapter 7), the Tribunal had to sift through masses of written documentation spread over 22 years. From these the counsel for the Tribunal team extracted 12,000 documents which were scanned into its database for reference throughout the Tribunal hearings (Waterhouse 2000, para. 1.11).

These few facts demonstrate the scale of the task which occupied the Tribunal members over the succeeding 16 months. A huge amount of evidence had to be sifted, assessed, analysed and presented in a way that would fulfil the terms of reference laid down by both Houses of Parliament. The Tribunal also had to satisfy those who had clamoured for a definitive answer to their questions and suspicions which had festered over a 10-year period between the first of the police investigations in Gwynedd in 1986 and the setting up of the inquiry in 1996. It is not surprising, then, that the report was a long time coming. The Tribunal presented an extensive summary report of 230 pages as well as the full, extremely weighty version comprising over 900 pages (including appendices). Having been handed over to the Secretary of State for Wales on 30 September 1999, the report had to wait a further four and a half months before it saw the light of day. It was presented to the House of Commons and ordered to be printed on 15 February 2000, three years after the first evidence was heard.

Pre-publication scares and alarms

The knowledge that the Waterhouse report had been delivered to the Secretary of State for Wales in September 1999 prompted a number of 'false starts' in the national press. Although the report had been completed and, reputedly, guarded closely in a strongroom in the Cabinet Office, the task of producing the extensive summary report, its subsequent translation into Welsh, and finding a parliamentary window of opportunity extended the delay in its being laid before Parliament. The delay heightened the fever of expectation and rumour surrounding the report.

Some intervening events raised the temperature further. The investigation and prosecution of a Social Services (Wales) inspector who had worked at a South Wales residential children's home between 1974 and 1980 fed continuing suspicions of cover-up at a high level – an issue which had led to demands for the inquiry in the first place. There were charges that the person involved – Derek Brushett – was highly placed within the Welsh Office, had the main responsibility for inspection of children's services for part of the period under investigation and was probably involved in advising ministers about the need for such an inquiry throughout the wrangling over demands for a judicial investigation. Brushett was arrested in August 1998, several months after the Tribunal had ceased sitting. There were demands for the Tribunal to reconvene to consider what part he might have played in the North Wales events and in the Welsh Office's response to them. Furthermore, when it was found that the Tribunal report referred only briefly to Brushett's arrest, suspension and imminent trial, this fuelled further accusations of cover-up in high places. In fact, the Tribunal was prevented from delving into the affair so as not to prejudice the criminal case against him. The Tribunal delivered its report in September 1999, two months before the conclusion of criminal proceedings against Brushett.

In December 1998, four months after Brushett's arrest and after the addition of further charges against him, the SSI(W) commissioned an independent audit of its working practices with particular reference to his responsibilities throughout his tenure at the Welsh Office. Dr Kevin McCoy, Chief Inspector of Social Services (Northern Ireland) and Roger Clough, Professor of Social Care at the University of Lancaster, reported to the Health and Social Services Committee of the National Assembly in March 2000 (McCoy and Clough 2000). In respect of Brushett, they found very little that was untoward in relation to the North Wales inquiry. There was no evidence that he had played a part in the handling of complaints or issues relating to Bryn Alyn, as had been suggested, or that he had had a central role in advising politicians about the need for an inquiry into the North Wales events. Furthermore he had played no part in presenting the Welsh Office case to the Tribunal.

In the event Brushett was convicted of a number of offences including sexual abuse and charges of cruelty, and in November 1999 he was sentenced to 14 years' imprisonment.[1]

Clearly the Brushett débâcle, the way it was treated in the press[2] and the scepticism among leading complainants and commentators were not conducive to an easy birth for a report which had spent so long in gestation.

The method

Given the welter of evidence brought before the Tribunal, just how did the members sift fact from fiction, half memory and hindsight? Amid claims from organisations like the Bryn Estyn Staff Support Group that complainants were manufacturing allegations to climb on to the compensation bandwagon, and counterclaims that 'children's homes were a gulag archipelago stretching across Britain' (Cllr Malcolm King quoted in an article by Roger Dobson in the *Independent on Sunday* 10 March 1996), the Tribunal had to devise some way of arriving at an objective assessment of events. The chairman devoted a chapter of the report to this issue (Chapter 6: 'The Tribunal's approach to the evidence'). In approaching its task, the Tribunal had a number of difficulties to contend with. Evidential problems included the lapse of time; the nature of the allegations; the credibility of the complainants; the dearth of complaints made at the time; gaps in agencies' records and other documentary material available; and gaps in the memories of many of the witnesses. Given these difficulties the Tribunal rejected any idea that it could give authoritative judgements on every individual complaint made to it.

The chairman referred also to the difficulties in relation to the Salmon Letter recipients and especially the judgements that had to be made about naming individuals, which we considered in some detail in Chapter 7. At the time of the hearing, the chairman of the Tribunal had been of the view that there would be limited anonymity granted in the written report. Where allegations against individuals were considered to be of a minor nature or were few in number, the Tribunal refrained from naming those people. Its naming policy did extend to exposing those people who had already been involved in related court proceedings; giving assessments of those against whom a number of more serious allegations had been made; naming those who had figured prominently in the evidence; identifying individuals in order to deal with current rumours and speculation; and naming and assessing the performance of many in management and supervisory positions in the various agencies who carried responsibility for children's services, handling complaints and responding to individual and organisational deficiencies. As in a court of law, oral testimony carried greater weight with the Tribunal members than written testimony since it was subjected to cross-examination.

The findings

There was some feeling that the North Wales Tribunal was meant to be the inquiry to end all inquiries into this shameful period of childcare in Britain. As we saw in Chapter 5, police investigations into current and historical abuse had mushroomed across the UK. There had also been several smaller scale inquiries. The use of a Tribunal of Inquiry to investigate matters in North Wales, while to some degree justified by events there alone, seemed to suggest that it would address the wider issues as well. In practice, however, the Tribunal kept very closely to its terms of reference in relation to child abuse in North Wales. Its recommendations do have wider relevance, but even in this respect, the Tribunal report is careful not to overstep the mark, resisting the temptation to recite those measures which government had already started to activate in its response to the Utting children's safeguards review (Utting 1997).

The report received plaudits, qualified support and brickbats but overwhelmingly it was greeted with shame and sorrow that a system set up to care for vulnerable children and young people could have harboured so much cruelty and neglect of their welfare. Its recommendations received widespread support in the press. Its greatest strength was to provide an authoritative public record of 22 years in the history of children's services in North Wales. The Tribunal told us the facts dispassionately and the effect was all the more harrowing for that.

The questions that the Tribunal sought to answer were as follows:

- What was the extent of abuse – sexual abuse in particular – throughout children's residential homes across the two counties?

- Was the sexual abuse organised by a network of paedophiles targeting those homes and their children?

- Was there a conspiracy to protect prominent people?

- How was it possible that widespread abuse – if it existed – could go undetected for so long?

- Were there failings among the responsible agencies – social services, the police, health authority and the Welsh Office – which prolonged the abuse suffered by vulnerable children and young people?

- What measures can we adopt to ensure that such a situation could not recur?

We consider the Tribunal's answers to these questions in the following sections.

Extent of the abuse

We outlined in Chapter 7 how the Tribunal made it clear at the outset that it accepted that children in care in Clwyd and Gwynedd had been abused physically and/or sexually on a major scale, and that this acceptance of the scale of abuse was initially a device to encourage reluctant witnesses to come forward – a reassurance that, whatever their past experiences in dealing with the legal system and other forms of authority, they could be confident of a listening ear from the Tribunal. The task of the Tribunal, however, was to quantify the extent of the abuse more precisely. The Tribunal considered the allegations relating to each individual home during its period of operation and undertook some assessment of where the major problems lay. Some complaints were discounted for further investigation because they were made against unidentified individuals; some were outside the Tribunal's terms of reference; others related to homes which closed early on in the period covered by the terms of reference; many were unsupported by any other body of evidence or complaints relating to the same home or individual. After this initial sifting the panel proceeded to examine in detail complaints relating to:

- nine out of the twenty-three local authority homes in Clwyd

- one of four voluntary children's homes in Clwyd

- three private sector childcare organisations in Clwyd

- one local authority residential special school in Clwyd

- one NHS adolescent psychiatric unit in Clwyd.

(a total of 20 establishments in the former county of Clwyd including the individual establishments run by the voluntary and private sector organisations)

- seven foster homes in Clwyd

- five of the ten local authority homes in Gwynedd

- two private sector childcare organisations in Gwynedd

(a total of nine establishments in the former county of Gwynedd including the individual establishments run by the private sector organisations)

- eight foster homes in Gwynedd.

Sexual abuse

CLWYD

The Tribunal's overall conclusions were that there was widespread sexual abuse of boys in local authority children's homes in Clwyd and some cases of sexual abuse of girls. The main local authority homes affected in the county were Bryn Estyn and Cartrefle, where Peter Howarth and Stephen Norris, both convicted of offences against a number of young boys, were senior officers. The Tribunal found examples of other serious offences against boys by both male and female staff in a further five council homes in Clwyd.

The private sector in Clwyd accounted for a further raft of sexual offences against boys and girls in care. John Allen was the main perpetrator in the Bryn Alyn Community and was convicted of a number of offences in 1995. Twenty-eight former residents made complaints against him to the Tribunal, though his conviction related to offences committed on six boys. In addition to Allen, three other members of Bryn Alyn staff were investigated for sexual offences against male and female residents. Two were convicted during the period under investigation; the third died before the conclusion of the police investigation into allegations against him.

Two other private sector operations were the scenes of further abuse against boy residents. Noel Ryan, of Clwyd Hall, and Richard Leake, of Care Concern's Ystrad Hall, were convicted in 1997 and 1999 respectively of a series of serious sexual offences. Richard Groome, a former officer in charge at a voluntary home and subsequently principal at Clwyd Hall, was due to be tried after the delivery of the Waterhouse (2000) report of offences against young boys. Two further individuals, who had run Gatewen Hall as a residential school prior to its acquisition by the Bryn Alyn Community, were also convicted of sexual offences in August 1999.

In respect of complaints of serious sexual abuse against two members of staff at a voluntary home, Tanllwyfan, the Tribunal took the view that those witnesses who gave evidence were in all likelihood telling the truth. Similarly it was accepted that sexual abuse had taken place at the adolescent psychiatric unit, though probably not at the residential school.

The Tribunal found that children in five of Clwyd's foster homes had been seriously sexually abused.

GWYNEDD

There were no proven findings of sexual abuse in Gwynedd's community or foster homes, but there were substantial concerns about allegations made in one of the private homes in the county.

Physical abuse

The Tribunal by and large took a somewhat different view of physical abuse than it did of sexual abuse, noting that it took a more overt form and that it posed more problems in terms of assessment and response to it. Nevertheless, the Tribunal was unequivocal about the need to eliminate such abuse and made important comments about the matter.

CLWYD

The Tribunal found that physical abuse was widespread in residential establishments in Clwyd. Staff in as many as six homes used physical force against children in contravention of the Community Homes Regulations and Clwyd County Council's own rules. The Tribunal was particularly critical of the lack of appropriate response to complaints about physical abuse, highlighting the case of Paul Wilson, a housemaster at Bryn Estyn, who was ultimately convicted of a number of assaults. It was somewhat less critical of other individuals who assaulted children in that it recognised their lack of training and qualifications.

> It was almost inevitable, therefore that bad practices would be perpetuated and that newcomers would absorb the existing customs and attitudes of the particular establishment to which they were first assigned. Thus, for example, bad habits such as the physical chastisement of children and lack of frankness in the recording of incidents were likely to be adopted by the newcomer unless very firm guidance was given by the Officer-in-Charge and other senior members of staff. (Waterhouse 2000, para. 30.37)

Much more criticism was reserved for all levels of management, therefore, for failure to establish firm ground-rules and to check that they were being followed.

GWYNEDD

The Tribunal's findings in relation to physical abuse in Gwynedd children's homes were that it was less widespread than in Clwyd, but certain individuals, such as Nefyn Dodd at Ty'r Felin, were seen to be both physically intimidating and punitive. Considerable criticism was levelled at management for failure to prevent the abuse that did take place.

> To sum up, the organisation and management of the community homes in Gwynedd were such that a degree of child abuse was almost bound to occur and the only cause for relief is that it did not occur on a greater scale than has been disclosed by evidence. (Waterhouse 2000, para. 45.24)

PRIVATE AND FOSTER HOMES

Turning to private establishments, the picture again was little different, with physical ill-treatment of children being widespread. Evidence was also heard of physical abuse of children in foster care in both Clwyd and Gwynedd.

In addition to actual abuse, the Tribunal had much to say about the general quality of care being offered in Clwyd and Gwynedd and not much of it was positive. The Tribunal took the view that the quality of care was below an acceptable standard in all the homes examined, both local authority and privately run.

Was there a paedophile ring in operation?

Was the sexual abuse that took place in homes in Clwyd organised by a network of paedophiles who were specifically targeting vulnerable young people in care? This was the central question which occupied the minds of those who fought for a judicial inquiry, and even though it was not spelt out explicitly in the Tribunal's terms of reference, it was an issue that occasionally reared its head during the hearings when counsel or members of the Tribunal took a detour from their primary course of establishing the facts to a more discursive consideration of their implications.

One of the problems facing the panel in determining whether a paedophile ring existed was that of securing a clear definition of such a ring.

Definitions of organised abuse were available in child protection guidelines and literature at the time of the hearings. In the *Working Together* guidelines issued in 1991, the term 'organised abuse' was defined thus:

> a generic term which covers abuse which may involve a number of abusers, a number of abused children and young people and often encompass [*sic*] different forms of abuse. It involves, to a greater or lesser extent, a degree of organisation. (DoH 1991a, para. 5.26.1)

Bibby (1996) arrived at the following working definition:

Organised abuse is the systematic abuse of children, normally by more than one male. It is characterised by the degree of planning in the purposeful, secret targeting, seduction, hooking and silencing of the subjects. Institutional and ritual abuse are but specialised forms of organised abuse. (p.5)

Bibby argues that for professionals, the key issue is that of understanding the processes of organised abuse, those of identifying, targeting, grooming and, eventually, 'hooking' a child. On this basis it is clear that those young people who suffered at the hands of Norris and Howarth in Bryn Estyn were the victims of organised abuse, but not so clear that they had fallen prey to a 'paedophile ring'.

However, concerns about paedophile rings were not confined to what took place inside residential institutions, but looked also to connections with groups outside the homes. The claims about the existence of this type of paedophile network were informed largely by Witness B, who had been in care in the late 1970s. His account was that he had been drawn into under-age homosexual activity in the Wrexham and Chester areas and that homes were being used as a source of vulnerable young people by a ring comprising senior members of staff and other individuals – prominent and otherwise – known to these employees. On his own account, in statements to the Tribunal, he claimed to have been sexually abused by 32 individuals (including 8 who were unnamed) and physically abused by 22. Witness B alleged that he and others had been passed around between paedophiles inside and outside the care system, with the collusion of Bryn Estyn staff. Such concerns operated on the minds of Clwyd County Council officers when they invited North Wales Police to initiate a wider investigation in 1991, but were not substantiated. The theory of a wider conspiracy was undermined by the fact that very few of the complaints of sexual abuse coming out of Bryn Estyn referred to more than one alleged abuser. Within that home, at least, there was no evidence that boys were being passed around between abusers. Indeed there was much to suggest the existence of a mutual antipathy between the two main perpetrators at Bryn Estyn – Howarth and Norris. Having considered such evidence and examined information about the recruitment of staff who were convicted of abuse subsequently, the panel concluded that

no evidence has been presented to the Tribunal or to North Wales Police to establish that there was a wide-ranging conspiracy involving prominent persons and others with the objective of sexual activity with children in care. Equally, we are unaware of any evidence to establish that there was any coherent organisation of men with that objective. (Waterhouse 2000, para. 52.07)

This was not the Tribunal's last word, however, on the matter of a paedophile ring. Having discounted the idea that the children's homes and their staff might be at the centre of such a ring, the members went on to consider the possibility of some such network operating across the broader gay community in Wrexham, Chester and along the North Wales coast and around the Chester outpost of the Campaign for Homosexual Equality, and concluded that a network of sorts existed:

> the cumulative effect of all the evidence has been to satisfy us that, during the period under review, a significant number of individual male persons in the Wrexham and Chester areas were engaged in paedophile activities of the kind described by Witness B ... These and other individuals were targeting young males in their middle teens and it was inevitable that some young persons in care should be caught in their web. The evidence does not establish that they were solely or mainly interested in persons in care but such youngsters were particularly vulnerable to their approaches for emotional and other reasons; and the abusers were quite prepared to prey on such victims, despite the risks involved ... Many, but not all, of these paedophiles were known to each other and some of them met together frequently, although there were strong antagonisms between individuals from time to time. Inevitably, some information about likely candidates for paedophile activities was shared, expressly and implicitly, and there were occasions when sexual activity occurred in a group. (Waterhouse 2000, paras 52.84–52.85)

Was there a conspiracy to protect prominent people?

The rumour factory surrounding the North Wales events had it that the reason that the whistleblowers were victimised by their employers and ignored by the authorities was that there were reputations at stake. Talk of the involvement of senior police officers and prominent members of the Establishment in 'the events' led naturally to allegations of the use of Masonic links to ensure that they did not see the light of day. This, it was suggested, was why the most senior CID officer in the North Wales force was given the task of investigating relatively minor assaults at a children's home in Gwynedd at the behest of the deputy chief constable in 1986. This was also said to be why an investigation into a petty theft at the home of a career paedophile was not expanded into a wide-ranging investigation into sexual abuse in North Wales children's homes upon discovery of some indecent photographs at the property. This, too, was said to account for the failure to prosecute a retired police officer (who was also a Freemason) who became the subject of allegations of sexual abuse during the Major Inquiry of 1991.

Set in such a context, allegations of the influence of Freemasonry seemed plausible. Much to the chagrin of some of the main protagonists, however, the issue never really took off. In his opening submission during the early days of the Tribunal, counsel for North Wales Police made a great flourish of announcing that none of the senior officers involved in any of the investigations under scrutiny and none of the officers at the very head of the North Wales Police during the relevant period, from assistant chief constable upwards, were Freemasons. Furthermore it was pointed out that the chief constable had issued a directive to staff in September 1984, encouraging existing members of Freemasonry to reconsider their membership in the light of trends towards more openness in the police and discouraging others from taking up membership of such organisations. Communications between the chief constable and Lord Kenyon, who was both Provincial Grand Master in North Wales and a member of the police authority at the time, reflected some conflict between the two about the former's position. There were additional rumours that Lord Kenyon had intervened on the part of his son, who was active in the gay scene in the Wrexham area and was at one point the subject of abuse allegations. This too was not substantiated by the Tribunal.

Failings in management, supervision and inspection (of the responsible agencies)

The Tribunal paid particular attention to the history of local authority management in general and social services management in particular across the two counties during the relevant period and the effect these had on the standard of care and response to problems with respect to children in care.

Clwyd County Council

The Tribunal found that a significant feature of the management and organisation of Clwyd County Council Social Services Department throughout the period under investigation was the state of almost permanent upheaval in which it found itself much of the time. In line with many social services departments across the UK, Clwyd was often undergoing organisational changes, notably in 1974, 1980 and 1990, largely involving shifts from centralised to devolved structures and back again. While the changes may have made sense on paper, their success was forced to depend largely on the availability of the necessary skills and expertise in house, since pressure on resources invariably prohibited the injection of new talent.

The Tribunal found that Clwyd's headquarters team was sadly lacking in childcare expertise throughout the review period. Its brightest stars were steeped in strategic management. Although able to design systems and job structures to facilitate high standards of care, they could not guarantee the quality of personnel to deliver it for all client groups. While new strategies for people who experienced learning difficulties or mental health problems received national attention and leadership, residential childcare appeared to be very much the poor relation. Thus the fate of children's services relied on the same middle-ranking officers who had presided over the earlier failures in the system.

Another problem highlighted by the Tribunal was the extent to which the local authority's senior officer, the chief executive, was insulated from problems arising within the social services department. Thus the Tribunal found that:

> Phillips [the chief executive] relied heavily upon the Director of Social Services and County Secretary and expected to be informed by one or both of them of any significant problems. (Waterhouse 2000, para. 28.51)

and that:

> As Deputy to Gledwyn Jones [Director of Social Services], John Jevons' [Deputy Director] understanding was that Mervyn Phillips as Chief Executive expected Chief Officers to manage their own departments and 'consume their own smoke'. (Waterhouse 2000, para. 28.54)

Things did change when Jevons became director himself, but this was not until 1990, by which time the convention of departments 'consuming their own smoke' had prevailed for nearly 20 years.

A similar convention could be observed further down the hierarchy in the social services department to prevent problems leaking beyond individual homes or, if that was not possible, from beyond middle management at HQ. At Bryn Estyn, the officer in charge, Grenville Arnold, went to great lengths to prevent rumours about Howarth's sexual proclivities from gaining wider circulation. There were also a number of instances of his persuading boys to withdraw complaints of serious physical assault and on at least one occasion of which there is documented evidence, he fabricated a completely fictitious account of how a serious injury was sustained. This was all in pursuance of a policy of containing problems within homes where possible and colluding with middle-ranking officers to stop them reaching the ears of senior officers and members. More often than not, complaints and problems stopped short of senior social services management as children were 'persuaded' by the use of threats of one kind or another that it was not in their interest to make too much of an incident. Where concerns about residential care did leak through the barrier of middle management to senior management, they frequently went no further. Although on occasions their response was to initiate a series of internal inquiries and reports between 1974 and 1991, the chief executive and members of the council remained blissfully unaware of serious and continuing problems in their children's residential operation.

The Tribunal clearly placed much of the responsibility for this state of affairs at the top of the hierarchy which set the tone for those lower down to keep the lid on things.

Gwynedd

The Tribunal found that although there were far fewer examples of serious abuse in Gwynedd, nevertheless, the quality of childcare services was very poor and that it shared many of the same management and organisational features as those found in Clwyd,[3] in particular the failure to monitor effectively the performance of staff with primary responsibility for children's residential care. The Tribunal heard evidence that members did not take much interest in children's services. With an increasing older population, councillors took more interest in residential care for older people than the needs of 'naughty' children. Their interest was occasionally awakened by representations from constituents who found the homes troublesome, but their primary concern was that establishments should not impinge too much on their neighbourhoods. This low priority given to children's services was evident in the county's expenditure record and was highlighted by the County Treasurer in the early 1980s and District Audit as late as 1993–4. The Tribunal doubted whether even the Social Services Committee or the director had made any serious attempt to gain extra resources for children's services during the relevant period, despite this patent under-funding.

The Tribunal found considerable rivalries between officers within Gwynedd Social Services Department. Failure to address these, and the high incidence of long-term illness among senior staff, led to a lengthy period of drift which particularly affected children's services. Roles and responsibilities were indistinct and temporary delegations were made which further muddied the lines of management and accountability in relation to children's homes.

These were highlighted in a report commissioned by the chief executive in 1981 which pointed, in particular, to shortcomings arising from the dual role held by Nefyn Dodd. He was both officer in charge at Ty'r Felin, the home which later became the centre of the Gwynedd allegations, and had been made de facto head of all children's homes on a temporary basis. Despite the warnings raised by this report, Dodd went on to hold this post on a temporary basis for another four years and was confirmed in the position in October 1985. Like his middle-ranking counterparts in Clwyd, Dodd kept a tight lid on dissent and complaints in the homes. Few controversial issues made it up the hierarchy and those that did were 'resolved' in Dodd's favour. Complainants and whistleblowers like Alison Taylor received short shrift.

Common failings

The Tribunal found that both counties demonstrated similar failings in terms of the quality of staff they employed and the care they provided during most of the relevant period. Homes were undifferentiated. Their role and purpose became blurred. Placements were rarely planned and bore little relation to the child's needs beyond the immediate need for shelter. Children would often spend many months in assessment centres where staff were not trained to undertake assessments. Recruitment was haphazard. Homes relied heavily on young, unqualified and inexperienced staff recruited informally on a casual basis to fill in gaps caring for very difficult young people. They received no induction, no training and no guidance on policies or practice pertinent to residential care. Managers failed to monitor and inspect homes and this clearly contributed to the failure to detect abuse at an earlier stage. The need for formal complaints systems was not widely recognised until the mid-1980s when problems in residential care generally were becoming more apparent. In so far as there were any mechanisms to complain, these relied on a relationship of trust existing between the child and the recipient of the complaint, most likely a member of staff. The general tenor of the regimes which existed in some homes militated against such trusting relationships. Nor was fieldwork support much in evidence in many of the cases before the Tribunal. It was recognised that field social work visits would be concentrated mainly around the time of the reception into care or admission to a home and discharge. There might be a long gap in between when children would receive little or no support. This was particularly the case for those who had been placed away from their home authority.

Overall, the Tribunal concluded that both local authorities had failed the children in their care. They had failed to give children the priority they deserved in their plans and programmes. They had failed to allocate adequate and appropriate management resources to monitoring and supervising children's residential care in particular. Frequent reorganisations in both counties had failed to provide for the proper coordination and oversight of children's services to the extent that a sense of 'drift' was created in terms of their management and control. Inadequate expertise in children's residential care at a senior enough level in social services gave the impression that children were a low priority as far as senior management was concerned. The services generally failed to provide skilled assessment of problems and needs, planned admissions to appropriate facilities, individual care plans, ongoing professional support, meaningful reviews and any hope of positive outcomes for young people. Rather they gave every appearance of providing *ad hoc* admissions to generic facilities which provided little more than containment in many instances. Even in this respect they failed miserably as many residents continued their offending behaviour while in care.

Response of North Wales Police

The Tribunal considered in some detail the role of the North Wales Police in responding to complaints and in carrying out three main investigations (Gwynedd 1986–8; Cartrefle 1990; Clwyd and Gwynedd Major Inquiry 1991–1993). In relation to the last-mentioned investigation, it looked at whether:

- the training and preparation of officers recruited were adequate
- the methods used to contact potential witnesses who were former residents of children's homes throughout the period and the treatment of witnesses who alleged serious abuse were reasonable
- the resistance to involving an outside force was justifiable despite the fact that allegations had been made against serving and former North Wales Police officers.

The Tribunal members were assisted in their task by Sir Ronald Hadfield, former chief constable in both the Nottinghamshire and West Midlands forces. He was appointed as 'Assessor to the Tribunal in respect of Police Matters'.

The Tribunal found that the North Wales Police had over a 15-year period conducted 20 inquiries in Clwyd which involved care workers, other employees or individuals involved in the North Wales 'paedophile' scene. The allegations involved, in various permutations, offences against young people who were, had been or would be in care at some stage during the period. These 20 inquiries resulted in 11 prosecutions and convictions for sexual offences, the remainder resulting in no further action. The Tribunal accepted that none of these investigations individually should have been expected to trigger a wider-ranging investigation across the care system without further complaints coming forward, though it did suggest that this number of allegations might have generated a greater degree of vigilance in social services management.

The Tribunal was critical of the police investigation in Gwynedd in 1986 which was set up in response to complaints by Alison Taylor. The 1986 investigation had been delegated to the Head of CID, who had taken it upon himself to conduct it with the assistance of only one junior officer. The inquiry he carried out was considered to have lacked depth and not to have been procedurally correct. The Tribunal report's final comment on this episode was as follows:

> Whether or not any criminal charge would have been brought if the defects referred to had not occurred is a matter of speculation; but a serious consequence of the way in which the investigation was conducted was that seeds of distrust of the North Wales Police were sown. (Waterhouse 2000, para. 51.17)

The two other police investigations received a clean bill of health from both Sir Ronald Hadfield and the Tribunal. The criticisms levelled at the investigating officer in the 1990 (Cartrefle) inquiry were that the events in that home and the conduct of Stephen Norris should have put the police on notice about the possibility of abuse at other homes in which he had worked. However, the Tribunal considered this investigation to have gone as far as it could and achieved a positive result.

With regard to the Major Inquiry which began in 1991, the Tribunal's overall conclusion was as follows:

> We are satisfied, on the basis of all the evidence that we have heard in the course of 14 months' hearings, that this investigation was carried out both thoroughly and efficiently. We have received no evidence to justify any suggestion that there was a 'cover-up' in respect of any part of it or to cast doubt upon the good faith of the police throughout the inquiry. (Waterhouse 2000, para. 51.46)

There had been several criticisms about some of the methods used in this investigation, including the following:

- The decision to approach ex-residents by means of cold-calling was said to be insensitive and traumatic for the most vulnerable witnesses, who had made great efforts to put their experiences behind them.

- In some cases, witnesses were approached by police officers who were known to them during their offending careers. This, too, was said to be insensitive and unlikely to create a relationship of trust and confidence.

- There were complaints from one particular witness (referred to as Witness B throughout the report) that officers had been downright abusive and offensive in their approach to him and that they had failed to record many of the complaints and statements made by him.

Both Sir Ronald Hadfield and the Tribunal members felt that 'cold-calling' may have been the 'least worst' option around but that exceptions might have been made in particular cases. Similarly the use of officers known to the witness was considered by the Tribunal to have been potentially helpful or unhelpful depending upon the individuals involved and the relationship existing between them. The Tribunal recognised that there were very few complaints about the way police officers treated witnesses. Many of the complaints of poor treatment came from Witness B who, it was acknowledged, was a difficult person to deal with. In view of these known difficulties, the Tribunal felt that he could have been treated more sensitively on occasions but did not accept the witness's charge that police had suppressed or failed to record any of his complaints or statements.

The matter of the involvement of an outside force was touched on in Chapter 7. The Tribunal accepted that the chronology of events and the pace of the investigation made any such option impracticable even if it were justified by the facts.

Overall, then, the performance of North Wales Police in its conduct of the last two investigations in 1990 and 1991–3 was deemed professional. With minor reservations about training and the treatment of a few witnesses, it was felt that the criticisms levelled by certain individuals were not justified. Nevertheless the Tribunal felt that there was one lesson which could be drawn from the experience, particularly in view of the fact that such wide-ranging historical inquiries were cropping up all over the UK. It recommended that an inter-agency review of the conduct of such investigations should be undertaken with a view to preparing appropriate practice guidelines for joint inquiries in the future.

Welsh Office

The Tribunal gave careful consideration to whether the Welsh Office itself should bear any responsibility for the treatment of children in North Wales homes during the period in question. After all, its Social Services Inspectorate had responsibility for inspecting local authority homes and for licensing and inspecting most of the private and voluntary establishments in Wales. The Tribunal considered carefully the various reorganisations within the Welsh Office between 1974 and 1994. It was noted that in 1979 resources allocated for the work of the Social Services Inspectorate (then called the Social Work Service) were greatly reduced by the incoming Conservative government elected on the back of promises to reduce taxes and state intervention.

Nevertheless, the Tribunal still found the actions of the Welsh Office to have been wanting in the following respects (see Waterhouse 2000, para. 47.47):

- It failed throughout the period under review to play a sufficiently interventionist part in the management and operation of county social services departments to ensure that appropriate standards were observed.

- It failed to plan the development of social services by setting clear aims and objectives and ensuring that they were understood.

- It failed to monitor adequately the performance of county social services departments in such a way as to promote the achievement of aims and the maintenance of standards.

- It failed to provide sufficient practical guidance to social services departments in a readily accessible form.

At the heart of these criticisms is the perception of the proper relationship, set out in statute and guidance, between the Welsh Office and local authorities. The Welsh Office was of the view that it had an advisory and guidance role in relation to social services departments in Wales, not a supervisory and instructive role. However, the Tribunal rejected this 'washing of hands' by the Welsh Office:

> To sum up, in our judgement there were serious failings by the Welsh Office in providing the leadership, guidance and monitoring that were necessary to ensure effective implementation of the new legislation relating to children in care that came into force at the beginning of the 1970s and the development of good practice. At least some of those failings were attributable, in part, to wider government policies; and there were other aspects of personal social

services policy, such as the All Wales Strategy for the Development of Services for Mentally Handicapped People, in which the Welsh Office gave a positive lead. For the future, however, the lesson must be that special attention will need to be given to the welfare of children in care in Wales by the Welsh Office and the Welsh Assembly in the wake of further local government reorganisation; and the limited size and resources of the 22 new authorities will be important factors to be considered when a childcare strategy is formulated. (Waterhouse 2000, para. 47.72)

The Tribunal's recommendations

Seventy-two recommendations emerged from the Tribunal's deliberations. As mentioned above, the Tribunal applied a self-denying ordinance by referring only to those recommended measures which were not already contained in government statements of intent, new proposals or existing bills going through Parliament (referred to elsewhere in this volume). As such, it is a relatively short list. Some of the recommendations require new legislation; others require only administrative action to implement. Many relate to pre-existing statutory requirements and practice guidelines which were being routinely ignored throughout the period under review. It might be thought that it would be unnecessary, for example, to reiterate the need for a child to have an appropriately qualified field social worker allocated throughout the period during which he or she is in care (Recommendation 10). Or, indeed, that any residential or fostering arrangements made for the child should allow for continuing supervision by the child's social worker (Recommendation 12). In what follows we have selected for attention those we consider to be key new recommendations.

Children's Commissioner

The Tribunal's recommendation of the appointment of a Children's Commissioner for Wales has received most attention. Many professional childcare bodies had been recommending such an appointment for some time. The body which represents the interests of children in care in Wales, Voices from Care, laid emphasis on this proposal in its submission to the Tribunal. While all agree that such a post should be independent of government, the permutations for the scope of the role of such a person are endless. The Tribunal outlines the duties that it would expect a Commissioner to fulfil:

(a)   ensuring that children's rights are respected through the
        monitoring and oversight of the operation of complaints and

whistleblowing procedures and the arrangements for children's advocacy;

(b) examining the handling of individual cases brought to the Commissioner's attention (including making recommendations on the merits) when he considers it necessary and appropriate to do so;

(c) publishing reports, including an annual report to the National Assembly for Wales.

(Waterhouse 2000, para. 56.05)

Plans to proceed with such an appointment are already under way. Under the terms of the Care Standards Bill, currently wending its way through the legislative processes of Parliament, a post of Children's Rights Director whose functions will relate only to looked-after children, will be created for England and Wales. However, the Welsh Assembly has sought an amendment to the Bill to allow for the appointment of a stand-alone Children's Commissioner for Wales with a much broader remit. It hopes to be able to appoint a Commissioner within the current year (2000–1) and has allocated £100,000 to cover the part year cost. In England, the forthright stance of the Welsh Assembly has fired Westminster MPs and the Commons Health Select Committee to argue the case for a champion of children's rights with a wider brief than that provided for in the Care Standards Bill (*Independent* 14 May 2000: Jo Dillon, 'Abuse row as Milburn blocks plan for a "children's commissioner"')

Establishment of an Advisory Council for Children's Services in Wales

Though not loudly trumpeted during the press bonanza following the release of the Waterhouse (2000) report, it is clear that the Tribunal members felt that such an advisory body would be a vital complement to the office of the Children's Commissioner. This was seen as having a proactive role along the lines of a think-tank on children's issues. Its role was envisaged as including:

(a) advising on government policy and legislation with regard to their likely impact on children and young people;

(b) commissioning research;

(c) disseminating information and making recommendations.

(Waterhouse 2000, para. 56.05)

Dedicated Complaints Officer for children in each social services authority

The Tribunal recommended that every such authority should be required to appoint a Complaints Officer solely for children, who should be outside the line management of any staff whose duties may be the subject of complaint by children. The duties of such an officer would include:

(a)   to act in the best interests of the child;

(b)   on receiving a complaint, to see the affected child and the complainant, if he or she is not the affected child;

(c)   thereafter to notify and consult with appropriate line managers about the further handling of the complaint;

(d)   to ensure that recourse to an independent advocacy service is available to any complainant or affected child who wishes to have it;

(e)   to keep a complete record of all complaints received and how they are dealt with, including the ultimate outcome;

(f)   to report periodically to the Director of Social Services on complaints received, how they have been dealt with and the results.

(Waterhouse 2000, para. 56.05)

In addition the Tribunal made recommendations about the design and application of complaints procedures which would render them accessible to vulnerable children. In view of the information that had come its way about past responses to complaints on the part of authorities, it also suggested that a child should not be moved after a complaint of abuse unless it is clearly in the child's best interests.

Whistleblowing procedures

The Tribunal recommended that each local authority should put in place procedures which would allow whistleblowers to make complaints and to have them investigated without fear of reprisal. Members also felt that consideration ought to be given to imposing a duty on staff to report abuse of which they become aware so that the failure to do so might become a disciplinary offence.

Application of disciplinary procedures

The Tribunal recommended the need to carry out disciplinary proceedings expeditiously and to bear in mind their primary responsibility to protect the welfare of the child (see Chapter 9 for more details on this).

Qualification and training

The Tribunal endorsed the recommendations on training contained within Utting's (1997) review of children's safeguards. In addition to these, it recommended that senior staff in children's residential settings should be professionally qualified or should, as a condition of appointment, undertake to become so within a specified period. Training in safe methods of restraint should be made a priority by central government as homes increasingly accommodate young people with the most challenging behaviour. In tune with most of its predecessors, the Tribunal repeated the plea to elevate the status of residential and field social work by undertaking a review of pay and career development within the sector, in order to guarantee a plentiful supply of qualified staff for all sectors of children's services.

Independent regulatory body

The Tribunal recommended the establishment of an independent body charged with the task of inspecting all settings in which children are accommodated away from home. At least one member of any such inspection team should have substantial experience and expertise in childcare. The Tribunal also called for the adoption of common standards of care across all sectors and settings offering services for children. The reports of inspections of local authority homes should be sent to the authority's chief executive in addition to the director of social services as a matter of course. The regulatory body should produce an annual report of its work, highlighting constraints and shortfalls in its performance of its task. This recommendation is generally in line with the proposals set out in the government White Paper *Modernising Social Services* (DoH 1998c).

Summary

In a sense there were few surprises in the Waterhouse (2000) report recommendations. Many of them were a restatement of issues which had failed to be addressed by central and local government after many previous inquiries and reports. Many others were already common currency among professional children's groups prior to the setting up of the inquiry. Yet more were already in the process of being implemented by government. What the Tribunal hoped to bring to these matters was a greater sense of urgency and, in telling the stories of many damaged and vulnerable adults who had been through the system in North Wales, it gave a glimpse of the future if real change is not effected forthwith.

Waterhouse: a fair assessment?

One of the major difficulties facing public inquiries into institutional child abuse is that of providing a balanced account and judgement of the events which led to their being established. There are many competing demands: those of the public to know the facts, those of the victims to have their accounts validated and the wrongdoers exposed, those of the alleged abusers and those responsible for managing them to receive a fair hearing, and those of the residential social work profession in general to be represented in context.

As we have seen in previous chapters, many public inquiries have failed to achieve this balance, though to some degree media representation of their findings has been to blame for this. Most inquiries have had negative impacts on individual social workers and the profession in general. In particular, they have been considered by those within the profession to have failed to emphasise the context within which social workers operate when assessing the quality of their practice. This was seen as a major issue in the first well-publicised inquiry of the modern era, that relating to the death of Maria Colwell (DHSS 1974). Such were the disagreements about providing fair representation that one of the panel members, Olive Stevenson, wrote a minority report which argued that some of the judgements made in the main report were not sufficiently informed by an understanding of the aims, goals and methods of social work intervention.

In this final section, therefore, we aim to assess briefly the success of the Waterhouse inquiry in achieving a balanced and informed picture.

As is clear from Chapter 7, the inquiry was determined to focus on establishing the facts as far as possible and its method of achieving this goal was by means of a cross-examination which enabled the chairman and the panel to make a judgement in relation to individual allegations of abuse and to the responses of managers and others to such allegations. As we have noted, the process was a painful one for many, but adopted by the Tribunal as the best practical means of establishing the facts. The report makes a series of detailed and balanced judgements about each of the incidents that was brought to its attention. In this respect, it clearly achieved what the public expected of it. It verified many of the allegations and dismissed others. As we have seen, it particularly rejected claims alleging conspiracies among high-ranking officials and the existence of paedophile rings within children's homes.

The Tribunal did go to great lengths to look at events in residential care in North Wales in their historical and political context, placing great emphasis on legislative and organisational change and on financial constraints. Thus a sense of context was clearly there. Nevertheless the Tribunal remained critical of those officers and administrators charged with responsibility for children's services in North Wales – whether in local authorities or in the Welsh Office – for placing too low a priority on children's residential services and for being too accepting of poor standards of practice.

With regard to residential social workers in the establishments where abuse was deemed to have taken place, the Tribunal differentiated between serious abusers (mainly sexual) and those accused of isolated physical assaults on children. It clearly recognised that many staff involved in these latter incidents were less culpable because of their youth, inexperience and lack of guidance and training in appropriate restraint techniques.

The chairman repeated at every opportunity his intention to place the events in context and to avoid the trap of judging them with the benefit of hindsight. His assessment of individuals took into account both the negative and the positive evidence about their conduct as well as the difficult job they had to fulfil with the minimum of guidance or leadership from above. Many witnesses who were judged to have 'lost their rag' on a few occasions were also credited with trying to provide a caring atmosphere for the children in their charge.

Despite these efforts to provide context and to make fair and balanced judgements, however, the overall impact of the inquiry remains a negative one, reinforcing a view that residential care in North Wales was an unhappy and dangerous experience for many children. Perhaps this was inevitable because the report had to deal with large numbers of allegations and some of its sections make dismal and shocking reading. Inquiries by their very nature are concerned with what goes wrong. They do not focus on the positives because they are not a direct part of their remit. When one considers, however, the number of homes which came within the remit of the Tribunal and the period of time in question, the amount of abuse, while still unacceptable, takes on a different light.

Concluding comments

In summary, therefore, the Tribunal achieved its main goals. It did make a reasonably balanced assessment of events, it highlighted systems as well as individual failures and paid careful attention to context. Nevertheless, the adoption of the adversarial process generated negative consequences. It put residential social work and social workers in the dock and on the defensive. It provided a very combative forum for some very sensitive issues to be played out. The input of some professional assessment from the residential social work side might have produced more realistic judgements about what was possible throughout the period under scrutiny. In our view, and that of the Tribunal, Sir Ronald Hadfield's assessment of the performance of North Wales Police took into account the operational realities of policing as well as the statutory framework and was all the more valuable for that.

Finally, the jury is out as to whether the Tribunal will ultimately have made any difference to the context of practice and the performance of practitioners.

Notes

1 A key matter of concern raised by the audit team about the handling of Derek Brushett's case was the fact that information about abuse allegations made against him to both the North and South Wales police in 1992 and 1994 had not been passed on to his employer, the Welsh Office, and became known to the North Wales inquiry only in April 1997. Brushett's duties were restricted shortly after the Tribunal's disclosure and became more restricted as further complaints were made over the succeeding months. He was not suspended from duty, however, until after his arrest in August 1998. In the light of these events, the audit team asked ministers to consider the feasibility of establishing a duty for agencies or individual staff members to share information about allegations of serious offences.

2. Headlines in the *Liverpool Daily Post* on 24 November 1999 read 'Jailed child abuser was on North Wales Tribunal team'.

3 The reasons for the lack of clear communication and poor management were somewhat different from those in Clwyd. Because the usual party political influences were non-existent in Gwynedd, the council was made up of Independents whose interests were territorial rather than political. There was no natural leader of the council who could spearhead strategic reforms which had become commonplace elsewhere. Instead, committee chairs presided over departmental fiefdoms and senior officers were more concerned to keep them happy rather than to contribute to the corporate good of the authority.

CHAPTER 9

Impact of Public Inquiries on Residential Care Now

Introduction

This chapter has two main aims – first, to describe the current policy and practice situation in residential care, and second, to evaluate the extent to which public inquiries have contributed to this state of affairs.

As has been seen, the extent of concern about abuse in residential care as reflected in public inquiries has intensified throughout the 1990s and still persists. The recommendations of inquiries have had some direct influences on practice – for example, the Pindown inquiry (Staffordshire 1991) led to an immediate response by the Department of Health instructing all local authorities to examine whether within their own services there were elements of the type of regime that was deemed abusive in Staffordshire. This led to the exposure of unsatisfactory practices in Bradford and Sheffield.

Mostly, however, the impact has been indirect. Inquiry recommendations have led to central government setting up reviews and research projects to establish whether the types of concern raised in particular cases are found more generally and, if so, to endorse the original recommendations.

This description makes the process seem fairly logical and straightforward. In reality, however, it has been far more complicated than this, mainly because new cases of abuse in residential care have continually been uncovered throughout this period. In a sense, there has been very little breathing space within which to establish effective responses as residential care has reeled from one scandal to another. To some degree, therefore, the policy-makers have been unable to make a great impact.

There have been two main sets of initiatives in the 1990s. One followed on from the first tranche of abuse revelations in the early 1990s (Utting 1991; Howe, Lady E. 1992; Warner 1992) which produced important recommendations about policy, management, staff recruitment, training and pay. The other responded to the continued pressure in the second half of the decade. This took the form of the children's safeguards review (Utting 1997) and the subsequent government response (DoH 1998d), which have produced much more wide-ranging initiatives in relation to inspection, monitoring and standard setting. However, despite these initiatives and the added impetus that one would expect from the publication of the North Wales Tribunal Inquiry report, as will been seen in what follows, the rate of actual change in residential care provision for children seems to have been very slow.

Nevertheless in the following sections, developments in the areas of recruitment and selection of staff, training, management of children's homes, responding to allegations and complaints, monitoring and inspection processes and the promotion of children's rights will be considered.

Recruitment and selection of staff

The Warner (1992) report, which was prompted by the conviction of Frank Beck for sexual offences against children in homes in Leicestershire in 1991, was set up primarily 'to examine selection and recruitment methods and criteria for staff working in children's homes' (Warner 1992, p.1).

The case of Frank Beck

The reasons for paying such close attention to recruitment stemmed from awareness of deficiencies in the appointment of Frank Beck which were later highlighted in the Leicestershire inquiry report (Leicestershire 1993).

Beck was appointed in 1973 to be head of a medium-sized home for adolescents with behavioural difficulties. A former Royal Marine, he was aged 31 at the time and had worked for two years as an unqualified residential childcare officer before completing a two-year social work qualifying course. He claimed to have had some experience in therapeutic work in residential childcare, which was considered to be a key requirement of the post. Although Beck was the only candidate for the post, technically the correct procedure was followed: he was supported by two written references and was interviewed by three managers from Leicestershire Social Services Department. In the course of the subsequent inquiry, however, it was found that one of Beck's referees, his tutor on the social work training course, harboured more doubts about him than he had felt able to divulge in a written reference, namely that he was a very single-minded, sometimes aggressive, individual who clashed frequently with other students and whose behaviour raised concerns among several of the other social work tutors. Similarly, it was revealed that the author of his second reference, the head of one of the homes in which Beck had been previously employed, felt that had she known that he was proposing to develop a therapeutic community, she would have pointed out his lack of experience, knowledge and training in such work. While the inquiry team felt that Beck's appointment was understandable in the circumstances, it was of the view that the selection process used was unlikely to highlight personality defects and his unsuitability for taking a lead in complex therapeutic work.

State of residential staffing in 1991

The Warner (1992) report conducted a survey of local authority recruitment practices for children's homes for its report in 1991. It painted a bleak picture, suggesting that little had changed since 1973. Levels of qualification were still very low (see next section) and staff turnover was high, with a significant minority being employed from recruitment agencies, particularly in the London area. Many staff were recruited in a casual and *ad hoc* manner and a large number of appointments were made from within authorities. Recruiting practices were inadequate, with over-reliance on the formal interview.

The Warner (1992) report argued that at a wider policy level there was need for key structural changes in order to attract a better calibre of candidate to residential social work: improved pay (as recommended in Lady Howe's (1992) report); better working environments; and improved supervision and support. It also argued that central government should instigate a recruitment campaign in the same way that it had with nurses between 1989 and 1991.

Achieving good practice in selection

The remainder of the Warner report's recommendations about recruitment focused on best practice at the ground level. Most of these recommendations were of a basic kind and could be applied to the process of recruitment to a large range of types of work. They included the need for clear job specifications, the need to advertise vacancies (externally in the case of heads of homes), the desirability of recruiting a pool of staff in advance, and the need to reduce the use of agency staff. Job specific application forms were recommended, and a variety of assessment methods including written exercises, and aptitude and personality tests. Visits by all short-listed applicants to the establishments to be worked in, the involvement of children in the selection process and the use of independent persons on interview panels were three further important suggestions.

The Warner report was particularly scathing about dominant practices in relation to giving references. As we noted earlier, Frank Beck's referees when he applied for a post in Leicestershire in 1973 were not as forthcoming as they might have been. However, the failures to express concerns then were nothing compared to events in 1987 when Beck, having resigned from Leicestershire Social Services Department following a series of allegations against him, was seeking other residential childcare positions in the London area. References from his ex-employers in Leicestershire were supportive and made no mention of the reasons for his resignation other than that he had found some of the authority's policies difficult to accommodate. No mention was made of several allegations against Beck of serious sexual harassment of, and sexual assaults on, both staff and residents in the period immediately prior to his resignation. Warner (1992) argued for a much more rigorous trawl of previous employers, more demanding questions being made of referees and the use of oral as well as written contacts.

Checking criminal records

The Warner (1992) report contained much useful information about the use of police checks on criminal records for prospective employees, a facility created in 1986. It recommended speeding up the process of carrying out checks and the need for guidance to be issued to the police about passing on any other relevant information that they might have about individuals in addition to cautions and convictions. It also recommended that the Crown Prosecution Service be required to divulge relevant information to be passed on by the police. In addition, Warner recommended greater use of central government department lists of persons considered unsuitable for working with children.

Responding to Warner and the safeguards review

Few could argue with the good sense of Warner's recommendations. But, to what extent have they been taken on board eight years later? Many of the concerns, issues and recommendations made by Warner were reiterated by the safeguards review published in 1997 (Utting 1997). The Social Services Inspectorate (1998) report *Someone Else's Children* showed that there had been little progress in recruitment and selection practices between 1992 and 1998. In the *Government's Response to the Children's Safeguards Review* (DoH 1998d), it expressed 'full compliance with the recommendations of Choosing with Care in the social services' and confirmed that it would 'announce action shortly' (DoH 1998d, para. 8.12). It also agreed with Utting (1997) that the recommendations of Warner (1992) should be applied to all other settings where children lived away from home.

More progress has been made in relation to the use of lists of persons deemed unsuitable for work with children by virtue of misconduct. The Protection of Children Act 1999 makes it mandatory to refer relevant information to the Department of Health. It also makes it mandatory for agencies proposing to offer individuals employment in childcare positions to check with the list and, if they are included, not to employ them. The position with regard to police checks is still unsatisfactory in that the great majority of non-statutory childcare organisations, including recruitment agencies, are still unable to check the criminal background of people they propose to engage. Finally, the list of approved practitioners recommended by Warner has not happened yet. A General Social Care Council with powers of deregistration of professionals has been proposed in the government White Paper *Modernising Social Services* (DoH 1998c) and is contained within the Care Standards Bill currently receiving its second reading before Parliament.

Training

The lack of training and qualifications among residential staff has continually been highlighted in inquiries. The Utting (1991) report commissioned a survey of 20 local authorities to determine the levels of qualification in childcare establishments. About 20 per cent of heads of homes were found to be unqualified; Warner (1992), who also conducted a survey, put this figure at 30 per cent. Similarly 70 per cent of the remaining staff were unqualified (40 per cent according to Warner). Voluntary and private homes were not in Utting's remit. However, Warner showed that in the early 1990s just under a third of residential care workers for children were employed in such settings and that the standards of training and qualification were lower overall than in the statutory sector. Utting (1991) recommended that all heads of homes should have professional qualifications within three years, that a third of all staff should also have such qualifications within five years, and that remaining staff should be registered for National Vocational Qualifications (NVQs), ultimately leading to full professional qualification. Utting also emphasised that post-qualifying training needed to be developed. The Warner report was largely in agreement with Utting. A major difference, however, was that it advocated a new form of professional qualification for residential workers that was more specialised and more flexibly administered than the Diploma in Social Work, which was (and remains) a more generalist form of training and qualification.

Residential Child Care Initiative

In September 1992, following Utting's (1991) recommendations, the Residential Childcare Initiative was established enabling 500 heads of homes and deputies to qualify for the Diploma in Social Work at nine universities across the UK. Crimmens (2000), however, quotes from a study by Karban and Frost (1998) which suggests the possibility of 50 per cent of staff qualified by this means being lost to residential care within two years of qualification. Crimmens (2000) also notes that in 1996, there was little evidence of improvement in the overall ratio of qualified staff in statutory residential childcare establishments, a fact confirmed by the *Messages from Research* review of residential childcare studies (DoH 1998a). If one considers these developments in a context of a shrinking statutory residential childcare sector (9000 children in homes in England in 1991 compared with 6500 in 1998) and a growing number of children placed in private and voluntary homes and boarding schools where progress is likely to be even slower, then it is clear that the rate of change has been woefully inadequate.

Disputes over the best form of training

The seepage of qualified staff from the residential sector is only one reason for the slow rate of progress. More could be done to stem the flow by tackling issues such as pay, conditions of service, the difficulties of the task and the overall low status of residential work. Another barrier seems to be the lack of agreement over the appropriate form of training for residential childcare workers. General social work training is not seen as particularly relevant, and vocational qualifications are seen by some as too narrow and task-focused. If anything, the pendulum has swung more in favour of vocational qualifications for residential childcare staff below the level of deputy heads of homes. Research (Whitaker, Archer and Hicks 1998) has come down in favour of more work-based, group-focused training. Under its recently initiated *Quality Protects Programme* (DoH 1998a), central government has set a target of all residential childcare workers being qualified at Level 3 of the NVQ Caring for Children and Young People by March 2002, and is encouraging local authorities to send heads of homes and deputies to newly established post-qualification childcare courses (DoH 1998b). These targets and goals are being supported by central government incentive funding.

We are still waiting, therefore, to reap the benefits of more childcare residential workers receiving training and education for the task they undertake. The low level of qualification and training before the 1990s was clearly unacceptable even then. The delay and confusion in responding to it in the 1990s in the light of the revelations made by the various inquiries are even less acceptable. There seems to have been too much argument about what sort of training is required, whether it is likely to be effective and how it can best be delivered. No doubt costs and the low status of residential care, which (as we saw in Chapter 1) have been key factors throughout its history, have contributed to the delay. Also (as we noted above) perhaps the persistence of abuse scandals has played a part in slowing down the response, as perhaps have the present government's plans under *Quality Protects* to review the full range of children's services, rather than giving urgent priority to residential care (DoH 1998a). What is clearly important, however, is that training needs to keep up with the times and equip practitioners for the job in hand. That job has increasingly developed into looking after and meeting the needs of small groups of often very deprived, disadvantaged and abused young people. To achieve this, it is clear that we need to move beyond the target of having everyone trained at a minimum level to having workers trained to tackle these demands in a positive, professional way – no mean task.

Management of children's homes

The Warner (1992) report was full of sensible advice about the management of children's homes. It pointed to the need for homes to have clearly articulated aims and objectives and to be adequately resourced to achieve these goals. Management's task is to clarify and make explicit these objectives, and to enable staff and residents to own and achieve them. For instance, more and more homes might focus on working with adolescents who have been traumatised or abused in some way before (or while) being in care (Warner's survey estimated that a third of all children in care had been sexually abused). Such children might need specialist psychiatric services, and they might have particular educational needs. Staff working with such children may need specialist psychological support. They may need particular training in issues of control and restraint. Warner's view was that issues like this should be central to the running of a home and resources should be organised in advance. Too often, the expectation is that children will 'behave' normally and when, understandably, problems linked to prior depriving or traumatising experiences arise, staff in residential homes are frequently ill equipped and insufficiently supported to deal with them. Another recommendation from Warner was the need for out-of-home line managers, preferably with residential care experience themselves, to work closely with heads of homes, providing regular supervision and periodic appraisal.

This formula for managing residential care establishments is a far cry from the situation found in homes which have been the subject of public inquiries. In many of these establishments, it was found that staff had little or no idea of the aims of the establishments in which they were working, little awareness of rules and regulations, and minimal guidance as to the limits of intervention. Heads of homes tended to receive little guidance and to manage largely by personal influence rather than by more structured management techniques. While the establishments inquired into were probably at the worst end of the spectrum, it is clear from the broader surveys carried out by Warner, and later by the Department of Health research teams who contributed to *Messages from Research* (DoH 1998a), that poorly structured homes in terms of goals and management are still fairly common. The DoH research found that approximately half of the homes involved in their projects were poorly managed in the ways outlined above. It also confirmed Warner's views about good management, finding that homes with clear goals and objectives where heads had good links with management in the wider social services departments were those most likely to provide the most successful in-care services for children.

These issues have not been directly tackled by central government. They are dealt with indirectly within the *Quality Protects* programme by a series of out-come-focused objectives in relation to children being looked after – namely to reduce the number of placements that children experience in any one year, to achieve minimum educational targets in terms of qualifications and attendance, and to achieve health targets such as having regular medical and dental assessments (DoH 1998b). In addition, there is the expectation (referred to in the previous section) of residential staff attending post-qualifying courses. Apart from this, however, there have been no specific requirements placed on managers despite the fact that in inquiries such as Pindown (Staffordshire 1991), Leicestershire (1993) and North Wales (Waterhouse 2000), poor management of the homes in question was seen as the key factor in preventing and discovering abusive practices.

Responding to allegations and complaints

Most of the inquiries into the abuse of children in residential settings have pointed to the great difficulties that children have experienced in making complaints about their treatment. In some cases they simply endured abuse without complaint because their abusers were the powerful figures in the establishment to whom one would normally complain. For some, particularly in relation to sexual abuse, fear, stigma and the likelihood of not being believed were key reasons for not taking matters further. It was notable in the North Wales Tribunal how few young people complained at the time they were being abused to other residential staff, their field social workers, their parents or the police.

Before the Children Act 1989

Nevertheless, there are also accounts of children making complaints, but not being listened to. In North Wales, for instance, it is fairly clear that incidents involving physical assaults by staff were frequently swept under the carpet with the young person involved being discouraged from taking matters further (Waterhouse 2000). Allegations of sexual abuse raised in Castle Hill (Shropshire 1992), Leicestershire (1993) and Edinburgh (1999) fell largely on deaf ears. Some explanation for this may lie in the facts, first, that the earlier allegations were made at a time when there was a lack of awareness of sexual abuse of children, and second, that there was not a strong culture of complaint and no requirement for local authorities to have formal complaints procedures prior to the implementation of the Children Act 1989.

After the Children Act 1989

By the beginning of the 1990s there were two mechanisms established for dealing with complaints by children. The first was under Section 26 of the Children Act 1989. In order to comply with this section, social services departments were required to establish a procedure for generating and responding to complaints via a panel with independent representation. The second means of responding to complaints was under the child protection procedures set out in the 1991 *Working Together* guidelines (DoH 1991a) which, as has been noted before, were revised in 2000 (DoH 2000a). These guidelines require allegations of abuse by children in care to be treated in the same way as other child protection concerns. They do, however, require the involvement of a person independent from the authority within which the allegation has arisen, and the NSPCC has been identified as a key agency in this respect. Most allegations of assault should be dealt with through this latter procedure, more general complaints about standards and care arrangements via the former.

Information about the way in which complaints have been handled in the 1990s is limited. Warner's 1991 survey found that in over 80 per cent of local authorities, there were arrangements for children to make complaints outside the line management structure. Half (50 per cent) of the homes had produced written guidelines about procedures; progress was being made to ensure that, in accordance with Community Homes Regulations 1991, children in care had access to pay telephones from which calls could be made in confidence (Warner 1992). How effective the procedures have been is open to question. Lyon (1997) found that there was very little use being made of procedures. Frost and Wallis (2000) found greater use being made of the system, but a lot of uncertainty on the part of children and young people as to what was considered serious enough to constitute a complaint, and dissatisfaction particularly with the feedback part of the process. There seems to be general agreement that children could benefit from more independent help with the complaints procedure, possibly via a children's rights officer. As we have seen, there has been some development in this respect in England and the North Wales Tribunal has gone further to recommend the appointment of a Children's Commissioner for Wales to oversee the system of complaints and to take an active role in pursuing complaints where deemed necessary.

As regards allegations dealt with through the child protection system, again there is little information about current developments. Barter (1999) reported on 36 investigations involving 76 children making allegations against 40 members of staff and 10 other residents. Just over half the allegations were upheld. This study raised several important issues, the most significant being the restrictive remit given to investigators, i.e. usually to investigate a specific incident in situations where a broad-based assessment of the quality of care might have been more beneficial. Criticisms were also raised about the lack of support given to those alleging abuse and to those complained against, and the lack of response to more general recommendations aimed at lessening the likelihood of further abuse taking place in future in the setting in question.

Whistleblowing

Another key issue raised by public inquiries relates to allegations of abuse made by members of staff against their colleagues, i.e. that of so-called whistleblowing. The North Wales Tribunal of Inquiry, as we have seen, was particularly concerned over this matter because of the treatment of Alison Taylor, whose persistence was a key factor in bringing concerns there to light. In its recommendations (as we saw in Chapter 8), this inquiry made a strong plea for whistleblowing to be facilitated. Indeed it recommended that consideration be given to treating the failure to report suspected physical or sexual abuse by another member of staff as a disciplinary issue (Waterhouse 2000).

The current position with regard to whistleblowing in residential care homes, according to Lane (2000), is that many authorities have devised their own procedures to encourage referrals and protect referrers. In its response to the safeguards review (DoH 1998d) the government has undertaken to remind governing bodies of all organisations of the need for procedures to enable staff to make complaints outside their normal line management.

Disciplinary actions

The treatment of staff complained against is another issue raised by inquiry reports. Warner was sympathetic to the need to ensure fair treatment of such staff, suggesting that those against whom allegations of abuse have been made should not be automatically suspended, but that careful consideration should first be given to the seriousness of the allegation (Warner 1992, p.1). The North Wales Tribunal of Inquiry recommendations are somewhat more robust in this respect, stressing that suspension is a neutral act in relation to innocence or guilt. It argues for a clear distinction to be made between bringing disciplinary proceedings against staff and initiating criminal charges via the police, stressing that the former is not conditional on the latter and that the standards of evidence required to support disciplinary action are less rigorous than those required for a successful criminal prosecution (Waterhouse 2000).

There have, therefore, been several developments towards creating a better climate for making and responding to complaints as a result of the findings of inquiry reports. How effective the new mechanisms will prove to be remains to be seen. The awareness of the potential for abuse in children's homes established during the 1990s is a key factor. Unless there is a backlash of concerns about false allegations (see Webster 1998), this new awareness should lead to earlier referrals about abuse and more positive responses.

Monitoring and inspection processes

Many of the public inquiries have pointed to the fact that external monitoring of practices within residential homes where abuse has taken place has been deficient. It has not been suggested that improved registration or inspection practices would necessarily have prevented the abuse taking place or that deficiencies in this area were contributory causes to the abuse. Nevertheless, there have been two main causes for concern raised, first, that regulations have not been followed, and second, that there are loopholes in the regulations.

Statutory reviews

Deficiencies in relation to statutory reviews of children in care have been a constant concern raised in inquiry reports. Prior to the implementation of the Children Act 1989 when new regulations were brought in, such reviews were meant to be held every six months. The North Wales Tribunal in particular found that many statutory reviews were held late and amounted to little more than paper exercises (Waterhouse 2000). The Review of Children's Cases Regulations 1991 have laid down a more rigorous procedure for the timing and conduct of reviews which should remedy some of these shortcomings, but much still depends on adequate methods of monitoring and inspection to ensure that the new requirements are followed.

Inspecting local authority establishments

Prior to the implementation of the Children Act 1989, local authority children's homes were subject to internal monitoring which consisted largely of visiting by elected council members, an approach which was considered by inquiries such as North Wales to have become routinised and to be more concerned with bricks and mortar than with the welfare of children. Another means of internal monitoring was that carried out by residential management teams, who were frequently over-reliant on heads of homes and whose objectivity might be less than desired – this was certainly the case in Staffordshire (1991) and Leicestershire (1993). The Department of Health had (and still retains) the power to inspect homes by means of its Social Services Inspectorate, but, in most of the cases inquired into, such inspections took place infrequently and were of a kind unlikely to uncover abuse because of the giving of prior notice. The Children Act 1989 brought in inspection units which, though funded by local authorities, retain a degree of independence from other aspects of residential care management. Such units are required to inspect care establishments twice a year and to report to directors of social services. Visits by elected council members are retained under the current system.

The present government has proposed in *Modernising Social Services* to make inspection of homes independent of local authorities altogether and to organise them on a regional basis (DoH 1998c). This move has clearly been a direct result of the impact of inquiry reports and is, therefore, aimed to some degree at reassuring the outside world that regulation and inspection have a much stronger element of independence. In fact, as much of the abuse inquired into has predated the implementation of the Children Act 1989, it could be argued that local authority inspection units have not had much chance to prove themselves. However, there are likely to be some benefits of the new system over and above the issue of objectivity. First, a regional approach is likely to provide more general consistency in applying standards than a more localised one. Second, the new system will operate a specialist approach to inspection (by service user type) which is preferential to the more generalist approach.

Inspecting other residential homes and schools

Another key area highlighted by inquiries – particularly North Wales (Waterhouse 2000) and the children's safeguards review (Utting 1997) – is the inconsistency of monitoring and inspection practices across the broad range of residential services for children over and above those administered by the local authorities (i.e. private homes, voluntary homes, independent and boarding schools). Legislation in respect of this wide range of establishments is very varied and reflects an *ad hoc* response to the development of different types of residential provision over time. The need for more consistent regulations for registration and inspection across the board is indisputable, and is now a stated aim of the present government. Currently, for instance, profit-making private children's homes for fewer than four children are subject to no registration or inspection requirements. Voluntary children's homes are not inspected by local authority inspection units, but directly by the Department of Health – such inspections are not as frequent as for private and local authority homes. Non-maintained special boarding schools are remarkably 'free' from external scrutiny; local authorities are merely required to satisfy themselves from time to time about the children's welfare. These are just a few of the many anomalies – for a very useful detailed account see Morgan (2000). Most of these loopholes are, according to the government's White Paper *Modernising Social Services*, being addressed (DoH 1998c). However, it should be noted that in some instances, the degree of delay is of great concern. The lack of external oversight of independent special boarding schools, for instance, was very clearly exposed in the Castle Hill inquiry as early as 1992 (Shropshire 1992).

The promotion of children's rights

The last area of practice and policy change resulting from the findings of public inquiries is that in relation to children's rights. Nearly all the inquiries have demonstrated that listening to children is of key importance if we are to discover and tackle child abuse. Most of the inquiries, however, have gone beyond seeing a child-sensitive approach simply as an instrument for uncovering abuse. They have clearly shown that failure to respect children as individuals and to underpin this respect with certain rights can contribute to the development of abusive environments, i.e. it can be the cause of abuse and not simply a factor hindering complaints. Children in residential care are particularly vulnerable to being harshly treated and abused because they frequently come into residential settings with deep-seated emotional and behavioural problems and difficulties which are very challenging to those who are required to care for them. Resolving these problems and seeing the child within are key issues for residential workers, and the assertion of children's rights can have a major contribution to achieving this.

It should be noted that recognition of the importance of children's rights in residential care preceded most of the inquiries and, therefore, is not directly attributable to them. For example, the Children Act 1989 promoted such rights by means of its representation and complaints clause and in its regulations for the review of cases. The Community Homes Regulations 1991 are also considerably influenced by children's rights thinking.

Nevertheless, there can be little doubt that the abuse uncovered by inquiries in the 1990s has greatly accelerated thinking and practice in this area. There have been considerable developments in the provision of children's rights and advocacy services. Willow (2000) reports that a quarter of all local authorities had established such services in their areas by 1999. The government in the same year established a national organisation to represent the voice of children in care, and has drafted legislation to ensure the rights of care leavers to continuing services after leaving care. As has been seen, the North Wales Tribunal of Inquiry has recommended the establishment of a Children's Commissioner in Wales with specific duties in terms of ensuring children's rights be asserted (Waterhouse 2000).

There are continuing debates about whether we have gone far enough in establishing children's rights. For some, the assertion of rights is the key issue in ensuring that children in care live an abuse-free existence and develop their full potential (see Stanley 1999; Willow 2000). Others are more cautious about over-reliance on individual rights as a means of developing policy (see Smith 1997). From this perspective, the establishment and pursuit of rights is one of the means of achieving social policy goals (in this case, the safety and protection of children in care), not the sole one.

Summary

This review of the impact of public inquiries on the details of residential childcare policy and practice shows that they do have influence even though it seems to take considerable time for this to become evident. This time-gap may to some extent be explained by the fact that there is a tension between change resulting from inquiries which, because of their rightful focus on negative and abusive practice, tends to be reactive, and change resulting from more studied long-term planning. In the particular case of residential care for children, most of the abuse inquiries postdated the Children Act 1989, but dealt with the situation that existed before it. This created tension between those who felt that the new regulations and laws were sufficient to tackle the problems identified by inquiries and those who felt that the discoveries of past abuse merited new legislation because the Children Act 1989 was passed in ignorance of the material that they had uncovered.

Nevertheless, despite the slow rate of progress, there is evidence of a considerable shift in policy (some of it still to be implemented) particularly in terms of staff selection and recruitment processes, responding to allegations of abuse, whistleblowing, monitoring and inspection and the promotion of children's rights. With regard to making residential care a more attractive option by raising its status, pay and training and with regard to the improvement of residential management, although there have been developments, there still seems to be much that remains to be decided and acted upon.

Possible dysfunctional consequences of inquiries

So far in the chapter, the focus has been on some of the more constructive impacts of inquiries. Would it were that this was the sum of the comment that could be made. However, that would not do justice to the complexity of the situation for there is a downside to the impact of inquiries, and for the remainder of this chapter, attention will be switched to some of these more negative effects.

A BLOW TO MORALE

There is clearly a concern (expressed in Chapter 5) that the overall impact of child abuse inquiries on residential care for children could be cripplingly negative. As we noted there, it is in the nature and remit of inquiries to focus on issues of poor practice. Therefore, inquiries are bound to cast a dark shadow over the services that they inquire into; this is true of inquiries into train crashes and the probity of Members of Parliament as it is of residential care for children. The unremitting nature of the focus on institutional abuse during the 1990s, however, has made it hard at times to see any positive aspects of residential care. This negative perception has been exacerbated by accounts of the poor outcomes of residential care experiences, such as the low educational achievement of children in care, the relatively high imprisonment rate of former care residents and, perhaps, most tellingly, the relatively high rates of former looked-after children who go missing, as highlighted by the West case in Gloucestershire (Gloucestershire ACPC 1995).

DECLINE IN QUANTITY AND RANGE

The major concern about the negative impact of inquiries is that it could have seriously dysfunctional effects. One key problem is that residential care will in all likelihood continue to be seen as a last resort option rather than as a positive placement. This could result in children, particularly older children, being less likely to be offered residential care services in the first instance, and being accommodated only in emergencies, after further damage may have been done to their own development and their relationships with their parents. A second problem is that local authorities may be loath to maintain, let alone expand, their childcare residential services, which in turn could lead to a further reduction in the range of residential care made available to children and young people. As we have seen, such provision has shrunk considerably since the mid-1980s. Many authorities already have very few residential childcare places, a trend made worse by the creation of smaller unitary authorities in the late 1990s. Some authorities such as Warwickshire and, until recently, Lewisham have operated without any residential facilities for children at all.

SHIFTING THE PROBLEM ELSEWHERE?

The net outcome of these developments may be greater reliance on foster care or other children's homes usually within the private or voluntary sector and often outside the geographical area of the authority in question.

The danger in these developments is that what may happen is that the problem of abuse may simply be transferred elsewhere. Private and voluntary childcare establishments have in the past had fewer trained staff and been less well regulated and inspected than local authority establishments, and, although these matters are currently being remedied, there is no reason to think that they will provide any better services than those that local authorities could themselves muster. Similarly, there are growing concerns that the potential for abuse in foster care is higher than previously thought (see Utting 1997). These concerns are based on the knowledge that more challenging children are being placed in foster care than before because of the decline in the use of residential care, and that foster carers are generally not as well equipped and supported as residential care workers to deal with such challenges. Foster care presents similar issues to residential care in relation to selection, inspection and dealing with complaints. Abuse of children by their foster carers formed part of the concerns of the North Wales Tribunal of Inquiry and was the subject of an inquiry in Derbyshire and Nottinghamshire (1990). There have also been concerns raised about abuse of foster children by other foster children (see Corby 1998). Hobbs, Hobbs and Wynne (1999) in a study of child protection assessments in Leeds found higher rates of referral involving abuse in foster care than in residential care.

IN DANGER OF BECOMING TOO DEFENSIVE?

A third potential dysfunction of inquiries is that residential social work may become over-bureaucratised and proceduralised and that residential social workers may become over-defensive to the detriment of the care and development of children living in their establishments. The experience of field social work in response to public inquiries is instructive in this respect (see Chapter 4). Faced with mounting criticism throughout the 1970s and 1980s of poorly coordinated inter-agency practice and of insufficient emphasis on the safety of the child within the family, child protection work became more and more tightly managed and bureaucratised (D. Howe 1992). However, by the mid-1990s government-sponsored research was highly critical of child protection interventions for being so focused on abuse prevention that the wider support needs of families with children in need were going unnoticed. Furthermore, the process of intervention was being experienced by parents as intrusive and insensitive (DoH 1995). Those responsible for overseeing and implementing residential work practice should learn from the lesson of field social work and avoid an overreaction towards safe practice where prevention and detection of abuse comes to dominate.

Concluding comments

It is worth noting that it could be argued that the negative consequences of inquiries are not their responsibility. Indeed if one examines inquiries in detail, one often finds that they are not as totally critical of the practices and policies that they are examining as reported by the media. The following quotation from the North Wales Tribunal of Inquiry, for instance, is not likely to be widely reported:

> Despite what we have said, however, a significant number of children regarded life in care, even at Bryn Estyn, as distinctly better than life at home and did not want to return to their family of origin. They were fed and clothed regularly

and preferred a more predictable life to the unstable and sometimes dangerous one that they had known. We do not subscribe to the view that children should be kept out of care at all costs, even though radical improvements in children's services may take some years to achieve. (Waterhouse, p.841)

The issue for residential workers and their managers, therefore, is to achieve a positively safe environment whereby abuse does not become a preoccupation, but where, if it should happen, both children and staff should feel safe to report it and assured in the knowledge that a protective response will follow immediately.

CHAPTER 10

Future of Inquiries into Residential Abuse

Introduction

In this final chapter we consider the future of residential child abuse inquiries in the light of the current concerns about such abuse. We review and expand on some of the key considerations looked at earlier, i.e. that of publicness versus privacy, the impact of the process of inquiries particularly on the participants, and the impact of inquiries on public policy. We also draw on parallels with the development of inquiries into child abuse in the community to see if there are any lessons to be learned from that experience. Finally, we consider some different approaches to inquiring into problems of key public concern drawing on material from Canada and South Africa.

The key question to be answered in this chapter is what type and form of inquiry is best suited to meet the concerns raised about abuse of children in residential care. There are usually such a wide variety of needs to be met by inquiries that it is unlikely that there is any perfect answer. Indeed, even though we would like to, we offer no single blueprint for the future. Rather, our aim is to highlight the ways in which different approaches to inquiries meet different needs.

Publicness versus privacy

Meeting public concerns

The first and foremost purpose of inquiries is to satisfy public concern about a particularly pressing issue. As we have seen, there are no hard and fast rules about this. Usually inquiries are held into the actions of public officials who are, unless they have committed criminal acts, to a large extent protected from outside criticism and interference. Inquiries are, therefore, a means whereby the actions of public officials can be challenged from outside. However (as we have also seen) inquiries are not readily conceded by those in authority and are usually a response to particularly serious issues, often following considerable public pressure. On some occasions, inquiries can be used by central or local government to settle a particularly tricky issue, or even to achieve certain political goals.

Protecting privacy

While the basic function of inquiries is of this public nature, there are competing concerns, the main one being in regard to the protection of the identity of officials during the process of an inquiry. The need to do this may be an issue both of fairness (i.e. to ensure that individuals are not adversely subjected to the full glare of media publicity before the inquiry has reached its conclusions) and of pragmatism (i.e. to ensure that individuals fully cooperate with the requirements of the inquiry). These factors have to be balanced against the demands of the public, which are usually for complete openness. As we saw in Chapter 7, these issues were hotly contested in the North Wales Tribunal of Inquiry which, despite representation by the press and broadcast media, resolved to place a ban on the reporting of names during the inquiry's hearings, except in the case of already convicted abusers.

Concerns about the publicity attached to inquiries have been a major factor for professionals (particularly social workers) in relation to cases of child abuse in the community. They have felt particularly exposed to unfair public criticism, because in many cases they have considered themselves to be going about their jobs in the required way. This was a particular concern in the 1970s and up to the late 1980s. However (as we have seen) only a relatively small number of such inquiries have been held in public. Also, since the late 1980s, except in the case of the Cleveland inquiry (Butler-Sloss 1988), public officials have not been named in reports. Thus, some protection has been afforded to professionals in these situations, and in many ways, this seems to be a reasonable compromise. In contrast, in varying degrees, public officials have been named in most of the inquiry reports into residential abuse.

Part 8 Reviews

Since 1988 there has been a considerable shift away from holding child abuse in the community inquiries that report to the public in favour of Part 8 Reviews (DoH 1991a).[1] The key official reason emphasised for this shift was the need to ensure that lessons from inquiries were more speedily incorporated into practice than under the then rather prolonged process characteristic of independent or statutory inquiries. A less clearly stated factor was that the number of cases of child deaths and serious injuries through abuse was persisting despite the best efforts of systems to prevent this, and that the publicity and bad press associated with larger scale inquiries had had negative effects on the morale and practices of child protection professionals.

The Part 8 Review system is (as we have seen) a more private approach. Area Child Protection Committees may, in consultation with the Department of Health, make their reports, or revised versions of their reports, available to the public if they consider there is sufficient public concern about the cases in question. While these arrangements may to some degree satisfy the needs of professionals to be protected from unfair public scrutiny, reduced publicity and the fact that reviews are carried out by the professionals themselves mean that these mechanisms may have become too private.

In theory, the Part 8 Review process is available for cases of residential abuse, but to date has not been widely used for this purpose. As we have seen, independent inquiries, and in the case of the North Wales Tribunal of Inquiry, those ordered by central government, have been more to the forefront. This is probably for the following reasons. First, abuse of children in residential care is still a relatively new issue. Second, such abuse raises more public concern because it deals mainly with state-employed officials who have themselves abused children rather than those who have failed to protect them. Third, and linked to this, residential abuse raises the concern that those managing abusing staff may have either played down concerns or actively covered them up. Such concerns do not lend themselves easily to self-administered reviews conducted largely in private without necessarily leading to a publicly available report. A fourth reason for residential abuse cases rarely being dealt with through the Part 8 Review system is that much of the abuse is not a single incident, nor is it usually confined to a single establishment or to a single abuser, and it often extends back over several years. Such situations do not lend themselves easily to the Part 8 Review format.

Summary

Judging from this overview of the issue of the publicness of inquiries, it is clear that their *raison d'être* is the extent of public concern – hence the importance of their being open to public scrutiny. In the case of abuse of children in the community, a more private system has been adopted for a variety of reasons. It may be that this is due to a degree of saturation resulting in a diminution of public concern, but other factors such as the adverse impact on professionals and public officials have no doubt played a large part in this. In our view, the public need to know about such cases should be better addressed, both on grounds of support for open government and, pragmatically, because individual child abuse cases are inevitably going to arouse public concern from time to time, and the issue of how reviews are conducted is likely to resurface.

In the case of residential abuse, the case for openness is more pressing in the current climate. Part 8 Reviews as they are currently arranged do not, and will not in our view, satisfy public concerns about this type of abuse.

Process of inquiry

The way in which inquiries are conducted is another key issue to be considered for the future development of inquiry processes. Public inquiries into abuse of children in the community were more frequently conducted on a quasi-judicial basis until the middle of the 1980s than afterwards.

Different forms of inquiry

Inquiries ordered by the Secretary of State under Section 98(2) of the Children Act 1975 (now replaced by Section 81 of the Children Act 1989) have all been chaired by lawyers, had powers of witness compellability, of enforcing the production of documents, and of requiring evidence to be taken on oath. Their style has been largely similar to that adopted by the North Wales Tribunal of Inquiry, whereby participants have been cross-examined by counsel for the Tribunal and by counsel acting on their behalf, the evidence being weighed up on the balance of probabilities by the inquiry chairperson and panel.

Many of the independently chaired inquiries sponsored by local authorities (usually in consultation with the Department of Health) have tended to follow the same type of format while lacking the full range of powers afforded by statutory inquiries. Some of the inquiries in this category, especially those led by non-lawyers, have opted for styles more similar to a third type of inquiry which has been increasingly used since the mid-1980, that conducted internally by local authorities, and since 1988 coming under Part 8 and Part 8 of the Department of Health *Working Together* guidelines (see note 1).

There has, therefore, been a wide range of styles employed starting with those that most equate with court proceedings, through those based largely on investigative interviews, to those largely carried out by review of documentation.

The pains of being a witness

The conduct of more formal inquiries is largely experienced as threatening by witnesses who feel on trial. To some degree this effect has been tackled by the use of Salmon Letters since 1966 (see Chapter 7) to inform witnesses beforehand of the complaints made against them and of the evidence supporting these complaints so that they can make preparations for their appearance.

However, as was clear in the North Wales Tribunal of Inquiry, there are major problems associated with the more formal quasi-judicial processes, in that, faced with cross-examination by two or more sets of barristers, those testifying feel themselves on trial and may as a result become defensive and less helpful to the Tribunal in its quest to establish the facts. This is particularly exacerbated in the case of residential abuse where the witnesses themselves or their colleagues are the alleged abusers. There are other factors which also contribute to defensive responses to this type of inquiry – the findings can be damaging to reputations and can lead to disciplinary hearings and dismissals. In the case of residential abuse, they can also lead to the commencement of police inquiries, claims for damages and compensation.

These factors apply to the more informal types of inquiry to a lesser extent, in that less weight is attached to their findings by the legal system, because of their more limited powers and greater reliance on the voluntary involvement of witnesses in their proceedings.

Clearly there are some important process lessons we can learn from the various inquiries, though it has to be said that many reports do not spend much time on issues of methodology.

Edinburgh inquiry 1999

The Edinburgh inquiry into the sexual abuse of children in residential care by two main abusers, which was a statutory inquiry under the Children (Scotland) Act 1995, raised some useful points about process. Despite having the range of powers referred to above, it took a less adversarial line than it might have (Edinburgh 1999). First, the panel decided to take evidence mainly in private and not to reveal names in the inquiry report, except in the case of those who had already been convicted. The panel members based this decision on the view that 'the failures of the past lay more with the system than with individuals' (p.11) and also on the view that this would encourage more openness. The panel placed its focus on the welfare of children rather than on the determination of guilt. They argued that

> for these reasons, we decided that it would be more appropriate for us to model our procedure broadly on a children's hearing as opposed to a judicial model. That is to say, we should try to engage the relevant parties in frank and full dis-

cussions in a relatively informal manner rather than mimic the formal procedures of a court. (Edinburgh 1999, p.12)

The general tenor of the Edinburgh inquiry was one of considerable empathy with the alleged victims of abuse, and the inquiry panel emphasised that it was concerned with past events primarily with a view to making improvements for the future. It is clear that an informal approach was chosen in order to maximise the chances of gaining information and in order to minimise the pain of the victims. The inquiry's concerns centred less on the abuse itself and more on the agencies' response to the abuse allegations. Its content and tone are quite different from that of the North Wales Tribunal of Inquiry, which focused much more on whether abuse had taken place, on whom and by whom.

Several factors may account for this difference. The abuse inquired into by the Edinburgh inquiry was not as widespread or as apparently complex as that dealt with by the North Wales Tribunal, which made its task somewhat easier. Arguably, the degree of public concern was lower as well. Certainly, there was an urgent political imperative placed on the North Wales Tribunal to get to the bottom of issues that had rumbled on for ten years. Also, there was a sense that the North Wales Tribunal would demonstrate central government's concern about residential abuse in general. Nevertheless, the sharp contrast between approaches is indicative of different emphases, with the North Wales Tribunal focusing more on guilt and culpability, and the Edinburgh inquiry more on the victims and their needs.

In thinking about the process of inquiring into residential abuse cases in the future, the model and style of the Edinburgh inquiry seem to have more to offer in terms of its treatment of victims and the more conciliatory attitude to residential work in general.

Impact on policy

As we made clear in Chapter 4, public inquiries have had a range of impacts on policy and practice in relation to the protection of children at risk in their own homes. The positives have been the raising of concern and awareness of child abuse, the development of better interprofessional systems of cooperation and, arguably, better protection of children. *Messages from Research* (DoH 1995) points to findings of a 70 per cent prevention of reabuse rate over two years among children identified as being at risk and worked with by child protection professionals. On the debit side has been the emergence of defensive practice, and the failure to support the broader needs of families because of professionals' preoccupation with abuse.

Critics of these inquiries have felt that they focus too much on what goes wrong at the individual level with too little consideration being given to wider issues such as social exclusion, poorly resourced authorities and lack of proper training of staff (see Hallett 1989). Thus the tendency is often to blame frontline workers and their supervisors for individual mistakes rather than the wider system. However, such criticism is not truly justified by a close reading of many inquiry reports. It is clear that both systems and individuals are seen to contribute to problems (see DoH 1991b).

When we turn to residential abuse of children, there is a different set of dynamics in operation because the abusers are social workers. In these circumstances, it is clear that individuals cannot escape blame and responsibility for child abuse. Nevertheless, there is much concern among some critics that all the attention should not be placed on pathological individuals, but that the system which allows abusers to be active should be carefully scrutinised (see Thomas 1990). Indeed, several of the inquiry reports into residential care have been particularly instructive in this respect making careful linkages between unsafe institutions and a context of shrinking resources and poor management; Staffordshire (1991), Leicestershire (1993) and the North Wales Tribunal of Inquiry (Waterhouse 2000) are very good examples of this.

As we made clear in Chapter 9, we do not yet know what the full impact of inquiries will be on residential care for children. The main policy thrusts will be diversion of children away from residential settings as far as possible, improvements in recruitment, training and management of staff, and the development of externally run mechanisms of inspection and dealing with complaints. There are some dangers that, as with abuse of children in the community, the outcome could be a more defensive form of practice which makes it difficult to meet children's broader needs.

What to do after North Wales?

A key issue for public inquiries into residential care is whether, as in the case of abuse in the community, they have in their present form now served their usefulness.

There does seem to be a case for rethinking what to do about further allegations of residential abuse in the past now that the North Wales Tribunal of Inquiry has reached its findings. As we have seen in the chapters which focus on this inquiry, it has performed a thorough task in establishing the truth of events in that part of the UK over a 20-year period. No doubt, there will be some who remain unsatisfied with its conclusions, but in some ways, in terms of fact finding, this is probably as good it gets.

It paints a picture which is likely to have been replicated in many other parts of the UK over this period, that of a shrinking and changing childcare residential sector between 1974 and 1996, largely staffed by unqualified care workers with low status within the social services department as a whole. It shows how in the late 1970s and early 1980s, there was a mix of community homes for deprived and delinquent children, and that, particularly in the homes looking after those coming into care for offending, standards were rough and ready, with a mixed philosophy of care and control. These homes were of medium to large size and had schooling on the premises. They were more institutionalised settings than the smaller children's homes, which tended to cater for deprived children in more family-type atmospheres.

The 1980s saw the closure of many of these larger homes, and the shift of many children from smaller homes into foster care. By the end of the 1980s, this fast shrinking residential sector consisted mainly of a relatively small number of children's homes, largely populated by older, often challenging, children from deprived, neglectful and abusive home backgrounds. The quality of care was variable, with some homes well run by resourceful individuals, but many characterised by lack of clear goals, and a pragmatic philosophy of managing on a day-to-day basis children who were perceived to be difficult, with frequent conflicts occasionally spilling over to violence. Levels of qualification and training had not improved much over the whole decade.

Within this turbulent climate, there were (as far as we know) a small number of individuals sexually abusing children, some abusing large numbers of children quite systematically. Lack of watchful external management, poor complaints procedures, lack of knowledge and awareness about sexual abuse generally, and the low status of the few children who did complain meant that these abusers could escape detection over long periods of time.

This sort of situation has begun to emerge in many parts of the UK. Many allegations of physical and sexual abuse are being made, mostly by adults after leaving care and often after many years of silence.

A key issue is how to respond to these revelations. Police investigations are still being actively pursued. There is a strong move to prosecute offenders wherever possible, though securing convictions is not easy given the time-gaps between some of the incidents of alleged abuse and the making of the allegations. Should such investigations be followed by more inquiries to find out in each area the reasons why children were abused and why the abuse remained undiscovered for so long?

In our view, this would not prove to be a useful exercise in that the findings of each inquiry would probably reach similar conclusions and make similar recommendations to those made by the North Wales Tribunal of Inquiry. However, it is also clear that the matter cannot just be dropped. This would do justice neither to the need of victims of abuse to have their pain recognised and compensated nor to the need of the public to be satisfied that the issue was being properly dealt with and not covered up. There is also a need for the residential care sector for children to be able to move forward, however, and not be held back by the failures of the past. Current research into residential childcare homes (see Sinclair and Gibbs 1998; Whitaker *et al.* 1998) points to much good work being done in difficult circumstances by dedicated staff. While the task of residential workers seems to be a daunting one, two-thirds of the residents think that staff are doing a good job (DoH 1998a).

Drawing a line under the past

It is crucially important, therefore, for the future positive development of residential care for children that some sort of line be drawn under the abuses of the past. A key question, however, is how can this be done in a way that does justice to the needs of those who have been abused.

It may well be that the answer is to take a more general and comprehensive stance than that provided by individual inquiries. So far, the pattern has been to respond to allegations of abuse which have aroused public indignation by setting up inquiries to get at the truth so that perpetrators can be disciplined and prosecuted, agencies be publicly called to account, victims have their say and be compensated and lessons be learned for future policy and practice.

In the case of allegations of abuse dating back more than ten years, most of these goals can be achieved without holding public inquiries. First, there is no indication that inquiries are needed to increase the likelihood of prosecutions of perpetrators. Most inquiries to date have followed police investigations which have become increasingly thorough and sophisticated during the 1990s. Second, many agencies have moved on from the times when much of the abuse was actually perpetrated and, therefore, focusing on their past practices and policies is probably not helpful. As for learning lessons, there are enough inquiries to be going on with at present, and it is unlikely that new lessons are likely to emerge. However, it should be stressed that these arguments are not being applied to situations where allegations of abuse are currently being made. Ways of carrying out 'new' inquiries will be considered below.

Compensating victims

One issue where inquiries into past abuse do seem to have a clear function is in relation to victims. While, as we have seen from the North Wales Tribunal of Inquiry, inquiries can be particularly stressful and challenging experiences for victims of abuse, there is also reason to believe that having the opportunity to give their evidence may have cathartic effects for some. Perhaps more significantly the findings of inquiries are often key factors in ensuring that victims receive financial compensation for the impact of abuse on them. Many victims of abuse are ineligible for Criminal Injuries Compensation because they themselves have criminal records or because of the time-gaps between the abuse taking place and the claim being made. Pursuing compensation from individuals through civil proceedings is also fraught with difficulty, as first, the proceedings tend to be protracted, and second, plaintiffs often have no money. An alternative is to sue the alleged abuser's employer (in many cases, the local authority) on the grounds of vicarious liability, but by and large suits of this kind have not been very successful (see Cobley 1998). Public inquiries, though themselves fairly protracted exercises, do seem ultimately to hasten the process of out-of-court compensation settlements on the part of local authorities. However, there can be little doubt that this is a messy, cumbersome and highly unsatisfactory way of tackling issues of compensation and one which can lead to all sorts of dysfunctional practices. As we saw in the North Wales case, the local authorities' insurers played a major part in encouraging the suppression of information because of their concerns about compensation claims.

South Africa and the Truth and Reconciliation Commission

In looking for a model for dealing more broadly with the past abuse of children in residential care in terms of moving forward, we were impressed by two approaches adopted in different countries. The first was that adopted in response to the gross violations of human rights that took place in South Africa during the apartheid regime, the National Truth and Reconciliation Commission. The second was the response of most of the states in Canada to widespread abuse of children in homes from as early as 1930.

We are mindful that, particularly in the South African case, we are dealing with a very different subject matter. Nevertheless, the purpose and philosophy of the Truth and Reconciliation Commission seemed to have relevance to the notion of drawing a line under the residential abuse of children revelations in that it too was trying to find a way forward without ignoring the past and it was concerned to compensate the victims both spiritually and financially. Archbishop Tutu summed up this philosophy as follows:

> having looked the beast of the past in the eye, having asked and received forgiveness and having made amends, let us shut the door on the past – not in order to forget it but in order not to allow it to imprison us. (South Africa 1999, vol. 1, para. 91)

Key emphasis was placed on publicly recognising the victims of crimes and their relatives and on providing reparation. The commission had more complex aims in relation to building a unified society in South Africa – particularly that of trying to achieve some form of reconciliation between perpetrators of violence and their victims and relatives. Clearly such aims are beyond our scope. However, the key message we wish to draw from the Truth and Reconciliation Commission's work is the notion of encouraging victims of abuse to come forward, to be heard, and to be compensated without experiencing all the pains of giving testimony at a public inquiry or in court. At the same time the notion of drawing a line under events would provide residential care with the opportunity to move forward.

The Canadian experience

In Canada, the abuse of children in residential care was revealed in nearly all states during the late 1980s and 1990s. Some of the allegations of abuse dated back as early as the 1930s. While most of the abuse in question was of a sexual and physical nature, concerns were also raised about the emotional and psychological pains of being reared in institutions and about the long-term effects ·of these experiences. The process of seeking prosecutions of alleged abusers in the criminal courts and making individual claims for compensation in civil courts proved unworkable. As a consequence, most of the states have decided ultimately to compensate all children making sustainable allegations of abuse while in residential care without processing claims through courts and without holding large-scale inquiries to confirm the allegations of abuse. In some states, compensation has also been made to those who can demonstrate that their in-care experiences alone (without direct abuse allegations) have resulted in their long-term harm.

The exception to this rule has been in Quebec, where the so-called Children of Duplessis have been denied the type of compensation settlements being made elsewhere. The system of caring for orphaned and deprived children in Quebec from the 1930s up to 1965 was of a very poor standard, particularly in the Depression years when poverty was widespread throughout Canada.

Concerns about the poor quality of care in these homes were raised in the late 1960s. A major issue was the high rate of transfer without diagnosis of children from care to psychiatric institutions, poor standards of education and a lack of rehabilitative programmes. Campaigners on behalf of the ex-residents of Quebec's residential care system made little headway until the 1990s, when allegations of sexual and physical abuse were added to the other concerns. In 1997 following a series of unsuccessful court cases, an Ombudsman's inquiry was held which recommended that no-fault compensation be awarded to those 'Duplessis orphans' who as children were improperly diagnosed as seriously retarded or mentally ill, those who experienced excessive physical abuse and those who were victims of sexual abuse (Quebec 1997). The government of Quebec has so far resisted taking this course of action, though it has set up a $3 million support fund to compensate the 'real prejudices' suffered by many of the 3000 orphans said to be surviving.

The Canadian experience is instructive in many ways, even though we are discussing a different culture and going further back in history than has so far been the case in relation to abuse in British residential establishments. The notion of dealing with claims for compensation out of court on a no-blame basis and drawing on state resources, offers food for thought. So too does the disputed issue of whether to compensate not only for serious abuses but also for the low quality of care and its impact on the long-term life chances of former residents of children's homes. For instance, many of the witnesses to the North Wales Tribunal had achieved poorly in terms of education, a relatively high proportion had served prison sentences and several argued that their ability to form close relationships had been severely impaired. It seems also that in most of the states in Canada, victims of abuse had been given apologies by the state, another concept that might be considered in Britain and one which has certainly not figured much in debates so far. We are not in a position here to make definite recommendations about matters such as these, but, given what has been happening during the 1990s in the UK, we are convinced, for the various reasons already stated, that a broader-based acknowledgement of victims' needs that is not reliant on the courts or a series of full-blown public inquiries should be considered in response to the large number of allegations of residential abuse that are still emerging.

Inquiring into contemporaneous residential abuse

Having argued the need to take steps to tackle past abuse in a positive way that serves the needs of abuse victims and allows residential childcare to move on and improve, there remains the issue of how to deal with new allegations of abuse that arise and the role and style of future inquiries in dealing with them. We hope that the need for inquiries into abuse cases will decrease. The developments that have taken place in residential childcare since the early 1990s (reviewed in Chapter 9) should reduce the likelihood of the sort of abuse which took place in the decades before that recurring, and they should enable swifter and more protective responses to follow where any abuse comes to light.

However, it is of considerable importance to ensure that where abuse occurs, there is a mechanism for investigating how it happened and how it was addressed by those with responsibility for dealing with it, particularly in cases where those alleging abuse feel that their concerns have not been adequately responded to. Currently there is provision for this under Part 8 of the *Working Together* guidelines (DoH 1991a). However, in several respects, these seem to fall short of some of the key requirements of an effective and trusted review or inquiry process, particularly in the case of residential abuse where professional workers are suspected abusers.

Some key principles

In our view, there are some key principles involved in achieving trust in an inquiry system. First, inquiries need to be carried out by an independent body so that it is clear that there is no issue of interest and, therefore, bias involved. Second, it is important that the findings of all inquiries are made open to the public, but with protection for the identity of individuals involved. Third, it is important that the findings of these inquiries are collated and made available both locally and nationally so that lessons can be learned from them. Fourth, it is important that such inquiries are held without delay. Fifth, inquiries should be empowered to recommend compensation for victims of such abuse. All but the last principle should in our view also apply to serious cases of abuse to children in the community.

We favour the notion of calling these processes 'inquiries' rather than 'reviews' because this term suggests a more comprehensive questioning process. The current system of Part 8 Reviews suffers in our view from not being a sufficiently public process, from not having in many cases a sufficiently independent element and from being over-concerned with procedure. In addition (as we saw in Chapter 8), little opportunity has so far been given for professionals to have access to the findings in order to learn from them. This latter concern has been particularly emphasised by Reder and Duncan (1999), who have made suggestions for remedying this by the setting up of regional child death review teams. While such teams would to some degree resolve this problem and at the same time incorporate into the process a more independent element, we consider Reder and Duncan's remedy to be over-dominated by professional concerns and lacking in regard to the public's need to know, which is especially, though not exclusively, important in relation to residential childcare abuse.

Towards a more effective system

Clearly, considerably more attention needs to be given to the processes, procedures and structures needed for an effective and trusted system of inquiry into child abuse than we have been able to devote to it. However, our concern has been to stimulate thinking about the complex issues that have been aroused by inquiring into residential child abuse during the 1990s culminating (as far as we know at this point in time) in the North Wales Tribunal of Inquiry. The experience has been an extremely painful one for all concerned, particularly for those who have been abused, but also for committed and hard-working residential care staff and their managers faced with the near-discrediting of their profession. There have, however, been some positive factors amid the pain, most obviously the opening up and tracking down of concerns about the abuse of children in care, particularly in relation to sexual abuse. Our main focus has been to examine in detail the process of inquiry into residential abuse, to consider the strengths and weaknesses of different approaches and to make recommendations for dealing with the remainder of current concerns and those that may arise in the future. The message that has most clearly come home to us is that there are no easy answers, and that inquiries are by and large fairly rough tools for dealing with the complicated issues raised by abuse of children in residential settings. We hope that to some degree by exploring the various avenues which we have in this book, we shall contribute at least marginally towards the development of a smoother and more effective process.

Notes

1   Although we refer to the review provision throughout this chapter as Part 8 Reviews, which were introduced in the 1991 *Working Together* guidelines (DoH 1991a), this form of review was first introduced as Part 9 of the 1988 guidelines (DHSS 1988).

APPENDIX 1

Public Inquiries into Child Abuse 1945–99

	Year	Name	Type of abuse*	Inquiry sponsor**	Area	Held in private/ public†	Inquiry type‡	Chair by profession	Recommendations/ findings
1	1945	O'Neill	P	Home Office	Shropshire	Pr	Stat	Lawyer	1. Need for coordination between agencies.
2	1967	Court Lees	R(P)	Home Office	Surrey	Pr	Stat	Lawyer	1. Found that punishment rules had been broken.
3	1973	Bagnall	P	LA	Shropshire				Not accessed.
4	1973	Brown/ Naseby	P	Regional Health Authority	West Midlands	Pr	Local A	Lawyer	1. Need for regional specialist child abuse team. 2. Need for better inter-agency coordination.
5	1974	Colwell	P	DHSS	E. Sussex/ Brighton	Pu	Stat	Lawyer	1. Need for coordination between agencies (note: minority report placing errors in context).
	1974	Colwell	P	DHSS	E. Sussex/ Brighton	Pu	Stat	Lawyer	1. Need for coordination between agencies (note: minority report placing errors in context).
6	1974	Piazzani	P	LA AHA	Essex	Pr	Local B	Local govt officer	1. Develop child protection system. 2. Need for improved health and social work cooperation.
7	1975	Auckland	P	DHSS	W. Riding Yorks/ Barnsley	Pu	Stat	Lawyer	1. Need to keep better track of offenders against children 2. Need for better supervision. 3. Need for more experienced social workers.
8	1975	Clark	P	Scottish Education Dept and Social Work Service Group	Perthshire	Pr	Stat	Lawyer	1. Low level of social worker experience.

	Year	Name		LA AHA Probation	Place		Local A/B	Independent chair (profession not clear)	Recommendations
9	1975	Godfrey	P	LA AHA Probation	Lambeth	Pr	Local A	Independent chair (profession not clear)	1. Need for better supervision. 2. Need for better inter-agency coordination. 3. Need for better record checks.
10	1975	Meurs	P	LA AHA	Norfolk	Pr	Local A	Local govt officer	1. Need for more resources. 2. Need for more training/supervision. 3. Need for greater involvement in child abuse issues by health visitors.
11	1976	Howlett	P	LAAHA	Birmingham	Pr	Local A	Lawyer	1. Develop child protection system. 2. Need for more training. 3. Need for more experienced social workers.
12	1977	Brewer	P	Area Review Committee	Somerset	Pr	Local B	Local govt officer	1. Develop child protection system. 2. Better communication needed between agencies. 3. Need for more training.
13	1977	H family	S	LA	Surrey	Pr	Local B	Director of social services	1. Need for less formal inquiries.
14	1978	Menheniott	P	DHSS	Cornwall	Pr	Stat	Social work service officers	1. Need for improved inter-agency liaison. 2. Need for better training.
15	1978	Peacock	P	LA AHA	Cambridgeshire	Pr	Local A	Health authority manager	1. Better system needed for tracking 'moving' families. 2. Need for training review.
16	1978	Spencer	P	LA AHA	Derbyshire	Pr	Local A	Lawyer	1. Need for specialist resources. 2. Develop child protection system. 3. Need for better qualified workers.
17	1979	Chapman	N	LA AHA	Berkshire and Hampshire	Pr	Local A	Lawyer	1. Need to give neglect a higher profile. 2. Need for specialist workers. 3. Need for better training.
18	1979	Trott	P		Humberside				Not accessed.
19	1979	Clarke	P	DHSS	Liverpool	Pu	Stat	Lawyer	1. Need for better investigative procedures.

	Year	P	DHSS	Place	Pu	Stat	Chair	Recommendations
20	1980	P		Wirral			Lawyer	1. Need to improve review of serious cases.
21	1980	P	LA	Birmingham	Pr	Local B	Social worker	1. Introduction of early warning register. 2. Guidance about 'no access' visits.
22	1980	P	LA AHA	Leicester	Pr	Local A	Local govt officer	1. Improvements needed to child protection procedures. 2. Need for training on misuse of drugs and impact on parenting. 3. Need for better inter-agency coordination.
23	1981	P	Area Review Committee	Essex	Pr	Local B	Chair of ARC Medic.	1. Need for regular medical checks.
24	1981	P		Walsall				Not accessed.
25	1981	P	Area Review Committee	Bradford	Pr	Local B	Chair of ARC Medic.	1. Focus on fostering arrangements. 2. Need for guidelines for foster parents with children at risk.
26	1981	P	LA	Calderdale	Pr	Local B	Lawyer	1. Focus on fostering arrangements.
27	1981	P	LA AHA Probation	Southwark	Pr	Local A	Lawyer	1. Better training needed. 2. Better inter-agency coordination needed. 3. Need for probation service to be involved in total care of family.
28	1981	P	Sheriff under the Fatal Accidents & Sudden Deaths Enquiry (Scotland) Act 1976	Not accessed	Pu	Stat	Lawyer	Not accessed.
29	1982	P	LA	Cambridgeshire	Pr	Local B	Chair of SS Committee	1. No grounds for formal inquiry. 2. Review of case conference system needed.

30	1982	Gates	P	LA AHA	Bexley	Pr	Local A	Lawyer	1. More control to be given to CP system. 2. Need for more training. 3. Need for more supervision.
31	1982	Fenlon	P		Cheshire				Not accessed.
32	1982	Aitken	P	Sheriff under the Fatal Accidents & Sudden Deaths Enquiry (Scotland) Act 1976	Not accessed.	Pu	Stat	Lawyer	Not accessed.
33	1982	Fraser	P	LA LEA AHA	Lambeth				Not accessed.
34	1984	Woodcock	P	LA	Hammersmith & Fulham	Pr	Local B	Social worker	1. Focus on fostering arrangements. 2. Lack of communication between agencies.
35	1985	Beckford	P	LA AHA	Brent	Pu	Local A	Lawyer	1. Better Health and Social Services cooperation needed. 2. More use of statutory inquiries. 3. Need for better social worker supervision and training.
36	1985	Hartwell	P	LA	Birmingham	Pr	Local B	Social worker	Not accessed
37	1985	Carthy	P	Area Review Committee	Nottinghamshire	Pr	Local B	Chair of ARC social worker	1. Need for better child protection awareness in hospitals. 2. Need for systems improvements.
38	1985	Leeways	R(S)	LA	Lewisham	Pr	Local A	Lawyer	1. Need for more monitoring. 2. Need for better complaints system. 3. Need for improved staff recruitment and development.
39	1986	Kincora	R(S)	DHSS (NI)	Belfast	Pu	Stat	Lawyer	1. Need for better qualified staff. 2. Need for better complaints system. 3. Need for better staff appraisal.
40	1986	Koseda	N	LA	Hillingdon	Pr	Local A	Social worker	1. Need for specialist approach. 2. Need for more training. 3. Police removal powers need clarification.

	Year	Name		Area Review Committee		Pr/Pu	Local	Chair of ARC	
41	1986	Salt	P	Area Review Committee	Oldham	Pr	Local B	social worker	1. Need to see the child.2. Need for medical examinations for children on supervision orders.3. Need for better training.
42	1987	Carlile	P	LA AHA	Greenwich	Pr	Local A	Lawyer	1. Health visitors to be child abuse focused. 2. Need for better resources generally. 3. Need for better training and supervision.
43	1987	Henry	P	LA	Lambeth	Pu	Local A	Lawyer	1. Need to have a more racially aware approach.2. Preference for private inquiries to be held.
44	1987	Mabey	P	Area Review Committee	Leeds	Pr	Local B		Not accessed.
45	1988	Plischkowsky	P	LA	Hampshire	Pr	Local B	Lawyer	1. Need to consider resource issues. 2. Need for health visitors to play a bigger role in child protection. 3. Need to monitor family moves.
46	1988	McGoldrick	P	AHA	Cumbria	Pr	Local A	Medic.	1. Need for more paediatric involvement in child protection cases.
47	1988	Cleveland	S	DoH	Cleveland	Pu	Stat	Lawyer	1. Need for specialist teams. 2. Better coordination between agencies. 3. Need for improved treatment of children and parents.
48	1988	Melanie Klein House	R(S)	LA	Greenwich	Pr	Local A	Social worker	1. Need for better staff training and recruitment. 2. Need to tackle issues of race. 3. Need to improve the physical and material environment.
49	1989	Aston	P	Area Review Committee	Southwark	Pr	Local A	Lawyer	1. Need to gain direct access to child. 2. Need for health visitors to be more involved. 3. Need for better supervision.

	Year	Name							Recommendations
50	1989	Johnson	P	Area Child Protection Committee	Islington	Pr	Local A	Lawyer	1. Need for organisational change. 2. Need for health visitors to be more fully involved in child protection work. 3. Need for better inter-agency liaison.
51	1990	Foster carer	P	LA	Derbyshire and Nottinghamshire	Pr	Local A	Lawyer	1. Need for improvement in foster parent selection and supervision. 2. Need for better inter-agency cooperation. 3. Need for better supervision.
52	1990	Fox	P	Area Child Protection Committee	Wandsworth	Pr	Local A	Social worker	1. Need for better case histories.
53	1991	Vergauwen	P	LA	Hackney	Pr	Local A	Nursing	1. Need to improve child protection system. 2. Need for better supervision.
54	1991	Pindown	R(P)	LA	Staffordshire	Pr	Local A	Lawyer	1. Need for better management. 2. Need for better complaints system. 3. Need for better recruitment of staff.
55	1991	Sukina	P	Area Child Protection Committee	Avon	Pr	Local A	Bridge Consultancy	1. Better training needed. 2. Better attention to records needed. 3. Better coordination needed between agencies.
56	1992	Orkneys	S	DoH	Orkneys	Pu	Stat	Lawyer	1. More careful interviewing techniques needed. 2. More involvement of parents needed.
57	1992	Gibelli	P	Area Child Protection Committee	Lambeth	Pr	Local B	Social worker	1. Need for better liaison between social services departments and hospitals. 2. Need for improved training. 3. Need for review of systems.
58	1992	Ty Mawr	R(P)	LA	Gwent	Pr	Local A	Lawyer	1. Need to close home. 2. Need to focus on improvements in staffing. 3. Need for improved formal visiting arrangements.

No.	Year	Name	Type	LA	Location	Pr	Local	Profession	Findings
59	1992	Scotforth House	R(P)		Lancashire	Pr	Local A	Lawyer	1. Need for an improved complaints system. 2. Need for more openness with parents.
60	1992	White	P	Area Child Protection Committee	Nottinghamshire	Pr	Local B	Social worker	Not accessed.
61	1992	St Charles Youth Treatment Centre	R(P)	DoH	Essex	Pr	Local A	Psychologist	1. Need for improved training. 2. Need for improved supervision. 3. Need for compliance with rules and regulations.
62	1993	Toni Dales ('Investigation into inter-agency practice following Cleveland ACPC's report concerning the death of Toni Dales')	P	Cleveland	South Tees area, Cleveland	Pr	Local A	National Children's Bureau (NCB)(Lead author: Paul Knight, NCB)	Not accessed
63	1993	Leicestershire	R(S)(P)	LA	Leicestershire	Pr	Local A	Lawyer	1. Need for better management. 2. Need for better staff supervision.
64	1993	Castle Hill	R(S)	LA	Shropshire	Pr	Local B	Social worker	1. Better recruiting methods needed. 2. Better complaints procedure needed. 3. Regular social work visiting needed.
65	1993	Lothian region: Finlayson/Newman report	R(S)	LA: Lothian Regional Council SSD	Lothian	Pr	Local A	Lawyer	Not assessed
66	1994	Oxendon House	R(P)(S) (alleged; report found staff not intentionally abusive)	LA	Bedfordshire	Pr	Local A	Social worker	1. Improved mechanisms for supervision and oversight of practices in homes. 2. Introduction of suitable professional support for therapeutic work with residents. 3. Better staff training.

67	1994	Multiple abuse in nursery classes	R(S)	LA	Newcastle upon Tyne	Pr	Local A	Lawyer	1. Need for better training for staff re child sexual abuse. 2. Need for better staff recruitment procedures.
68	1995	Paul	N	Area Child Protection Committee	Islington	Pr	Local A	Bridge Consultancy	1. Need for better training. 2. Need for improved inter-agency cooperation. 3. Need for better staff supervision.
69	1995	West	P	Area Child Protection Committee	Gloucestershire	Pr	Local A	Bridge Consultancy	1. Need to listen to children. 2. Need for better record keeping. 3. Need for better coordination.
70	1995	Islington	R(S)	LA	Islington	Pr	Local A	Social worker	1. Need for better staff recruitment and management. 2. Need for better record keeping. 3. Need for better training and supervision. 4. Need for review of council's equal opportunities policy.
71	1995	Meadowdale	R(P)	LA: Northumberland County Council	Northumberland	Pr	Local A	Social worker	1. Need for improved residential services for children with disabilities. 2. Need for better staff training, management and supervision. 3. Need for improved complaints system.
72	1996	Beckett	P	Area Child Protection Committee	Nottinghamshire	Pr	Local B	Social worker	1. Need to explore links between mental health problems and child abuse. 2. Need for better training and supervision of frontline workers. 3. Need for more comprehensive assessments.
73	1997	Neave	P	Area Child Protection Committee	Cambridgeshire	Pr	Local A	Bridge Consultancy	1. Need for seeking out children's views. 2. Need to establish risk thresholds. 3. Need to devise stratagems for working with hostile families.

	Year	Name	R(P)(S)	LA		Pr (and not published ?)	Local A		
74	1997	Sunderland (Witherwack House)	S, P	LA: Sunderland SSD	Sunderland	Pr	Local A	NSPCC	This report was the last in a series: SSI Feb. 1992; Emlyn Cassam May 1992; NSPCC Oct. 1992
75	1998	Caerphilly (James report)	S, P	LA: Caerphilly County Borough Council	Caerphilly (formerly in Mid-Glamorgan County Council area)	Pr	Local A	Social worker	1. Better links between schools and SSD re. at risk children. 2. Greater awareness re. legal powers of social workers re. uncooperative parents. 3. More rigorous recruitment of staff for child protection work.
76	1998	Hackney	R(S)	LA: London Borough of Hackney	Hackney	Pr	Local A	Social worker	1. Corporate action to ensure that councillors are aware of and capable of fulfilling their statutory duties. 2. Improved departmental organisation and performance for dealing with allegations of abuse. 3. Improvements in Working Together guidelines especially re. cases of organised abuse.
77	1998	Shieldfield Nursery, Newcastle upon Tyne	S	LA: Newcastle City Council	Newcastle	Pr	Local A	Social work academic	Report published but later withdrawn on advice of LA's libel lawyers.
78	1999	Edinburgh: Edinburgh's Children	R(S)	LA: City of Edinburgh Council	Edinburgh	Pu	Stat. (Section 6B, Social Work (Scotland) Act 1968)	Lawyer (children)	1,135 recommendations covering status of child protection across the LA; development of children's strategies and service plans; recruitment, vetting and exit interviews; training; supervision; investigation of complaints; whistleblowing 'Children's Commissioner for Scotland etc.
79	1999 (second interim report)	Lambeth: Lambeth Independent Child Protection Inquiry	R(S)	LA: Lambeth LBC	London Borough of Lambeth	Pr	Local A	Social worker	This was not a final report. Findings, however, surround the overall past 'organisational incompetence' of Lambeth Council and its SSD.

	Year		P	Area Child Protection Committee		Pr	Local A	Bridge Consultancy	
80	1999	Caerphilly: 'Neglect and developmental Delay: Part 8 Case Review; Overview report re. case 1/99 in Caerphilly'	P	Area Child Protection Committee: Caerphilly ACPC	Caerphilly	Pr	Local A	Bridge Consultancy	1. Need for improved inter-agency recording systems. 2. Need for an audit of child protection registers. 3. Need for more involvement of children in child protection processes.
81	1999	Aliyah Ismail	Neglect and SA (Neglect by statutory authorities)	Area Child Protection Committee: Harrow ACPC	London Borough of Harrow	Pr	Local A (external reviewer was appointed to work with the Case Review Committee of the ACPC)	Childcare expert	1. Insufficient sharing of information between agencies. 2. More focus needed on risk assessments on older children. 3. Child prostitution to be seen as a child protection issue.

APPENDIX 2

Chronology of Events Leading up to Announcement of North Wales Tribunal of Inquiry

Date	Event
February 1986	Alison Taylor, an officer in charge working for Gwynedd Social Services Department, complained to a local councillor and to North Wales Police of abuse and management deficiencies in a local children's home, Ty'r Felin. This triggered the 1986 investigation by North Wales Police. No prosecutions followed but the investigating officer claimed to have warned the director of social services of dubious conduct on the part of another officer in charge, who also managed the county's children's residential service.
December 1986	An ex-resident of Ty'r Felin children's home went to the police with similar allegations of abuse witnessed at the home. A new investigation was initiated but did not result in any prosecutions. Meanwhile Alison Taylor was told to stay away from work and was subsequently formally suspended.
January 1987	In Clwyd, David Gillison, a social worker and former Bryn Estyn employee, was convicted of offences of indecency with a male resident of a Clwyd home. He was jointly charged with an ex-resident of four Wrexham community homes. His 'cousin', Jacqueline Thomas, a care worker at Chevet Hey children's home, was also convicted in August 1986 of sexual offences against a boy under 16 in care.
November 1987	Alison Taylor failed to attend a disciplinary hearing and was dismissed by Gwynedd County Council.
September 1989	Park House (Butlins) Panel report was finalised and presented to the director of social services. The panel, under the chairmanship of a senior officer of the National Children's Home, was set up following complaints of inadequate supervision on a group holiday after a 13-year-old female resident of Park House had had unlawful sexual intercourse with a 16-year-old boy at the holiday camp. They found failings in the management of residential care across the county but the matter was not reported to the Social Services Committee or council.
21 April 1990	A young woman, resident at a Deeside hostel, complained to police about sexual abuse by the warden, Frederick Rutter, also an ex-employee of Clwyd children's homes. He was suspended by his housing association employer on 18 May and resigned on 12 June 1990. Rutter was prosecuted and convicted in July 1991 (see below).
15 June 1990	A young male resident of Cartrefle children's home revealed to a care worker that he had been abused by the officer in charge. The officer in charge was suspended on return from leave and North Wales Police was informed.

5 October 1990	The officer in charge of Cartrefle, Stephen Norris, was convicted after pleading guilty to charges of indecency against three boys. He was sentenced to three and a half years' imprisonment. At the conclusion of the trial, Clwyd's ACPC commissioned a review of the children's cases under the 1988 *Working Together* guidelines.
April 1991	John Jevons is appointed director of social services for Clwyd.
17 July 1991	The county secretary, Andrew Loveridge, wrote to North Wales Police regarding 'events, findings and suspicions against a number of persons' and invited them to investigate.
30 July 1991	Frederick Rutter was convicted of four counts of rape and two of indecent assault and sentenced to twelve years' imprisonment.
2 August 1991	North Wales Police began its inquiry into allegations of abuse within Clwyd's children's homes under the direction of Det. Supt Peter Ackerley.
26 September 1991	A Harlech TV programme, *Wales this Week*, featured complaints by Alison Taylor and others about abuse within Gwynedd's homes. The director of social services, Lucille Hughes, asked the chief constable to investigate the allegations.
1 December 1991	The *Independent on Sunday* featured an article by freelance journalist, Dean Nelson, which alleged widespread abuse in homes in Gwynedd and Clwyd, the involvement of a retired police officer and police attempts to cover up the failures of senior police officers and local authority officials.
2 December 1991	The separate police inquiries under way in Gwynedd and Clwyd were merged into a single Major Inquiry under Det. Supt Peter Ackerley.
15 March 1992	Seventeen people were arrested and interviewed by police in Clwyd. These included five serving members of staff in Clwyd Social Services Department.
June 1992	A libel writ was issued against the *Independent on Sunday* by the retired police officer named in the December 1991 article.
4 September 1992	The chief constable called for a full public inquiry into the North Wales investigation as soon as the trials were completed.
7 September 1992	A Welsh Office press release quoted the Under-Secretary of State Gwilym Jones' intention to hold a public inquiry once the legal proceedings had run their course in North Wales.
21 October 1992	Delivery of the report on Rutter and submission to Clwyd's Children and Families subcommittee.
27 October 1992	The final draft of the Cartrefle Panel report was delivered in July 1992. Following advice from the insurers and the Crown Prosecution Service, a summary report and commentary were submitted to the Social Services Committee.
November 1992	Harlech TV programme in which allegations against a retired police officer are repeated, causing Harlech TV to be joined in the libel action by that individual.

10 February 1993	Her Majesty's Inspector of Constabulary formally recommended to the North Wales chief constable that an outside force should take over the investigation. The idea was rejected on the grounds that it was unnecessary and impractical.
September 1993	Stephen Norris, having been released from jail, was rearrested and charged with further offences at Cartrefle and Bryn Estyn. On 22 September he was convicted at Mold Crown Court of offences including indecent assault and buggery against six boys. He was sentenced to seven years' imprisonment on 11 November.
12 January 1994	Clwyd's Social Services Committee approved the appointment of an independent panel of inquiry under the chairmanship of John Jillings, former director of social services for Derbyshire County Council.
8 July 1994	Peter Howarth, former deputy principal of Bryn Estyn children's home, was convicted of offences including indecent assault and buggery against seven boys. Sentenced to ten years' imprisonment.
28 November 1994	Paul Wilson, former residential child care officer at Bryn Estyn, pleaded guilty to offences of physical assault against three boys. Sentenced to fifteen months, suspended for two years.
6 December 1994	The verdict in the retired police officer's libel trial went against the newspapers and TV company. The plaintiff won substantial damages.
9 February 1995	Trial of John Allen, former head of the Bryn Alyn Community, for offences of indecent assault against a number of ex-residents. Allen was convicted and sentenced to six years.
May 1995	The Secretary of State for Wales appointed Nicola Davies QC to examine documentation relating to the North Wales allegations and to determine whether a further inquiry was required.
December 1995	Nicola Davies reported to the Secretary of State and recommended against a further inquiry which 'would have been of historical value only', but in favour of an examination of childcare policy, practice and procedures to establish whether new primary and secondary legislation and guidance was having the desired effect of raising standards. Adrianne Jones, former director of social services for Birmingham City Council, was appointed to undertake the work.
22 February 1996	Clwyd County Council received the Jillings report. Advice was sought from counsel on the likely consequences of publication.
26 March 1996	At its last full council meeting before local government reorganisation in Wales, Clwyd County Council agreed to note the contents of the Jillings report and to refer the matter of its publication and a recommendation for a public inquiry to the Welsh Office.
1 April 1996	Dissolution of Clwyd and Gwynedd County Councils and the handing over of powers to the six new unitary authorities in North Wales.

7 April 1996	The beginning of a campaign by the *Independent* newspaper and its Sunday stablemate to bring the contents of the Jillings report into the public domain and to press the Secretary of State for Wales to hold a judicial inquiry into the North Wales allegations. The campaign ran throughout April and May 1996 with a series of articles entitled 'Victims of the Abusers'.
5 June 1996	Letter from (Clwyd) successor authorities to William Hague as Secretary of State seeking a meeting 'to jointly find a way forward to ensure that we work together to restore and maintain confidence in the public agencies dealing with childcare within North Wales and beyond', i.e. to deal with the non-publication of the Jillings report and respond effectively to Adrianne Jones' report and continuing public concern. It suggested that the Welsh Office either place the Jillings report on deposit in the House of Commons Library or institute 'an immediate full judicial inquiry into childcare in North Wales and elsewhere for the period 1974–1996'. The local authorities referred to their own financial situations: 'The imposition of a directed inquiry (under the [Children Act 1989]) would be of little value and that has been amply demonstrated by Clwyd County Council's attempt to conduct the Jillings Inquiry. The path to publication has raised more questions than answers. The resources of local authorities would not be able to withstand the cost of such an inquiry without a drastic cut in services currently provided; this being hard on the heels of the financial difficulties and uncertainties created by local government reorganisation.'
17 June 1996	The Secretary of State for Wales receives the Adrianne Jones report and announces the appointment of Sir Ronald Waterhouse, a recently retired High Court judge, to chair a Tribunal of Inquiry (under the 1921 Act) to look into the allegations surrounding child abuse in North Wales. At the same time, his colleague, Stephen Dorrell, the Secretary of State for Health, announced the children's safeguards review under the chairmanship of Sir William Utting.
4 February 1997	After a number of preliminary hearings and opening submissions, the Tribunal heard its first live evidence from a complainant.

References

Aldridge, M. (1994) *Making Social Work News.* London: Routledge.

Allen, M., Baroness Hurtwood (1945) *Whose Children?* London: Simpkin Marshall.

Barker, A. (1994) 'Enriching Democracy: Public Inquiry and the Policy Process.' In I.Budge and D.McKay (eds) *Developing Democracy.* London: Sage.

Barker, A. (1997) 'The Inquiry's Procedures.' In B. Thompson and F. F. Ridley (eds) *Under the Scott-Light: British Government Seen through the Scott Report.* Oxford: Oxford University Press.

Barter, C. (1999) 'Practitioners' Experiences and Perceptions of Investigating Allegations of Institutional Abuse.' *Child Abuse Review 8,* 392–404.

Beck, U. (1992) *Risk Society: Towards a New Modernity.* London: Sage.

Bedfordshire County Council (Roycroft, B. and Witham, L.) (1994) *Oxendon House: A Case to Answer?* Bedford: Bedfordshire County Council.

Behlmer, G. (1982) *Child Abuse and Moral Reform in England 1870–1908.* Stanford, CA: Stanford University Press.

Beitchman, J., Zucker, K., Hood, J., Da Costa, G. and Akman, D. (1991) 'A Review of the Short-term Effects of Child Sexual Abuse.' *Child Abuse and Neglect 15,* 537–556.

Beitchman, J., Zucker, K., Hood, J., Da Costa, G., Akman, D. and Cassavia, E. (1992) 'A Review of the Long-term Effects of Child Sexual Abuse.' *Child Abuse and Neglect 16,* 101–118.

Ben-Tovim, A., Elton, A., Hildebrand, J., Tranter, M. and Vizard, E. (eds) (1988) *Child Sexual Abuse within the Family: Assessment and Treatment. The Work of the Great Ormond Street Team.* London: Wright.

Berridge, D. and Brodie, I. (1996) 'Residential Child Care in England and Wales: the Inquiries and After.' In M. Hill and J. Aldgate (eds) *Child Welfare Services: Developments in Law, Policy, Practice and Research.* London: Jessica Kingsley.

Bibby, P. (ed) (1996) *Organised Abuse: the Current Debate.* Aldershot: Aldgate.

Birkinshaw, P. (1985) *Grievance, Remedies and the State,* 2nd edn. London: Sweet and Maxwell.

Boswell, J. (1990) *The Kindness of Strangers: the Abandonment of Children in Western Europe from Late Antiquity to the Renaissance.* Harmondsworth: Penguin.

Bowlby, J. (1952) *Maternal Care and Mental Health: A Report Prepared on Behalf of the World Health Organization as a Contribution to the United Nations Programme for the Welfare of Homeless Children,* 2nd edn. Geneva: World Health Organization.

Brent, London Borough of (1985) *A Child in Trust: the Report of the Panel of Inquiry into the Circumstances Surrounding the Death of Jasmine Beckford.* London Borough of Brent.

Bridge, Child Care Consultancy Service (1991) *Sukina: An Evaluation of the Circumstances Leading to her Death.* London: The Bridge.

Bridge, Child Care Consultancy Service (1995) *Paul: Death from Neglect.* London: The Bridge.

Bridge, Child Care Consultancy Service (1997) *Report on the Professional Judgements and Accountability in Relation to Work with the Neave Family.* London: The Bridge.

Bridge, Child Care Consultancy Service (1998) *Dangerous Care: Working to Protect Children.* London: The Bridge.

Bridge, Child Care Consultancy Service (1999) *Neglect and Developmental Delay: Part 8 Case Review Overview Report re: Case 1/99 in Caerphilly.* London: The Bridge.

Burlingham, D. and Freud, A. (1942) *Young Children in War Time: a Year's Work in a Residential Nursery.* London: Allen and Unwin.

Butler, D. and Butler, G. (1987) *British Political Facts.* London: Macmillan.

Butler-Sloss, Lord Justice E. (1988) *Report of the Inquiry into Child Abuse in Cleveland 1987,* Cm 412. London: HMSO.

Campbell, B. (1988) *Unofficial Secrets.* London: Virago.

Cane, P. (1986) *An Introduction to Administrative Law.* Oxford: Clarendon.

Cartwright, T. (1975) *Royal Commissions and Departmental Committees in Britain.* London: Hodder and Stoughton.

Clyde, Lord (1992) *Report of the Inquiry into the Removal of Children from Orkney in February 1991,* HoC 195. London: HMSO.

Cobley, C. (1998) 'Financial Compensation for Victims of Child Abuse.' *Journal of Social Welfare and Family Law 20*, 221–235.

Corby, B. (1993) *Child Abuse: Towards a Knowledge Base.* Buckingham: Open University Press.

Corby, B. (1998) *Managing Child Sexual Abuse Cases.* London: Jessica Kingsley.

Corby, B., Doig, A. and Roberts, V. (1998) 'Inquiries into Child Abuse.' *Journal of Social Welfare and Family Law 20*, 377–395.

Council on Tribunals (1998) Annual Report 1997/8. London: The Stationery Office.

Crimmens, D. (2000) '"Things Can Only Get Better!" An Evaluation of Developments in the Training and Qualification of Residential Child Care Staff.' In D. Crimmens and J. Pitts (eds) *Positive Residential Practice: Learning the Lessons of the 1990s.* Lyme Regis: Russell House Publishing.

Cunningham, H. (1991) *The Children of the Poor: Representations of Childhood since the Seventeenth Century.* Oxford: Blackwell.

Curtis, Dame M. (1946) *Report of the Care of Children Committee*, Cmd 6922. London: HMSO.

Davies, N. (1995) Child Abuse North Wales: *Examination of Papers by Miss Nicola Davies Q.C. Conclusions and Recommendations.* London: HMSO.

Department of Health and Social Security (1974) *Report of the Committee of Inquiry into the Care and Supervision Provided in Relation to Maria Colwell.* London: HMSO.

Department of Health and Social Security (1975) *Report of the Committee of Inquiry into the Provision of Services to the Family of John George Auckland.* London: HMSO.

Department of Health and Social Security (1979) *Report of the Committee of Inquiry into the Actions of the Authorities and Agencies relating to James Darryn Clarke*, Cmnd 7739. London: HMSO.

Department of Health and Social Security (1980) *The Committee of Inquiry into the Case of Paul Stephen Brown*, Cmnd 8107. London: HMSO.

Department of Health and Social Security (1986) *Child Abuse – Working Together: A Draft Guide to Arrangements for Inter-agency Cooperation for the Protection of Children.* London: HMSO.

Department of Health and Social Security (1988) *Working Together: a Guide to Inter-agency Cooperation for the Protection of Children from Abuse.* London: HMSO.

Department of Health and Social Security (Northern Ireland) (1985) *Report of the Committee of Inquiry into Children's Homes and Hostels.* Belfast: HMSO.

Department of Health (1991a) *Working Together under the Children Act 1989: a Guide to Arrangements for Inter-agency Cooperation for the Protection of Children from Abuse.* London: HMSO.

Department of Health (1991b) *Child Abuse: a Study of Inquiry Reports 1980–1989.* London: HMSO.

Department of Health (1995) *Child Protection: Messages from Research.* London: HMSO.

Department of Health (1998a) *Caring for Children Away from Home: Messages from Research.* Chichester: Wiley.

Department of Health (1998b) *The Quality Protects Programme: Transforming Children's Services, LAC(98)26.* London: Department of Health.

Department of Health (1998c) *Modernising Social Services: Promoting Independence, Improving Protection, Raising Standards.* London: The Stationery Office.

Department of Health (1998d) *The Government's Response to the Children's Safeguards Review*, Cm 4105. London: The Stationery Office.

Department of Health (1999a) *Working Together to Safeguard Children: a Guide to Inter-agency Working to Safeguard and Promote the Welfare of Children. Consultation Draft.* London: Department of Health.

Department of Health (1999b) *Framework for the Assessment of Children in Need and their Families: Consultation Draft.* London: Department of Health.

Derbyshire and Nottinghamshire County Councils (1990) *Report of the Inquiry into the Death of a Child in Care.* Derbyshire and Nottinghamshire County Councils.

deYoung, M. (1997) 'Satanic Ritual Abuse in Day Care: an Analysis of 12 American Cases.' *Child Abuse Review 6*, 84–93.

Dingwall, R. and Eekelaar, J. (1984) 'Rethinking Child Protection.' In M. Freeman (ed.) *State, Law and Family: Critical Perspectives.* London: Tavistock.

Dominelli, L. (1986) 'Father-daughter Incest: Patriarchy's Shameful Secret.' *Critical Social Policy 16*, 8–22.

Edinburgh, City of (Marshall, K., Jamieson, C. and Finlayson, A.) (1999) *Edinburgh's Children: The Edinburgh Inquiry into the Abuse and Protection of Children in Care.* Edinburgh City Council.

Falkov, A. (1996) *Study of Working Together 'Part 8' Reports: Fatal Child Abuse and Parental Psychiatric Disorder.* London: Department of Health.

Finkelhor, D. and associates (eds) (1986) *A Sourcebook on Child Sexual Abuse.* Newbury Park, CA: Sage.

Finkelhor, D., Williams, L. and Burns, N. (1988) *Nursery Crimes: Sexual Abuse in Day Care*. Newbury Park, CA: Sage.

Finlayson, A. and Newman, A. (1993) *Listen – Take Seriously What They Say: A Review of Present and Planned Arrangements for Responding to Complaints From Young People in Care, with Recommendations for Further Action*, September 1993. Edinburgh: Lothian Regional Council.

Franks, Lord O. (1957) *Report of the Committiee on Administrative Tribunals and Inquiries*. London: HMSO.

Franks, Lord O. (1983) *Falkland Islands Review: A Report of a Committee of Privy Counsellors Presented to Parliament by the Prime Minister*. Cmnd 8787. London: HMSO.

Frost, N. and Wallis, L. (2000) 'Empowering Children and Young People? The Possibilities and Limitations of the Complaints System.' In D. Crimmens and J. Pitts (eds) *Positive Residential Practice: Learning the Lessons of the 1990s*. Lyme Regis: Russell House Publishing.

Gallagher, B. (1999a) 'Institutional Abuse.' In N. Parton and C. Wattam (eds) *Child Sexual Abuse: Responding to the Experiences of Children*. Chichester: Wiley.

Gallagher, B. (1999b) 'The Abuse of Children in Public Care.' *Child Abuse Review 8*, 357–365.

Gelles, R. and Cornell, C. (1985) *Intimate Violence in Families*. Beverly Hills, CA: Sage.

Gloucestershire Area Child Protection Committee (1995) *Part 8 Case Review Overview Report in Respect of Charmaine and Heather West*. Gloucester: Gloucestershire ACPC.

Government Views on the Recommendations of the Royal Commission on Tribunals of Inquiry and the Interdepartmental Committee on the Law of Contempt as it affects Tribunals of Inquiry (1973) Cmnd 5313. London: HMSO.

Greenwich, London Borough of (1987) *A Child in Mind: the Protection of Children in a Responsible Society. The Report of the Commission of Inquiry into the Circumstances Surrounding the Death of Kimberley Carlile*. London Borough of Greenwich.

Gwent County Council (1992) *Ty Mawr Community Home Inquiry*. Gwent County Council.

Hackney and City of London Area Child Protection Committee (1991) *Report of the Daniel Vergauwen Review Panel*. London: Hackney and London ACPC.

Hallett, C. (1989) 'Child Abuse Inquiries and Public Policy.' In O. Stevenson (ed.) *Child Abuse: Public Policy and Professional Practice*. Hemel Hempstead: Harvester Wheatsheaf.

Harris, N. (1987) 'Defensive Social Work.' *British Journal of Social Work 17*, 61 –69.

Harrow Area Child Protection Committee (1999) *Part 8 Review: Summary Report*. London: Harrow ACPC.

Hendrick, H. (1994) *Child Welfare: England 1872–1989*. London: Routledge.

Hennessy, P. (1986) *The Great and the Good*. London: Policy Studies Institute.

Heywood, J. (1978) *Children in Care: the Development of the Service for the Care of the Deprived Child*, 3rd edn. London: Routledge and Kegan Paul.

Hill, M. (1990) 'The Manifest and Latent Lessons of Child Abuse Inquiries.' *British Journal of Social Work 20*, 197–213.

Hobbs, G., Hobbs, J. and Wynne, J. (1999) 'Abuse of Children in Foster and Residential Care.' *Child Abuse and Neglect 23*, 1239–1252.

Home Office (1947) *Report of the Committee of Inquiry into the Conduct of Standon Farm Approved School and the Circumstances Connected with the Murder of a Master at the School on February 15th. 1947*, Cmd 7150 (session 1946–7). London: HMSO.

Home Office (1959) *Report of the Inquiry Relating to Carton Approved School*, Cmnd 937 (session 1959–60). London: HMSO.

Home Office (1967) *Administration of Punishment at Court Lees Approved School*, Cmnd 3367. London: HMSO.

Howe, D. (1992) 'Child Abuse and the Bureaucratization of Social Work.' *Sociological Review 40*, 3, 491–508.

Howe, Lady E. (1992) *The Quality of Care: Report of the Residential Staff's Inquiry*. London: Local Government Management Board.

Hunt, P. (1994) *Report of the Independent Inquiry into Multiple use in Nursery Classes in Newcastle upon Tyne*. City Council of Newcastle upon Tyne.

Ingleby, Viscount O. (1960) *Report of the Committee on Children and Young Persons*, Cmnd 1191. London: HMSO.

Islington, London Borough of (White, I. and Hart, K.) (1995) *Report of the Management of Child Care in the London Borough of Islington*. London Borough of Islington.

James, G. (1994) *Department of Health Discussion Report for ACPC Conference: Study of Working Together 'Part 8' Reports*. London: Department of Health.

Jones, A. (1996) *Report of the Examination Team on Child Care Procedures and Practice I, North Wales.* London: HMSO.

Jones, J. (1994) 'Towards an Understanding of Power Relationships in Institutional Abuse'. *Early Childhood Development and Care 100,* 69–76.

Karban, K. and Frost, N. (1998) 'Training in Residential Child Care: Assessing the Impact of the Residential Care Initiative.' *Social Work Education 17,* 287–300.

Kempe, C., Silverman, F., Steele, B., Droegemueller, W. and Silver, H. (1962) 'The Battered Child Syndrome.' *Journal of the American Medical Association 181,* 17–24.

La Fontaine, J. (1994) *The Extent and Nature of Organised and Ritual Abuse: Research Findings.* London: HMSO.

La Fontaine, J. (1998) *Speak of the Devil: Tales of Satanic Abuse in Contemporary England.* Cambridge: Cambridge University Press.

Lambeth, London Borough of (1987) *Whose Child? The Report of the Public Inquiry into the Death of Tyra Henry.* London Borough of Lambeth.

Lambeth, London Borough of (Barratt, J.) (1999) *The Lambeth Independent Child Protection Inquiry.* London Borough of Lambeth.

Lambeth, Lewisham and Southwark Area Review Committee (1989) *The Doreen Aston Report.* London: Lambeth, Lewisham and Southwark ARC.

Lancashire County Council (1992) *The Scotforth House Inquiry.* Lancaster: Lancashire County Council.

Lane, D. (2000) 'Often Ignored: Obvious Messages for a Safe Workforce.' In D. Crimmens and J. Pitts (eds) *Positive Residential Practice: Learning the Lessons of the 1990s.* Lyme Regis: Russell House Publishing.

Leicestershire County Council (Kirkwood, A.) (1993) *The Leicestershire Inquiry 1992: Report of an Inquiry into Aspects of the Management of Children's Homes in Leicestershire between 1973 and 1986.* Leicester: Leicestershire County Council.

Le Quesne, Sir G. (1988) Barlow Clowes. *Report of Sir Godfrey Le Quesne Q.C. to the Secretary of State for Trade and Industry.* HC 671. London: HMSO.

Levi, M. (1993) *The Investigation, Prosecution, and Trial of Serious Fraud: Research Study No. 14.* London: HMSO.

Lewisham, London Borough of (1985) *The Leeways Inquiry Report.* London Borough of Lewisham.

Lyon, C. (1997) 'Children Abused within the Care System: Do Current Representations Procedures offer the Child Protection and the Family Support?' In N. Parton (ed.) *Child Protection and Family Support: Tensions, Contradictions and Possibilities.* London: Routledge.

McClure, R. (1981) *Coram's Children: The London Foundling Hospital in the Eighteenth Century.* New Haven, CT: Yale University Press.

McCoy, K. and Clough, R. (2000) *Safety in Practice: an Audit of the Work of the Social Services Inspectorate (Wales).* Cardiff: National Assembly for Wales.

Macfarlane, K. and Waterman, J. (1986) *The Sexual Abuse of Young Children.* New York: Holt, Rinehart and Winston.

Mahood, L. (1995) *Policing Gender, Class and Family.* London: UCL Press.

Masterman, C. (1911) *Inquiry into the Management and Discipline of the Heswall Nautical School,* Cmd 5541. London: HMSO.

Merrick, D. (1996) *Social Work and Child Abuse.* London: Routledge.

Middleton, N. (1971) *When Family Failed.* London: Victor Gollancz.

Miller, A. (1985) *Thou Shalt Not Be Aware.* London: Pluto Press.

Monckton, Sir W. (1945) *Report on the Circumstances which led to the Boarding-Out of Dennis and Terence O'Neill at Bank Farm, Minsterley, and the Steps taken to Supervise their Welfare,* Cmd 6636. London: HMSO.

Morgan, R. (2000) 'Positive Residential Practice: the Contribution of Inspection.' In D. Crimmens and J. Pitts (eds) *Positive Residential Practice: Learning the Lessons of the 1990s.* Lyme Regis: Russell House Publishing.

Munro, E. (1996) 'Avoidable and Unavoidable Mistakes in Child Protection Work.' *British Journal of Social Work 26,* 795–810.

Myers, J. (1994) *The Backlash: Child Protection under Fire.* Thousand Oaks, CA: Sage.

National Society for the Prevention of Cruelty to Children (1999) *Out of Sight: NSPCC Report on Deaths from Abuse 1973–1998.* London: NSPCC.

Nelson, B. (1984) *Making an Issue of Child Abuse: Political Agenda Setting for Social Problems.* Chicago: University of Chicago Press.

Northumberland County Council (Kilgallon, W.) (1995) *Report of the Independent Review into Allegations of Abuse at Meadowdale Children's Home and Related Matters.* Morpeth: Northumberland County Council.

Nottinghamshire Area Child Protection Committee (1996) *Overview Sub-Committee Report Concerning the Deaths of Tracy and Clare.* Nottingham: Nottingham ACPC.

Parker, R. (1983) 'The Gestation of Reform: the Children Act 1948.' In P. Bean and S. Macpherson (eds) *Approaches to Welfare.* London: Routledge and Kegan Paul.

Parsloe, P. (1978) *Juvenile Justice in Britain and the United States: the Balance of Needs and Rights.* London: Routledge and Kegan Paul.

Parton, N. (1979) 'The Natural History of Child Abuse: a Study in Social Problem Definition.' *British Journal of Social Work 9,* 431–51.

Parton, N. (1985) *The Politics of Child Abuse.* London: Macmillan.

Parton, N., Thorpe, D. and Wattam, C. (1996) *Child Protection, Risk and the Moral Order.* London: Macmillan.

Pelton, L. (1978) 'Child Abuse and Neglect: the Myth of Classlessness.' *American Journal of Orthopsychiatry 48,* 608–617.

Pinchbeck, I. and Hewitt, M. (1973a) *Children in English Society Volume 1: From the Tudor Times to the Eighteenth Century.* London: Routledge and Kegan Paul

Pinchbeck, I. and Hewitt, M. (1973b) *Children in English Society Volume 2: From the Eighteenth Century to the Children Act 1948.* London: Routledge and Kegan Paul.

Police Complaints Authority (1993) *Inquiry into the Police Investigation of Complaints of Child and Sexual Abuse in Leicestershire Children's Homes.* London: Police Complaints Authority.

Pollock, L. (1983) *Forgotten Children: Parent–Child Relations from 1500 to 1900.* Cambridge: Cambridge University Press.

Pringle, K. (1992) 'Child Sexual Abuse Perpetrated by Welfare Personnel and the Problem of Men.' *Critical Social Policy 36,* 4–19.

Quebec, Government of (1997) *27th Annual Report of the Quebec Ombudsman (1996–7) 'For Fair and Just Government'.* Quebec City.

Reder, P. and Duncan, S. (1999) *Lost Innocents.* London: Routledge.

Reder, P., Duncan, S. and Gray, M. (1993) *Beyond Blame: Child Abuse Tragedies Revisited.* London: Routledge.

Rimmer, J. (1985) *Yesterday's Naughty Children: Training Ship, Girls Reformatory and Farm School. A History of the Liverpool Reform Association founded in 1855.* Manchester: Neil Richardson.

Rowe, J. and Lambert, L. (1973) *Children Who Wait.* London: Association of British Agencies for Fostering and Adoption.

Rush, F. (1980) *The Best Kept Secret.* Englewood Cliffs, NJ: Prentice-Hall.

Russell, D. (1984) *Sexual Exploitation: Rape, Child Sexual Abuse and Workplace Harrassment.* Beverly Hills, CA: Sage.

Russell, D. (1986) *The Secret Trauma: Incest in the Lives of Girls and Women.* New York: Basic Books.

Salmon, Lord Justice (1966) *Royal Commission on Tribunals of Inquiry: Report of the Commission,* Cmnd 3121. London: HMSO.

Seebohm, F. (1968) *Report of the Committee on Local Authority and Allied Personal Social Services,* Cmnd 3703. London: HMSO.

Shahar, S. (1990) *Children in the Middle Ages.* London: Routledge.

Shropshire County Council (Brannan, C., Jones, R. and Murch, J.) (1992) *Castle Hill Report Practice Guide.* Shrewsbury: Shropshire County Council.

Sinclair, I. and Gibbs, I. (1998) *Children's Homes: a Study in Diversity.* Chichester: Wiley.

Skinner, A. (1992) *Another Kind of Home: a Review of Residential Care.* Edinburgh: HMSO.

Smith, C. (1997) 'Children's Rights: Have Carers Abandoned Values?' *Children and Society 11,* 3–15.

Social Services Inspectorate (1988) *Report of an Inspection of Melanie Klein House CHE by the Social Services Inspectorate.* London: Department of Health.

Social Services Inspectorate (1991a) *Report of an Inspection of Grove Park Community Home by the Social Services Inspectorate.* London: Department of Health.

Social Services Inspectorate (1991b) *Report of an Inspection of St Charles Youth Treatment Centre by the Social Services Inspectorate.* London: Department of Health.

Social Services Inspectorate (1995) *Learning Lessons: a Report Based on the Information Drawn from Three Seminars Organised by the Social Services Inspectorate, North of England Policy and Business Division looking at the Part 8 Review process.* London: Department of Health.

Social Services Inspectorate (1998) *Someone Else's Children: Inspections of Planning and Decision-making for Children Looked After and the Safety of Children Looked After.* London: Department of Health.

Social Services Inspectorate (Wales) (1991) *Accommodating Children: a Review of Children's Homes in Wales.* Cardiff: Welsh Office.

South Africa, Republic of (1999) *Report of the National Truth and Reconciliation Commisssion.* London: Macmillan.

Spock, B. (1966) *Baby and Child Care.* London: New English Library.

Staffordshire County Council (Levy, A. and Kahan, B.) (1991) *The Pindown Experience and the Protection of Children: the Report of the Staffordshire Child Care Inquiry 1990.* Stafford: Staffordshire County Council.

Stanley, N. (1999) 'Institutional Abuse of Children: an Overview of Policy and Practice.' In N. Stanley, J. Manthorpe and B. Penhale (eds) *Institutional Abuse: Perspectives Across the Life Course.* London: Routledge.

Surrey County Council (1977) *H Family: Report of an Investigation by the Director of Social Services and the Deputy Town Clerk.* Guilford: Surrey County Council.

Taylor, Lord Justice P. (1989) *The Hillsborough Stadium Disaster.* Cmd 1989. London: HMSO.

Thomas, G. (1990) 'Institutional Child Abuse: the Making and Prevention of an Un-Problem.' *Journal of Child and Youth Care 4,* 1–22.

Thompson, S. (1993) *From Policy to Issue Network: the British Offshore Safety Industry and the Role of the Public Inquiry. Newcastle University Discussion Papers in Politics No. 1.* Newcastle upon Tyne: Newcastle University.

Thorpe, D. (1980) *Out of Care: the Community Support of Juvenile Offenders.* London: Allen and Unwin.

Utting, Sir W. (1991) *Children in the Public Care: a Review of Residential Child Care.* London: HMSO.

Utting, Sir W. (1997) *People Like Us: the Report of the Review of the Safeguards for Children Living Away from Home.* London: HMSO.

Vick, G. (1945) *London County Council Remand Homes: Report of the Committee of Inquiry,* Cmd 6594. London: HMSO.

Wade, E. C. S. and Bradley, A. W. (1985) *Constitutional and Administrative Law,* 10th edn. London: Longman.

Wagner, G. (ed) (1988) *A Positive Choice: Report of the Independent Review of Residential Care.* London: HMSO.

Walton, M. (1993) 'Regulation in Child Protection: Policy Failure?' *British Journal of Social Work 23,* 139–156.

Wandsworth, London Borough of (1990) *The Report of the Inquiry into the Death of Stephanie Fox.* London Borough of Wandsworth.

Warner, N. (1992) *Choosing with Care: the Report of the Committee of Inquiry into the Selection, Development and Management of Staff in Children's Homes.* London: HMSO.

Waterhouse, Sir R. (2000) *Lost in Care: Report of the Tribunal of Inquiry into the Abuse of Children in Care in the Former County Council Areas of Gwynedd and Clwyd since 1974,* HC 201. London: The Stationery Office.

Webb, S. and Webb, B. (1909) *The Break-Up of the Poor Law: Being Part One of the Minority Report of the Poor Law Commission.* London: Longmans, Green.

Webster, R. (1998) *The Great Children's Home Panic.* Chichester: Wiley.

Whitaker, D., Archer, L. and Hicks, L. (1998) *Working in Children's Homes: Challenges and Complexities.* Chichester: Wiley.

Wild, N. (1986) 'Sexual Abuse of Children in Leeds.' *British Medical Journal 292,* 1113–1116.

Willow, C. (2000) 'Safety in Numbers? Promoting Children's Rights in Public Care.' In D. Crimmens and J. Pitts (eds) *Positive Residential Practice: Learning the Lessons of the 1990s.* Lyme Regis: Russell House Publishing.

Winetrobe, B. (1997) 'Inquiries after Scott: the Return of the Tribunal Inquiry.' *Public Law* Spring. 1997, 18–31.

Woodhouse, D. (1995) 'Matrix Churchill and Judicial Inquiries.' *Parliamentary Affairs 48,* 24–39.

Wraith, R. and Lamb, G. (1971) *Public Inquiries as an Instrument of Government.* London: Allen and Unwin.

Subject Index

Author Index